The Houses That Sears Built

Everything You Ever Wanted to
Know About Sears Catalog Homes

The Houses That Sears Built

Everything You Ever Wanted to Know
About Sears Catalog Homes

Rosemary Thornton

Gentle Beam Publications
Alton, Illinois

Published by
Gentle Beam Publications
P. O. Box 1392
Alton, IL 62002

ISBN: 0-9715588-1-7

Printed in the United States of America
February 2004
Second Edition

This book is available at quantity discounts for bulk purchases.
For information, contact Gentle Beam Publications.

Table of Contents

This book is dedicated to my dear Mom,
Betty Brown Fuller
who left for heaven on January 1, 2002.

I finally did it, Mom. I finished the book.
How I wish you were here to rejoice with me.

As Abraham Lincoln said, of his own dear mother:
"All that I am or hope to be I owe to my angel mother.
I remember my mother's prayers and they have always followed me.
They have clung to me all my life."

iv

Introduction

By Christmas 2001, the manuscript for the first edition of "*The Houses That Sears Built*" was 95% complete. I flew from St. Louis to Virginia for the holidays to visit my mother. But while I was in town, she passed on suddenly. It was a terrible shock.

A few weeks later, my marriage of 24 years ended abruptly. I packed a few things and moved into an apartment.

In the weeks that followed, this manuscript was completed and published. I decided to change some other things about my life, too. I dropped 30 pounds, grew out my hair and bought a new wardrobe. I looked and felt like a different woman; like a person who'd been given a new springtime and a second chance.

I worked some mighty long hours in those first post-divorce months, lecturing, traveling and promoting my book. My goal was to make Sears homes my full-time vocation. And it worked. In a short time, book sales were off and running.

That was about two years ago. Since that time, *The Houses That Sears Built* has sold several thousand copies and has appeared in the *Christian Science Monitor*, *The New York Times*, *Old House Journal* and about 40 other publications, as well as WGN-TV, CBS's *Sunday Morning News*, A&E's *Biography* and PBS's *History Detectives*.

As a result of the book's popularity, I have received about 1000 emails and letters from people willing to share their stories and memories about Sears homes.

In these last two years, I've traveled thousands of miles, seeking and finding Sears homes. I've given more than 150 lectures throughout the country. My knowledge of Sears homes has increased exponentially and I want to share all the new information I've learned; hence, this major revision.

I hope you enjoy this new book. Burying myself in research and writing (again) and revising this book was *intense*, but it was also a labor of love. It always has felt like the work I was born to do.

Come with me as we explore this topic even further and let me show you what I've learned. ☺

Rose Thornton

Acknowledgments

Before I wrote this book, I never spent much time reading the acknowledgments in other people's books. Having completed this manuscript, I now understand how much an author relies on the kindness and generosity and support of other people. I hope you'll read my "gratitude list" - otherwise known as the "acknowledgments."

This book came into being, largely because of the encouragement of LaWanda Smith. In the Winter of 1999-2000, LaWanda and I spent many happy hours together, driving around Wood River, Illinois and rediscovering that community's large collection of Sears homes.

And I owe a huge debt of gratitude to Carolynn Bettis, whom I met one day at the Carlinville Public Library. Like LaWanda, Carolynn was supportive, enthusiastic and helpful and became a dear friend.

Long after this book is gone and forgotten, I'll remember the kindness of Dick Warner and Elaine Trowbridge, whom I met through e-Bay. Dick outbid me one night on a Sears Modern Homes catalog. I sent him an e-mail and explained my book project. I asked if he'd be willing to sell me a copy of the catalog. He wrote back and said, "I'll be in touch." Within 30 days, he and Elaine had mailed their personal collection of Sears Modern Homes catalogs to my home. How do you repay such kindness and trust? A simple thank-you in the front of a book seems so inadequate, but *thank-you Dick and Elaine.*

And then there's Dale Patrick Wolicki, Architectural Historian (Bay County Historical Society). I met Dale the same way I met Dick – online – bidding on old kit home catalogs. He shared numerous rare documents with me, refusing to accept any payment, saying only, "Just write a good book and get the facts right." He freely shared information he'd spent years uncovering and researching.

Thank-you also to Kit House Historian Rebecca Hunter, who has dedicated a tremendous amount of time and effort to creating a nationwide database of information about Sears houses. She, like Dale, freely shared her hard-earned lessons and became a dear friend.

A huge thank-you to Ken and Deb Holmes, of Old House Web. They encouraged me to write that first article about the Sears homes in Carlinville, Illinois and published excerpts of this book on their site, www.oldhouseweb.com, and filled my e-mail box with a steady stream of supportive and enthusiastic notes.

And thanks to my brother, Tom Fuller, who taught me how to use computers, word processing programs, printers and cameras; and then let me borrow *his* computer, *his* printer and *his* camera.

And a thank-you to my three dear daughters, Crystal, Anna and Corey, who always remembered to ask, with a smile and sincere interest, "how's the book coming, Mom?" When I was discouraged or disheartened, they were supportive and encouraging. They've been wonderful and patient and forbearing.

A heart-felt thank-you to my ex-husband, Tom Thornton, for the good things. And there were many good things.

Last but not least, a special thank-you to the people who read my book and took the time to send me a note. Those first weeks and months after my divorce - living alone for the first time in my life - were tough. Sitting on the floor of my apartment in the wee hours, I often felt overwhelmed and terrified. On those long, sleepless nights, I'd read through my "happy mail" – a collection of letters from readers who wrote to say that they loved my book.

One such letter writer said he read my book seven times in a row. Many people reported that they had caught my passion for these awesome old houses. Several readers said they loved my casual writing style and laughed out loud while reading. Others said they read the book cover to cover and could not put it down.

My favorite letter came from a recently divorced woman. She said that my book and this new joy of searching for Sears homes had helped heal her broken heart.

Sears homes and the whole of mortal experience are quite transitory in the big scheme of things, but the kindness and love that was shown to me through those dear letters will endure forever.

Thank you for taking the time to write. Thank you for the supportive, encouraging words - and the love behind the words – that helped me find my way through some very challenging times.

And, in the words of Handel, SDG.

It's recorded that Handel wrote SDG at the bottom of all of his music. SDG is an abbreviation of the Latin phrase, "Soli Deo Gloria," or "To God alone, all glory." Finding obscure information, researching, documenting, and organizing thousands of pages of materials was very challenging for me. Throughout this project, I prayed frequently and diligently, asking God to teach me and lead me. Whatever good this book imparts and whatever blessings may come are practical proofs of Her infinite love. ☺

Chapter 1

What is a Sears Catalog Home?
(And Why Are They So Intriguing?)

The home we picked out – the Hammond – had a kitchen that was 8 x 10 feet so I asked the salesman (at the Sears Modern Homes Sales Center in Chicago) if we could make the kitchen bigger. He suggested that we make the back of the house two feet wider, so the kitchen, dining room and a back bedroom would all be two feet wider.

This of course changed all the precut lumber and the original plans. They had to make a new set of blueprints and specially cut all the material.

My dad, who had accompanied us to Chicago, asked the salesman how much these changes would cost. We all held our breath while the salesman did the figuring and it seemed like it took him forever. Finally, he told us that the extra square footage would cost an additional $67. We went with the extra two feet.

> *Reminiscence of Joseph Origer*
> *Sears Modern Home "The Hammond"*

A few months ago, I was sitting at my computer in the wee hours, bidding online for a rare Sears Modern Homes catalog. I'd been buying these old catalogs for about five years now, but I'd never seen this one before. In the last seconds of the auction, I was outbid. This small, thin 95-year-old catalog – once offered for *free* to interested customers – sold for $450. *(By comparison – the cheapest kit home in that catalog was Modern Home #142 which sold for $495*!)

Throughout the country, interest in Sears homes continues to grow.

In Battleground, Indiana (near West Lafayette), a Sears Modern Home was recently re-created as part of a museum exhibit that offers an interpretive display of a working farm. To build the Sears "Hillrose," an American Foursquare, architects intently studied old Sears catalogs, working to recapture and re-create a mail order house that was first offered in the 1910s.

On August 12, 2003, *The Sun Sentinel*, a South Florida newspaper, reported that a local architect was making arrangements to move a 1930s Sears home to save it from demolition. The article stated that the cost to relocate the three bedroom Cape Cod would be about $100,000.

In the historic community of Carlinville, Illinois, the local chamber of commerce has created an entire

NINE ROOMS AND BATH

Honor Bilt

The Hillrose
No. 3015 "Already Cut" and Fitted.
$3,141⁰⁰

This house can be built with the rooms reversed. See page 3.

At the price quoted we will furnish all of the material to build this nine-room house, consisting of lumber, lath, Oriental Slate Surfaced Shingles, mill work, porch ceiling, siding, flooring, finishing lumber, console, china closet, medicine case, building paper, eaves trough, down spout, sash weights, hardware and painting material. We guarantee enough material to build this house. Price does not include cement, brick or plaster.

Can be BUILT COMPLETE with high grade hot water heating plant, plumbing, electric wiring and lighting fixtures, including ALL material and ALL labor, for $6,880.00.

See Description of "Honor Bilt" Houses on Page 7.

FIRST FLOOR PLAN.

SHED — KITCHEN 12'0"X12'0" — PORCH
PANTRY 13'4"X3'9" — WASH RM. 10'8"X5'0" — CHINA
BED ROOM 13'6"X11'6" — DINING ROOM 18'0"X11'4"
CLO.
LIBRARY 13'6"X11'6" — LIVING RM. 15'0"X15'0"
PORCH 26'0"X10'0"
30'0" / 46'0"

THIS modern country residence was awarded first prize in a contest participated in by one hundred of our country customers.

First Floor A beautiful massive door leads into the living room in which we provide a console with a large mirror. A pair of French doors lead from the living room into the library. Sliding doors lead to the dining room from the living room. A convenient china closet, that is often used as a serving cupboard, connects with the pantry, the dining room side having a glass door. The pantry is large and is easily reached from dining room or kitchen. Adjoining the dining room is a large bedroom. Workmen entering this house from the rear porch pass into the washroom, which is connected by a door with the dining room. Another desirable feature is the shed to the left of the kitchen, also outside stairs leading to the basement, which is made of cement. The main stairway to the second floor starts from the living room. The kitchen has maple flooring. Rooms are 9 ft. high.

Second Floor On this floor are four bedrooms, a hall and bathroom. All rooms have closets. The two front bedrooms are lighted by four windows each and the two rear bedrooms by two windows each, fresh air in all rooms being obtained from two sides so that ventilation is perfect. The bathroom has maple flooring. Rooms on this floor are 8 feet 2 inches high.

Basement Basement well lighted under the entire house, 7 feet from floor to joists with concrete floor. We furnish our best "Quality Guaranteed" mill work, shown on pages 118 and 119. Interior doors are five-cross panel, with trim and flooring to match, all yellow pine, in beautiful grain and color. Windows are made of clear California white pine, with good quality glass set in with best grade of putty. Porches have fir edge grain flooring.
Paint for three coats outside, your choice of color. Varnish and wood filler for two coats inside for doors and trim. Chicago Design hardware, see page 120.
Built on a concrete foundation. No. 1 yellow pine frame construction with narrow bevel clear cypress siding.

SECOND FLOOR PLAN.

ROOF
BED ROOM 13'6"X8'0" — BED ROOM 12'8"X8'0"
DOWN — HALL 9'6"X6'6" — BATH 9'0"X6'4"
BED ROOM 13'6"X11'6" — BED ROOM 12'8"X11'6"
ROOF

OPTIONS

Sheet Plaster and Plaster Finish to take the place of wood lath, $251.00 extra. See page 114.
Clear Red Oak for Floors, Trim and Doors in the living room, dining room and library, $170.00 extra.
Storm Doors and Windows, $133.00 extra.
Screen Doors and Windows, black wire, $64.00 extra; galvanized wire, $68.00 extra.
This house can be built on a lot 40 feet wide.
For prices of Plumbing, Heating, Wiring, Electric Fixtures and Shades, see page 115.

Built at Dixon, Ohio, Grand Chain, Ill., Houghton, N. Y., Antwerp, Ohio.

Our Guarantee Protects You—Order Your House From This Book
Price Includes Plans and Specifications.

"The Hillrose" has been re-created and built in Battleground, Indiana (near West Lafayette) as part of an interpretive display of a working farm. The first floor of Indiana's newest Hillrose matches the floor plan above (as pictured in the 1922 Sears Modern Homes catalog). The second floor has a different layout (than above) and is used as administrative offices.

tourism event around that town's "Standard Addition," a collection of 152 Sears homes that fill 12 blocks. Their annual Christmas festival draws thousands of tourists from hundreds of miles.

On September 13, 2001, *The Washington Times* carried an article about Sears homes entitled, "Bygone bungalows by the book," which reported that a modest Sears home in Chevy Chase recently sold for $816,000.

In my part of the country (Southwestern Illinois), Sears homes are plentiful and sell for about $50,000 - $85,000. Hopefully, these prices will increase as folks become more aware of these architectural treasures.

But let's back up a bit. You may be wondering, what is a Sears catalog home?

Put simply: It is a kit home purchased out of a Sears mail order catalog.

In the early 1900s, you could order just about anything from a Sears catalog: Plows, obesity powders, electric belts (the 1900s Viagra cure), sewing machines, cook stoves and complete houses.

In 1895, Sears Roebuck and Company issued its first building materials catalog and began selling lumber, hardware and millwork and other building materials, in addition to the tens of thousands of items already offered in their general merchandise mail order catalog.

In 1908, a headline appeared on page 594 of their general merchandise catalog which read, "*$100 set of building plans free. Let us be your architect without cost to you.*"

Customers were invited to write in and ask for a copy of Sears new "*Book of Modern Homes and Building Plans*," which featured house plans and building materials.

That first Modern Homes catalog was issued in 1908 and offered more than 40 different house designs, ranging in price from $495 to $4115. (*As of this writing, seven different editions of the 1908 Sears Modern Homes catalog have been found.*) In addition to the kit homes, Sears offered plans and building materials for a do-it-yourself kit schoolhouse! Price - $11,500

Sears' timing was perfect. In 1900, only 8000 cars were on America's roads. Eight years later (1908), the "Model T" was introduced. By 1910, 460,000 automobiles were registered and licensed. People were heading to the suburbs and Sears had just the house for them.

After receiving the Modern Homes catalog and selecting a house design, buyers were asked to send in $1 and by return mail, they'd receive a Bill of Materials List and full blueprints. When the buyer placed the actual order for the home-building materials, the $1 would be credited toward their purchase.

Let's assume that, after a careful study of the Modern Homes catalog, you chose to purchase Modern Home #111, known in later years as *The Chelsea*.

A few weeks after the order was placed, two boxcars containing 30,000 pieces of house would arrive at a nearby train depot. If you purchased an "Already-cut and fitted home" (first offered in 1914), the framing members – joists, rafters and studs - were precut and ready to be nailed into place. Each piece of lumber was stamped with a letter and numbers to facilitate assembly.

YOU CAN BUILD THIS ELEGANT CONCRETE AND FRAME CONSTRUCTION NINE=ROOM $4,000.00 HOUSE For $2,135⁰⁰

By Using Our Plans, Specifications and Bill of Materials Which We Will Send You For a Temporary Deposit of $1.00 and Which We Apply as Cash on Your Order For Mill Work, Making the Plans Cost You Nothing, as Explained on Page 2.

MODERN HOME No. III

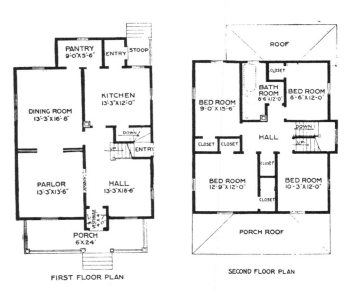

Modern Homes #111 (The Chelsea) as pictured in the 1908 Sears Modern Homes catalog. Sears estimated that a builder would charge $450 to assemble these 30,000 pieces. Also pictured: The 1908 Sears Modern Homes catalog.

A 75-page leather-bound instruction book, with the homeowner's name embossed in gold on the cover, gave precise directions on the proper placement of those 30,000 pieces of house. The book offered this somber (and probably wise) warning: *"Do not take anyone's advice as to how this building should be assembled."*

In 1908, Sears estimated that a carpenter would charge $450.00 to erect your spacious two-story foursquare, with its hipped roof and a lone shed dormer in the attic. However, Sears also promised that a man with an elementary understanding of construction techniques would be able to assemble the house.

According to their calculations, a painter would want $34.50 to paint the two-story house. The plasterer's bill would be around $200, they figured, which included nailing up 840 square yards of wooden lath and applying three coats of plaster.

Masonry (block, brick, cement) and plaster were not included in the kit, but the Bill of Materials List advised that 1300 cement blocks would be needed for the basement walls and foundation.

The salutary effects of living in a modern home were extolled throughout the pages of the Sears catalogs. Beyond the financial freedom and comfort in old age that owning a Sears home would surely bring, Sears promised that their modern homes would improve the health, morals and well-being of its occupants.

The term "Modern Home" was part of the vernacular in the early 1900s. It was a descriptive term indicating that a house had modern amenities (that we take for granted today), such as a primitive, centralized heating system, electricity and indoor plumbing. In some cases, the houses were more modern than the communities in which they were built.

Electricity and municipal water systems were not available in every locale where Sears homes were sold. To meet this need, Sears offered bathroom-less houses well into the 1920s. And for about $30, you could always purchase a dandy outhouse. This also explains, in part, why Sears sold heating, electrical and plumbing equipment separately, and not as part of the kit.

Sears began offering mortgage loans for their houses in 1911. Easy payment plans made homebuying attainable for the masses and qualifying for a Sears home mortgage was about as difficult as falling off a log. A 1920s Sears mortgage application asked a few simple questions about the house and lot, but only asked *one* financial question: "What is your vocation?" If you could answer that question, you qualified for a mortgage.

World War I, the war to end all wars, ended in 1918 and soldiers returning home found a severe housing shortage. Housing analysts estimated that 1-2 million homes were needed immediately. The constant flood of immigrants pouring in through Ellis Island also exacerbated the housing shortage.

At a time when skilled labor and quality lumber (both of which were needed to build homes),were in short supply, Sears was ready and waiting with their Sears Modern Homes catalog. A kit home, which contained everything you needed to build a house, solved the problem of lumber shortages. Precut lumber obviated the need for skilled carpentry. (That's assuming, of course, that the buyer had an "elementary understanding of construction techniques.")

The sale of Sears Modern Homes skyrocketed in the 1920s. The Sears Modern Homes catalogs of the early 1920s were the largest, peaking at 144 pages, with each catalog offering more than 90 different house designs, in addition to garages, outhouses and chicken coops.

The Greatest Building Proposition!

4. EASY PAYMENT PLAN

If you own a good, well located building lot free and clear from debt, and have some cash on hand, you can buy from Sears, Roebuck and Co. an "HONOR BILT" Modern Home, consisting of Lumber, Lath, Mill Work, Sash Weights, Hardware, Nails, Paint, Building Paper, Eaves Trough, Down Spout and Roofing Material, Plumbing Goods, Heating Plant and Lighting Fixtures, on easy payment terms, and in some instances we will advance part of the cash for labor and material, such as brick, lime and cement, which we do not furnish.

A small payment each month as you would pay rent makes you the owner of a good home in a few years. Interest charges 6 per cent per year. Your interest becomes less each time you make a payment.

THIS IS THE WAY OUR MONTHLY EASY PAYMENT PLAN WORKS OUT:

Suppose you want to own a house to cost $4,500.00 complete, not including lot, and pay for it in five years.
1. Cost of building lot..$ 500.00
2. Cost of building material and freight charges......................$2,500.00
3. Cost of labor and masonry material................................2,000.00
   Cost of house (built complete).....................................4,500.00
   Cost of lot and house completed...................................$5,000.00
Here is what Sears, Roebuck and Co. will do in this case:
1. Ship the material according to our monthly payment plan...........$2,500.00
2. Advance you cash to help you pay for the construction of the building.....500.00
                                                          Total........$3,000.00
This means that if you own a lot costing $500.00 free from debt, and have $1,500.00 in cash, you can put up a $4,500.00 house with our assistance and pay us back a little each month, about equal to your rent.

Here is what would be required of you in this case:
1. Show clear title for building lot costing $500.00. (See explanation below.)
2. Send us with your order a payment of $75.00, which is 2½ per cent of $3,000.00, the amount due us for material and cash advanced. This is the additional charge we make to cover the expense of handling the transaction and compensate us for expenses we do not have in connection with our cash with order business.
3. Make small payment of $30.00 or more including interest each month on $3,000.00 due us as shown above. You may pay more than your regular monthly payment whenever you desire or even take up the loan in full before it is due.
4. Install plumbing including bathtub, closet and lavatory if you select an "Honor Bilt" Modern Home in which a bathroom is provided for in our plans. If there is no sewerage system near your lot the plumbing can be connected to a cesspool or septic tank.

Explanation: The above is just an example to give you an idea of our LIBERAL EASY PAYMENT PLAN. It is not necessary that your lot cost exactly $500.00. It may cost more. Likewise, it is not necessary that your labor and masonry material cost exactly $2,000.00. This may be more or less, depending upon the conditions in your locality. If you feel that you can comply with our few simple requirements, just **FILL IN THIS INFORMATION BLANK** and we will be glad to give you figures for your particular case **WITHOUT OBLIGATION** on your part.

EASY PAYMENT PLAN INFORMATION BLANK

1. Which of our Modern Homes do you like best?............................Price, $...............
2. Shall we include heating, plumbing, lighting or Goodwall sheet plaster? Check items wanted.

HEATING   **LIGHTING**
☐ Hot Water.   To burn Hard Coal ☐   ☐ Electric Fixtures   ☐ Goodwall Sheet Plaster.
☐ Steam.   or Soft Coal. ☐   ☐ Plumbing.
☐ Warm Air Furnace.

3. Do you own the lot or land on which you intend to build?...............What size?........x.........

4. How much did it cost? $...............Is it free and clear of debt?...............

5. How much cash have you   How much can you
   to put in the deal? $...............   pay each month? $...............

6. What is your occupation?...............

7. About when do you expect to start building?...............

Your Name...............

Postoffice...............State...............

Rural Route...........Box No...........Street and No...............

SEARS, ROEBUCK AND CO., CHICAGO-PHILADELPHIA
128   2d Ed

The financial application for a Sears mortgage was pretty simple and asked only one question about personal income: "What is your occupation?" (1924 catalog)

According to *Catalogs and Counters, A History of Sears, Roebuck and Company*, the sales of Sears homes crested in 1929. That year, sales volume hit $12,050,000. In 1930, that number slid down to $10,658,000 and in 1931, it dropped to $8.4 million.

As the economic waves of the Great Depression fanned out further and faster, sales of Sears Modern Homes continued to plummet.

By 1931, Sears had sold 57,000 of these "Modern Homes" throughout the country. And in 1932, the Sears Modern Homes department began operating at loss, for the first time since 1912. The company's annual report stated that sales of their Modern Homes had dropped 40% in one year. For the next few years, there would be stops and starts, but the losses of 1932 marked the beginning of the end.

Two years later, in 1934, Sears' annual report to stockholders stated that the Modern Homes department had been closed. The report also stated that sales for 1933 were a meager $3.6 million. (Source: *Catalogs and Counters, A History of Sears, Roebuck and Company.*)

In 1934, Sears liquidated more than $11 million of their home mortgages. At a time when the average Sears house cost well under $3,000 (and mortgages were typically a fraction of that amount), this was a staggering sum. Foreclosing on – and evicting – Sears' best customers from their own homes became a public relations nightmare.

The next year, in 1935, the Modern Homes department was reopened, but the days of Sears "Easy Payment" home mortgages were over.

Also in 1935, Sears seriously considered entering into a partnership with General Houses, Incorporated, based in Chicago. General Houses, Inc. specialized in steel, prefabricated, easy to assemble houses. The low-priced, non-traditional, futuristic houses that General Houses, Inc. would build for Sears were all steel and had flat roofs. The prefab steel housing craze that swept the country in the mid-30s turned out to be a flash in the pan. Sears' relationship with General Houses was over before it ever really began. By 1936, that partnership was officially dissolved because, as one national magazine quipped, "the air temperature inside and outside of a 'General House' is pretty much the same."

An era in housing comes to an end.

In the 1920s, the first ten pages of Sears Modern Homes catalogs were filled with pictures and promises, proudly extolling the multitudinous virtues of living in a Sears home. By 1940, the bold promises had disappeared. The 1940 Modern Homes catalog contained two pages of subdued assurances, informing buyers that Sears homes were a sound value and met FHA guidelines. It had only 53 pages and 38 house designs, many of which looked remarkably similar to one another.

Prices were no longer listed. An enclosed letter stated that, due to differences in regional economies, buyers should write and ask for a quote on the cost to erect a modern home in their locale.

$1 Brings You a Complete Set Of Any of Our Building Plans WORTH $100.00

Not a charge for the plans but just a temporary deposit for our protection.

We will apply this $1.00 as cash on any order you send us for Mill Work or Building Material amounting to $10.00 or more; thus our valuable Plans (Blue Prints), Specifications and complete Bill of Materials for any house illustrated in this book

≡ COST YOU NOTHING ≡

Write us at once for the plans of the house that suits you. After carefully studying the perspective views, that is, the exterior views of the finished houses and reduced illustrations of the floor plans as shown in the various pages of this book, select the house you would like to know all about, then take the order blank which comes with this book, or if at any time you have no order blank, use any plain sheet of paper, write down the number of the house which you will find right below the illustration of the finished house, plainly write your name and address, enclose $1.00, in the form of an express or postoffice money order, bank draft or the currency in a registered letter, and mail the letter to us. Upon receiving it we will at once send you the **complete set of building plans (blue prints), specifications and bill of materials, together with our mill work certificate for $1.00, as shown below.** We will accept this certificate as cash for one dollar ($1.00) on any order you send us for mill work or building material amounting to ten dollars ($10.00) or more. Thus the plans will cost you nothing whatever.

THERE IS NO OTHER CONDITION WHATEVER ATTACHED TO THIS OFFER.

No.   CHICAGO, ILL._____190__   ONE DOLLAR

SEARS, ROEBUCK MILL WORK CERTIFICATE AND COMPANY

THIS IS TO CERTIFY that we have received from
Mr._____ P. O._____ State_____
R. F D No. or Box No._____ Invoice No._____ ONE DOLLAR in exchange for on complete set of
building plans, specifications and bill of materials for Modern Home No._____

This Certificate, if accompanied by an order for mill work or building material, such as windows, doors, moulding, etc., amounting to ten dollars ($10.00) or more, will be accepted by us as one dollar ($1.00) in cash.
This Mill Work Certificate is not transferable and good only to the person whose name is written hereon and not good if altered or defaced in any way.

SEARS, ROEBUCK & CO.,
By *Richard W Sears* Pres.

READ OTHER SIDE

This is a copy of the Mill Work Certificate we send you at the same time we mail you the plans you order. Be sure to enclose $1.00 with your order for these plans in accordance with our offer on this page. We do not accept these plans back for exchange or for refund of $1.00 in cash. We give you credit for the $1.00 only according to the terms of the offer on this page.

Why We are Compelled to Ask a Temporary Deposit of $1.00

Our building plans are immensely popular and we receive thousands of requests for them day by day. They are very valuable and we want to place them in the hands of only those who intend to build. We would gladly have offered them without condition whatever, but unfortunately there are great numbers of curiosity seekers, youths and other people who would order these valuable plans (blue prints), specifications and complete bill of materials, with no intention of using them for building purposes, if we should furnish them without any conditions whatever. If we did not require a deposit of $1.00 as evidence of good faith, we would therefore be put to a great deal of unnecessary expense, as you can plainly see. As a protection to ourselves, therefore, we must require $1.00 deposit with each order for plans. Remember, the $1.00 is not a charge for the plans but merely a temporary deposit. When we send you the plans, we also send you a certificate for $1.00 which we consider as cash when you send it to apply on any order for mill work or building material amounting to $10.00 or more. **Thus the plans cost you nothing whatever.**

SELECT THE HOUSE THAT SUITS YOU; give the number of the house, enclose $1.00 as above described, and we will at once send you a complete set of plans (blue prints), specifications and full itemized typewritten bill of materials, together with our $1.00 Mill Work Certificate for your $1.00 deposit. Send this certificate with any order for mill work or building material amounting to not less than $10.00 and we will count it as $1.00 cash. These are the only terms on which we furnish plans.

After selecting a house design from the Modern Homes catalog, buyers were asked to send in $1 and by return mail they'd receive a Bill of Materials List and full blueprints. When the buyer placed an order for the house, the $1 would be credited toward the purchase. (1908 catalog)

Between 1908 - 1940, Sears sold *about* 75,000* homes by mail order in all 48 states. They offered about 370** different styles of homes during those 32 years. Unfortunately, sometime after the Sears Modern Homes department closed, their sales records, promotional information, catalogs and other ephemera were destroyed.

Future generations would rediscover these Sears homes that our parents and grandparents bought and built. And we'd fall in love with them all over again.

---

* Sears sold about 75,000 homes during their 32 years in the home business, *not* 100,000 as is frequently (mis)quoted in the media.

** *"Houses by Mail: A Guide To Houses from Sears, Roebuck and Company,"* by Katherine Cole Stevenson and H. Ward Jandl is a useful guide for identifying the different styles of houses that Sears offered. *"Houses by Mail"* lists 447 different designs. My estimate is *approximately* 370 different designs, largely because of different methods of tabulating. More on that later.

Chapter 2

"Hang Your Saw On a Nail All Day"
Sears Homes and Their Unique Place in American Architecture

My dad used to joke about our little Puritan (Sears house). He said the postman brought it.

When my mother died in 1918 (in the flu epidemic), she left behind five children, ages 10, 8, 6, 4 and an 18-month old toddler. At the time, we were living in a poor area – kind of a slum – and to get us out of that, Dad decided to get us into a home of our own in a different neighborhood. In 1924, we moved into our new home.

I know that if it had not been for Sears and their kit homes, my dad could never have afforded to have a home of his own. It was so good for us to have that little home. Everything in it was shiny and bright and clean.

Reminiscence of Ruth Sward
Sears Modern Home "The Puritan"

Richard W. Sears' decision to sell homes through his mail order catalog was a stroke of genius on several levels. It was an idea whose time had come.

Sears had a distinct and important advantage over their primary competitor in kit homes - Aladdin - which started their business in Bay City, Michigan in 1906. One out of every four Americans were *already* faithfully perusing Sears' mail order catalogs in 1908 when Sears offered their first "*Book of Modern Homes and Building Plans.*" Sears' 1908 general merchandise catalog stated that "one-half of all the families in the United States - outside of the larger cities - have sent to us for goods."

In the early 1900s, parents often taught children how to read using the Sears, Roebuck catalog and the family Bible. In some rural homes, those were the only two books in the household.

Owning a home was everyone's dream at the turn of the century, but financially, that dream was out of reach for many young families. Sears "homes through mail order" tapped right into the heart of that innate desire for homeownership and concurrently, lowered the cost of construction with mass production, while maintaining excellent quality.

The kit home that Sears offered included house plans (blueprints), hardware (door knobs, locks, hinges), millwork (doors, windows, moldings), building materials (paint, putty, rain gutters, nails, roofing) and lumber (framing lumber, flooring and siding). If desired, you could purchase your lumber *locally* instead of ordering it from Sears. This was an option for Sears homebuyers throughout the 32-year history of the Modern Homes program and explains (in part) why some Sears homes do not have stamped lumber.

By 1914, Sears was offering "Already-cut and fitted houses" which meant the kits came with the framing lumber *precut* and ready to be nailed into place. An advertisement on the back cover of the 1918 Modern Homes catalog went so far as to say that no sawing was needed to build a precut Sears home and that you could "hang your saw on a nail all day." While this was an overstatement, the fact is, precut lumber in kit homes saved the average do-it-yourself homebuilder inestimable hours of measuring and sawing (and the inevitable heartache of mistakes and mis-cut lumber).

The 1916 Modern Homes catalog promised that their "Already-cut and fitted" homes could be ordered, erected and ready for occupancy in less than 90 days. One homebuilder wrote back to Sears and reported, "It took us just six days to get the house ready for the plaster," adding, "My carpenter's bill was only $168 for this big house."

In the 1922 catalog, under the heading, "The Most Difficult Job Made Easy" was this statement: "Every piece cut and fitted ready for its place. You only need a hammer and nails to put up the framework of your house."

To fully appreciate the value of precut lumber, you have to go back in time to the early 1900s. Electricity was in its infancy. In some cities, electricity was turned off each night at 11 p.m. for six hours of repairs and maintenance! In 1910, only 10% of homes had electricity. By 1930, that number had jumped to 70%. (Source: *Electrifying America: Social Meanings of a New Technology*, David E. Nye.) As late as December 1917, *American Carpenter and Builder Magazine* was still describing electric lights as a <u>luxury</u> that a builder should incorporate into a modern city home.

To cut a piece of lumber with a handsaw required time, strength and a degree of expertise (for a good square cut). Electric saws and the heavy duty wiring to handle the amperage draw were a thing of the future. In fact, the electric handsaw (a portable circular saw) wasn't widely available until 1925. A fascinating news item in the February 1925 *American Carpenter and Builder* heralded the "new invention" with this commentary: "The portable circular saw does the sawing for 15 carpenters."

Imagine someone pressing a handsaw into your hands and pointing you toward 620 pieces of framing lumber! (The lumber list for Modern Home #111 included 380 2 x 4s and 240 2 x 6s.) The 1929 Gordon Van Tine catalog (another kit home company), stated "by actual count, there are 2,940 handsaw cuts made in preparing the lumber for the framing of an average five room bungalow." Note – that is not strokes, but actual *cuts*!

In 1921, Sears conducted an "experiment' building two Rodessas (small frame homes) side by side at the site of the Sears mill in Cairo, Illinois. One house was erected using Sears' precut lumber. The second house was built using traditional construction techniques; no precut lumber. The precut house was fully assembled in 352 carpenter hours and the non-precut home was completed in 583 carpenter hours.

The 1929 Sears Modern Homes catalog featured a blow-by-blow description of the "race" to build the little Rodessas:

Hand saw is badly beaten: No carpenters ever worked harder or faster but to no avail. Every hour shows them further behind. Here at 509 hours they have accomplished what took only 281 hours the modern "Honor Bilt" way.

And further on:

The old ordinary hand-saw method of construction loses the race by 231 hours. See the pile of wasted lumber!

For the next ten years, Sears promoted this contest in the front pages of their catalogs as unquestionable proof that Sears precut kit homes were an exceptional value in construction. What they <u>didn't</u> emphasize was that a full-time carpenter or builder would have utilized steam engines (or in later years electric table saws) at the construction site. Nonetheless, it proved a powerful point: Precut lumber was well worth the extra cost for the amateur homebuilder.

An interesting aside: I've visited Cairo several times and was surprised to find several Rodessas – sometimes in pairs – throughout the city. Rodessas were popular, but not <u>that</u> popular. After pondering this for a bit, it hit me. Sears was apparently <u>practicing</u> building these Rodessas in anticipation of this 1921 experiment out at the mill.

The introduction of Sears' "Easy Pay" mortgages and the super-easy loan qualification process made homeownership affordable and attainable for the masses. Based on the testimonials in the back pages of the Modern Home catalogs, the average Sears homebuilder created a 20 – 30% equity position by building a kit home (even *after* paying the estimated carpenter's fee of $168).

The do-it-yourself factor – the idea that you could buy and build your own *Modern Home* - was solidly American. It *must* have had a special appeal for a generation that remembered Grandma's soddie on the plains or maybe spent several days at a relative's log cabin in the far west (beyond the Mississippi River). It's possible that the Midwestern men and women who built Sears kit homes in the early 1900s were raised in housing that would be considered extremely primitive by today's standards. In 1917, *American Carpenter and Builder Magazine* reported that "watertight roof, walls and floor are an essential feature of a modern city house." As a point of reference, Laura Ingalls Wilder's "*Little House*" books described life on the plains in soddies and tiny cabins in the 1870s.

Why did Sears decide to get into the kit home business?

Dick Sears' decision to sell kit homes was based in part on gut instinct as well as some primitive marketing research. Homeowners, he knew, consistently bought more merchandise than non-homeowners.

At first blush, you might be inclined to describe a non-homeowner as a "renter," but that was not the case 100 years ago. Many young families lived with their elders – their parents or even grandparents. Multi-generational housing was the norm. That's one reason why old homes have so many interior and exterior doors – compartmentalization. Plenty of doors created more privacy for all the different family members trying to get along under one roof.

Boarding houses were also very common 100 years ago. In either case, young families living with Mom and Dad or young marrieds living in a boarding house didn't have the space or the need for extra merchandise and furnishings. Sears knew that getting these folks into a home of their own would create new customers and boost sales.

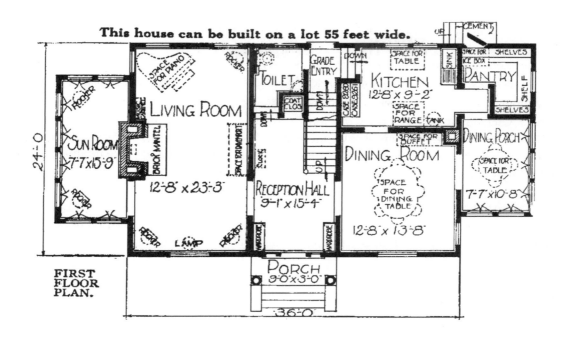

This house can be built on a lot 55 feet wide.

FIRST FLOOR PLAN.

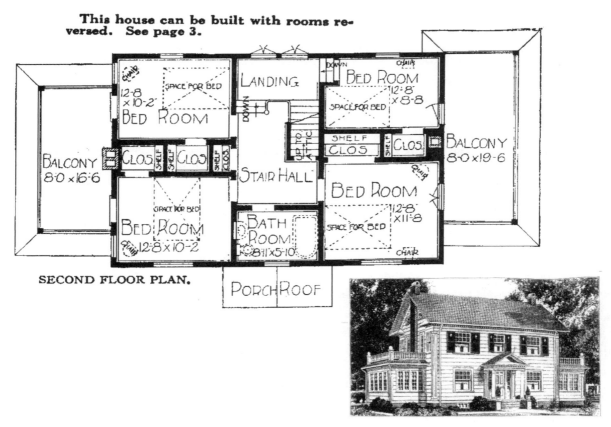

This house can be built with rooms reversed. See page 3.

SECOND FLOOR PLAN.

Look at the floor plan of "The Lexington" (a 2-story Colonial) and you'll see dotted lines, suggesting ideal placement for davenports, rockers, beds, dressers and even lamps.

By encouraging and enabling more Americans to become homeowners, he'd be *creating* a new market for the 100,000 items in his 1200-page, four-pound mail order catalog.

Look closely at the floor plans in Sears Modern Homes catalogs and you'll see itty-bitty dotted lines showing ideal placement for a graphophone (also known as a phonograph), davenport, piano, library table, beds, dressers and more.

In the late 1920s, Sears hired Miss Mayer, an interior decorator, to figure out the ideal placement for all those itty-bitty dotted lines. Part of her job was to ascertain how much furniture could be stuffed inside a four-room house with bedrooms that measured 8 x 9 feet.

The 1925 Modern Homes catalog made a hard pitch for furnishing the house with Sears' merchandise. A two-page advertisement in the middle of the catalog showed interior views of the Alhambra, a Spanish-flavored American four-square. The caption read,

> Our department of interior decorating will offer suggestions upon request just how to completely furnish The Alhambra or any other home in this book. There is no charge for this service to "Honor Bilt" customers. All the furniture, rugs, lamps, etc., illustrated above are taken from our Big General Catalog, "The Thrift Book of a Nation."

The marketing scheme was successful, as is evidenced by testimonials like this:

> I have just recently completed building one of your "Honor Bilt" Modern Homes and want to tell you how well I am satisfied. I saved over $2000 in building this house. You might also like to know that it is furnished with Sears Roebuck rugs, furniture, curtains, wall paper and fixtures. In buying my furniture from you, I saved over half. (1929 Sears Modern Homes catalog)

Avoid everything that is superfluous: Changing tastes in American architecture

The early 1900s saw dramatic changes in architectural tastes. A growing understanding of the germ theory was changing the way Americans designed and built houses. The introduction of electricity and the invention of modern cleaning devices (such as vacuum cleaners) created an almost insatiable desire to rid the house of dust and dirt and hidden germs.

The ostentatious and dust-bunny-collecting Queen Anne, with its ornate woodwork, fretwork and gingerbread fell from favor with a resounding thud.

In the book, "*Household Discoveries and Mrs. Curtis' Cook-Book*," (a popular book of the era) was this statement:

> Simplicity, harmony and durability are the keynotes of the modern tendency. The general intention seems to be to avoid everything that is superfluous; everything that has a tendency to catch and hold dust or dirt. Wooden bedsteads are being replaced by iron or brass; stuffed and upholstered furniture by articles of plain wood and leather. Bric-a-brac, flounces, valances and all other superfluous articles are much less fashionable.

It was the dawning of a new era in American ideals and opinions about home design. Alan Gowans' *"The Comfortable House: North American Suburban Architecture"* is a 214-page treatise on the dramatic shift in housing tastes between 1890-1930 and his book gives an in-depth explanation on the ideology that motivated those changes.

In the first decade of the new century, *Ladies' Home Journal* consistently featured a majority of articles centered on homeownership. The February 1911 issue of *Ladies' Home Journal* was devoted to the new housing style: Bungalows. One headline said, "The Bungalow, because of its easy housekeeping possibilities is becoming more popular every year and bungalows show what can be done with a little money wisely spent." The same issue featured these articles:

When you build a little house (common mistakes to avoid)
How I built this house for $700
The Bungalow - from $250 - $2500
What I did with an old farmhouse
Two houses built for less than $1500
What can be done with old houses
A fireproof house for less than $4000
If a woman must earn her living at home (A house planned by a woman to meet this need.)

It seems as though that the ladies were ahead of the men on this bungalow thing. Whilst *Ladies' Home Journal* was promoting bungalows, *American Carpenter and Builder* described them as "tiresome."

Craftsman houses and odd bungalows will have their day. People may like them now, but it is an extreme type and will become tiresome in course of time. The uncompromising squareness in the craftsman style, with its small wall space does not permit of much artistic decoration (June 1913).

By the 1910s, bungalows and other small homes were undeniably the future and Victorian homes now seemed like architectural dinosaurs; old, troublesome, oversized, cluttered and stuffy. Victorian societal rituals, such as "calling cards" had necessitated the oversized reception hall (foyer) and now the ritual ceased and the huge foyer disappeared from new construction. ("Calling cards" were like business cards, but bore only the bearer's name and address. It was the Victorian equivalent of leaving someone a voice-mail message. It was quite gauche to not reply when someone "called on you at home" – visited you – and left their calling card.)

Front parlors gave way to living rooms, and dining rooms were no longer separate, distinct rooms. In the new bungalow, only a colonnade or archway separated the living and dining room. Kitchens were made smaller and more efficient with an increased emphasis on organization. Walk-in pantries were replaced with cupboards. Breakfast nooks – where the family could enjoy simple meals without the formality of the dining room – became very popular.

"Everyman's House" by Caroline Bartlett Crane told the story of a tiny, but extremely well-designed house built in Kalamazoo, Michigan in the early 1920s. Architects and builders interviewed and surveyed women, asking how *they* thought a home should be organized. The kitchen in this house was 9 x 10 feet and was the "hub" of the house.

Crane stated, "Three-meals-a-day remains woman's most exacting job. They tie her to the stove and the clock, at the hub of the house and of the household circle. Between these fixed engagements she makes brief excursions – duty calls - to the front door, the back door, the furnace and the telephone. The daily round, we call it! This is her life" (p. 58). *Author's note: Ugh.*

Younger families had new ideas about housing and a modest home could be a "first home" instead of the only home. This new generation of homeowners understood that the first home could provide a financial stepping stone to a better house in the years ahead.

In 20 years, American architecture had gone from large and fancy to compact and simple.

According to *"Victorian America; Transformations in Everyday Life"* (Thomas J. Schlereth), 500 new subdivisions opened in the Los Angeles area between 1903-1914, featuring bungalows as the primary housing style.

In 1915, *American Carpenter and Builder* incredulously reported that an entire community in Gary, Indiana had been created with this building restriction: Bungalows only! It went on to say, "When the lots are all improved (with houses on each lot), there will be approximately four miles of Bungalows."

Americans wanted compact, simple, affordable homes and they welcomed the opportunity to build their own small comfortable home on the lot of their choice.

Again, with perfect timing, the marketing genius of Sears, Roebuck and Company had discerned the need of the American people and with the introduction of Sears Modern Homes, Richard Sears met that need in a new, modern way.

1908 was a landmark year for Sears Roebuck and Company for other reasons, as well. Richard W. Sears, the former railway station clerk from Redwood Falls, Minnesota, retired on November 1, 1908.

After leaving his position as President of Sears Roebuck, he remained with the company as Chairman of the Board, but never attended any meetings. For the next few years, he took care of his sick wife, traveling and trying to find the right combination of climate and medicine that might bring relief from her chronic ailments. Richard Warren Sears died in 1914 at age 50. (For more information on Richard W. Sears, see Chapter Three.)

In 1903, *Ladies' Home Journal* solicited stories from people who had overcome financial adversities and bought or built their own house on tiny incomes. Several of these stories were published each month in a continuing series in the *Journal*.

Some stories had headings such as, "How a wife did it herself," and "Bought her own home with nine children and $800 a year income." These stories paint a vivid word picture of how much toil and sacrifice pre-World War I families endured to have a home of their own.

The following story appeared in the October 1903 *Ladies' Home Journal* and was the winning entry for the magazine's series, "How some families have saved for their own homes."

It's a wonderful story that really demonstrates the sacrifice involved in purchasing a home at the turn of the last century. The wages mentioned in this piece lend some additional insight to the dollar values of the day, and help explain the low prices of homes offered in the Sears catalogs.

We planted a garden and my husband worked it himself. He [arose] every morning at about four and worked [in the garden] until time to go to the shop - about two hours. We'd sell the vegetables at market, keeping only a minimum for ourselves.

We could not afford to buy a sewing machine, so I rented an old-fashioned hand machine at $3 a year and had to turn the wheel with one hand and guide the work with the other. I would sew every night (taking in work for hire) never retiring earlier than one o'clock. I got up at five every morning.

So much work came to me that [many] nights, I would sit up until daybreak, snatch an hour's nap, then get up to cook breakfast My husband would get up when I retired, work his garden, split the wood, build a fire in the kitchen stove, bring in enough water for the day (we had no well) and then set the coffee pot to boil. I did the washing and ironing and made my own soap.

Three years thus rolled away. My husband's wages went up to $8 a week but we still practiced the most rigid economy and cut off some of our necessities. Our cow had a calf and when he was one year old, we killed him and sold the meat.

To clothe my little boy, I took my husband's cast-off clothing, turned it wrong side out and cut out the best portions, making the boy's clothes.

At the end of seven years, my husband's wages had increased to $9 a week. After seven years of struggle and extreme economy, toil and labor, today finds us with a comfortable home, horses and cows.

As for myself, before my marriage I never knew the value of money as I was the petted daughter of a rich man.

Chapter 3

The Amazing Mr. Sears:
A Brief Look at The Handsome Genius and His Store

Don't be afraid you will make a mistake (on your order). We receive hundreds of orders every day from young and old who never before sent away for goods. Tell us what you want in your own way, written in any language. We have translators to read all languages.

1908 Sears Roebuck catalog

Richard Warren Sears is one of my favorite characters in American history. He was a marketing genius, a fascinating entrepreneur and a true family man. Throughout his life, he maintained a deep and profound devotion to his family.

Sears' father was a farmer and a blacksmith. When Sears was about 16 years old, his father died and Richard Warren Sears went to work to support the family.

In the mid-1880s, whilst working as a railway station agent in Redwood Falls, Minnesota, Sears paid $50 for a shipment of watches that arrived at the train station and had been refused by a local merchant. Selling them to other railway agents and passengers, Sears turned $50 worth of watches into $5000 in a few months.

His timing could not possibly have been any better.

With the advent of the steam locomotive and reliable passenger rail service, people could now travel hundreds of miles each day, but there was a problem with all this expeditious movement. In the early 1880s, the United States had 300 different time zones.

Many rural communities relied on "sun-time." If you wanted to know what time it was, you gazed upwards at the sky. Or, if you were traveling westward, you deducted one minute for every 12 miles. (Hope you're good at ciphering!) Travelers heading east made the opposite calculations.

In November 1883, railway companies established four time zones to help manage and standardize the complex train schedules. As folks adapted to the new time zones, watches became a hot commodity.

In 1886, 23-year-old Sears invested his $5000 cash profit into a new watch business and called it the "R. W. Sears Watch Company." He advertised his watches in regional newspapers and in a short time, he moved the business from Minneapolis to Chicago.

Occasionally the watches came back needing repairs or adjustments, so in 1887, Sears decided to hire someone to help him in this new venture. A young watch repairman from Hammond, Indiana responded to

Sears' help wanted ad and was hired immediately. The watch repairman's name was Alvah Curtis Roebuck. Richard Sears and Alvah Roebuck became good friends and eventually became partners in the business venture which they named, "Sears Roebuck and Company."

Around 1891, Sears and Roebuck published their first mail order catalog, offering jewelry and watches within its 52 pages. By 1893, the little watch and jewelry catalog had grown to 196 pages and offered a variety of items, including sewing machines, shoes, saddles and more. One year later, another 300 pages were added, creating a 507-page mail order catalog.

In 1895, Alvah Roebuck decided he wanted out. The 31-year old watch repairman felt that his physical health was collapsing under the strain of this new enterprise. The business was growing too fast and the enormous burden of debt combined with Sears' wild ways of doing business were too much for mild-mannered, methodical Alvah. He asked Sears to buy his one-third interest in the company for $25,000.

Of course, Sears didn't have that kind of cash on hand, so he offered Chicago businessmen Aaron Nusbaum and Julius Rosenwald (Nusbaum's brother-in-law) a one-half interest in the company. The price - $75,000, or $37,500 each. Six years later, in 1901, Rosenwald and Sears decided to buy out Nusbaum and offered him $1 million for his share of the business. Nusbaum refused and asked for $1.25 million, which he received. (Pretty tidy profit for six years!)

Following a nationwide depression in 1907, Rosenwald and Sears were at loggerheads on the best course of action to weather the economic storm. This disagreement seemed to highlight their radically different methods of doing business.

On November 1, 1908, 44-year-old Richard W. Sears emerged from a terse closed-door meeting with Rosenwald and announced that he would resign as President from his own company. Sears' reason for retiring: He "didn't see the work as fun anymore." A short time later, Sears sold his stock for $10 million dollars. There was another reason for his departure. Sears wanted more time to take care of his ailing wife, who had suffered from ill health for years.

In September 1914, at the age of 50, Sears died, having turned $50 worth of pocket watches into a multi-million dollar mail order empire. His estate was valued at more than $20 million.

Awesome trivia about Sears, Roebuck and Company

Knowing that many households would have both his catalog and the Montgomery Ward catalog, Sears purposefully designed his catalog a little shorter and narrower than the Ward catalog. He knew that when the housewife was tidying up the home, the Sears catalog, being smaller, would be stacked *on top* of the Ward's catalog. (*Source*: *Mr. Sears' Catalog*, The American Experience, 1991 VHS.)

At its peak in 1915, the general merchandise catalog contained 100,000 items in 1200 pages and weighed four pounds. In 1896, annual sales were $1.2 million and by 1914 they hit $101 million. (*The Good Old Days*; *A History of American Morals and Manners as Seen Through the Sears Roebuck Catalogs.*)

Local merchants and owners of general stores were up in arms at the low prices Sears offered in his catalog and the bold promises that buyers could save money by "eliminating the middle man." Of course, the "middle man" that Sears wanted to eliminate was the owner of the general store! In more than a few towns, children were promised a free movie ticket for every Sears catalog they brought into the local store. The catalogs were then piled high and ceremoniously burned in a massive bonfire.

During World War I, the Sears Roebuck catalog was the "book" most requested by American soldiers recovering in overseas hospitals. Julius Rosenwald sailed to France in the midst of the "Great War" (WWI) with four huge wooden crates, each filled with Sears catalogs, for distribution to the "American boys lying in a hospital." (*The Good Old Days*; *A History of American Morals and Manners as Seen Through the Sears Roebuck Catalogs.*)

The book "*Sears Roebuck and Company: 100th Anniversary*" relates that a Sunday School pupil was asked "Where did the Ten Commandments come from?" and the child replied, "From the Sears, Roebuck catalog."

According to "*Sears, Roebuck, USA: The Great American Catalog Store and How It Grew*" a Sears customer wrote and asked to return several bottles of patent medicine she'd purchased from Sears, explaining that the medicine had originally been intended for her husband and he'd since passed on. The clerk who received the inquiry responded by asking the woman if she'd like to see a copy of Sears' *Tombstone Catalog*.

The famous Chicago radio station, WLS, actually began as a promotional tool for Sears. In fact, WLS stands for "World's Largest Store." The station signed on in 1924 with farm reports and weather information. Sears sold the radio station in the fall of 1928.

In the 1930s, Sears sold live baby chicks through their mail order catalogs. The chicks cost ten cents each and safe, live delivery was promised.

In November 1952, Sears announced it would sell the "Allstate" - a small car with a 100-inch wheel-base, capable of 35 mpg. The little car with a four or six cylinder engine cost $1395 - $1796. Two years later, Sears stopped selling the cars, having sold about 1500. The reason: Sears was ill-prepared to handle the problem of trade-ins.

Chapter 4

What Were Sears Homes Made of?
Amazing Facts, Interesting Details and Curiosities About Sears Homes

If you order this house from us and construct it according to our "Honor-Bilt" specifications, you will have a home in every sense of the word. We guarantee everything that goes into the construction of our "Honor-Bilt" Modern Homes to be the best of its kind. We want every (buyer) to be a satisfied customer and we aim to give him a house that will last a lifetime.

1918 Sears Modern Homes Catalog

Let's pretend that it is the fall of 1908 and about ten days ago, you mailed in an order form and $1 to Sears, Roebuck and Co., and in today's mail, you received your requested materials: Specifications and Bill of Materials List and also the blueprints for Modern Home #111. Settling into an easy chair you adjust your reading glasses and begin to peruse the paperwork.

The 10-page "List" (printed in tiny purple print on 11 x 14-inch paper) is a complete inventory of the materials that will come with your Sears kit home. You begin to feel a little overwhelmed, as you visualize yourself standing next to this mountain of lumber and doors and windows and nails and paint. You may even imagine yourself gazing at this massive pile and wondering, "where do I begin?"

According to the Specifications and Bill of Materials List, your kit home will include 25 doors and 28 windows, as well as 750 pounds of nails and 27 gallons of Seroco paint and varnish. (Seroco was an acronym for Sears Roebuck Company.) You'd also receive 400 feet of sash cord, 72 sash (window) weights (weighing a total of 460 pounds), 200 feet of galvanized gutters and 325 feet of crown moulding. There'd also be 240 balusters, 36 risers and 37 treads (for basement and primary staircase), 6 dozen coat hooks, ten pounds of wood putty and one doorbell.

In the first years of the Modern Homes department, the Bill of Materials List included a back page titled "Lumber Bill" which listed the specific quantities of framing lumber the homeowner needed to purchase at the local lumber yard. (As mentioned in Chapter Two, lumber was not always supplied by Sears and especially in the early years, framing lumber was often obtained by the *homeowner* at a local mill.)

The 1908 Bill of Materials List said the following framing lumber was needed to build Modern Home #111 (The Chelsea):

4 pcs. 6" x 6" x 7-foot posts
3 pcs. 6" x 8" x 10-foot girders
120   2" x 4" x 18-foot inside studding
130   2" x 4" x 20-foot rafters and collar beams

132   2" x 4" x 20-foot wall studding
70   2" x 6" x 16-foot ceiling joists
4   2" x 6" x 24-foot hip rafters
175   2" x 6" x 14-foot floor joists

But wait, there's more:

600   linear feet 1" x 2" bridging and strips
3000 feet 6-inch #2 D&M sheathing
3500 feet 6-inch #3 SIS roof boards and floor lining
20,000 shingles (cedar shingles for the siding and/or roof)

In 1908, Sears estimated that a carpenter would charge $450 to assemble this house and a housepainter would charge $34.50 to apply those 27 gallons of varnish and paint. In the 1920s, Sears estimated that other skilled labor would cost about $1 an hour.

About 192 cubic yards of earth would have to be excavated, at a cost (Sears estimated) of 25 cents per cubic yard, for a total of $48. In the early 1900s, basements were usually excavated using a horse-drawn scoop. Sometimes, mules were used, yoked together in pairs to pull the scoop – a large, flat-bladed shovel. And that was the *fast* way to dig out a 7-foot basement. I've received more than a few letters from the descendants of Sears homebuilders who remember helping Mom and Dad dig out their basement by *hand* – using only shovels, picks and wheelbarrows (and child labor).

Sears estimated that the average man could erect a "Modern Home" in about 90 days, in good weather. That was, of course, assuming that you did not intend to make your own cinder blocks. After all, you'd need 1300 cinder blocks for The Chelsea's basement.

In Chapter Two, I mentioned that Sears houses were a hit because their bungalows met three basic and important housing needs; They were affordable, practical and hygienic. Sears pitched one particular type of home as being *more hygienic* than the others: The house made of concrete block.

In the 1908 catalog, Sears said this about block homes:

This elegant house is constructed with 8 x 16-inch concrete blocks, a building material which is almost identical in appearance with hand finished stone and is considered even more durable. It makes a house more sanitary than the average house, is perfectly dry at all seasons of the year, cool in summer and warm in winter. Concrete construction is no longer in the experimental state. *(Author's note: How can a house built of concrete blocks be described as "elegant"?)*

But it gets even better. The catalog also states:

Not only can concrete houses be erected at one third less the cost than any other stone structure, but you can buy a Wizard concrete building block machine from Sears' (only $42.50), and make a sufficient number of blocks in spare time during the dull season of the year and thus save on the cost of building material.

The Wizard block making machine was a big hit for many years in the general merchandise catalogs.

$1,995.00 AND OUR BUILDING PLANS

WILL BUILD, PAINT AND COMPLETE, READY FOR OCCUPANCY, THIS MODERN NINE-ROOM $3,000.00 HOUSE

SEND A TEMPORARY DEPOSIT OF $1.00 AND WE WILL SEND THE PLANS, THEN APPLY YOUR $1.00 AS CASH ON YOUR ORDER FOR MILL WORK, MAKING THE PLANS COST YOU NOTHING, AS EXPLAINED ON PAGE 2.

MODERN HOME No. 52

A Few Points About This $3,000 Concrete House
WHICH WE ENABLE YOU TO BUILD COMPLETE FOR $1,995.00.

This Handsome Nine-Room Concrete residence and structure, which could not be duplicated for less than $3,000.00 if built in the old fashioned way with natural stone, can be built for $1,995.00, according to our plans and specifications which cost you nothing, as explained on page 2. This elegant house is constructed with 8x16-inch concrete blocks, a building material which is almost identical in appearance with hand finished stone and which is considered even more durable and gives better satisfaction. It makes a house that is more sanitary than the average house, is perfectly dry at all seasons of the year, cool in summer and warm in winter. Concrete construction is no longer in the experimental state. Some of the most costly and largest residences and office buildings erected during the last ten years have been made of concrete and have proven to be superior to frame or stone buildings in every respect.

Concrete Houses Can Be Erected at One-Third Less than any kind of stone structures. They can be built in less time, with much lower priced labor than other kinds of buildings. With one of our Wizard or Buckeye Concrete Building Block Machines (which are fully described and illustrated in our Special Concrete Building Block Machinery Catalogue, free on request) anyone can make a sufficient number of blocks in spare time during the dull season of the year to erect his own buildings, and thus save the cost of labor on building material. Our $1,995.00 price includes the cost of hired labor, so that if you did the work yourself in making the building blocks, you could make your building for even less.

Read on Page 2 How We Can Furnish Building Plans and specifications for any one of the many houses shown in this book. These plans are made by a corps of the best and most experienced licensed architects in this country who have carefully studied the requirements of our trade and every plan we offer is so carefully and accurately laid out that unnecessary waste of material and labor is entirely avoided. On pages 28 to 35 we illustrate in reduced size a full set of blue prints and working drawings to give you some idea of the very careful way we set everything forth. Note how carefully every detail has been worked out. It is so simple in every way that any carpenter or ordinary workman can understand.

If You Are Interested in Building, if you want to save one-third to one-half of the entire cost on your future home, read our liberal offer to you on these building plans and specifications. We fully explain there our great building plan proposition. After you have read page 2, go through this book and select the house which meets your requirements in every particular, tell us the number of the house you want to know more about, and if you will send us your order according to our simple offer on page 2, we will send you a complete set of plans and specifications, which will itemize every piece of material and give you an approximate cost for labor. In fact, we will give you all and more information than you would be able to get from an architect in your home town who would likely charge you $100.00 to $150.00 or more for his expert advice. Besides saving you the entire cost of architect's fees for plans and specifications, we save you one-third of the cost of your mill work, including windows, doors, moulding, casing, stair work, grilles, flooring, etc. We would also save you from 25 to 50 per cent on the cost of your plumbing material, your hot water or hot air furnace heating system (whatever you wish to use), your water supply outfit, paints and varnishes and building hardware. In fact, we can save you on every item which enters into the construction of your house.

We Invite Comparison. Please compare our $1,995.00 nine-room concrete house, which is illustrated on the opposite page, with houses in your locality which have cost all the way from $2,000.00 to $3,000.00, note the size of the houses, then also note that ours is a full two-story house with a large attic, compare the arrangement and size of rooms, then also make a careful comparison of the doors and windows and see if they in any way compare with those shown on this page. If still in doubt then send for the plans of this building and our Special Mill Work Catalogue and we feel sure that you will be immediately convinced beyond doubt that we can save you all we claim.

On Pages 22, 45 and 56 we show three different houses ranging in price from $705.00 to $1,995.00 and illustrate certain kinds of materials, mill work, etc., in a similar manner to those shown on this page, simply to demonstrate to you the average kind of material that goes into our houses. You will note that materials specified in our $705.00 houses are equal to what is usually specified in houses at a much higher price. The same rule holds good on every house shown in this book. If you are interested in this $1,995.00 concrete house or any other house shown on the pages of this book, don't delay but write us at once, using the enclosed order blank, plainly stating the number of house you desire to know more about, enclose a temporary deposit of $1.00, and we will send you our complete set of plans (blue prints), specifications and bill of materials by return mail, and apply the $1.00 on your order for millwork making the plans cost you nothing, as explained on page 2.

The 1908 Modern Homes catalog stated that concrete block houses were "almost identical in appearance with hand finished stone. [A concrete block] house is more sanitary than the average house." Sears featured many block houses (like this) in their early catalogs. (1908 catalog)

The text for the ad claimed "We know of several instances where one man has made a perfect block on the Wizard in one minute's time." Further on, the ad's text stated that such a rapid rate was not sustainable, but simply presented an example of the possibilities.

In reality, one man, working steadily, could expect to make about 50-70 cinder blocks per day. At that rate, it'd take him 26 days (50 a day) to make enough cinder blocks for the *basement* of The Chelsea. If he opted to build an entire house of block, it'd take a lot longer than 26 days.

In Alan Gowans' book, "*The Comfortable House*," he states that concrete block construction was a Sears' specialty. I tried to contact Mr. Gowans to learn more about this, and was saddened to learn that he has since passed on. In my own house-hunting experience, I haven't seen too many Sears homes built entirely of concrete block. Yet Sears certainly did promote block houses in the early catalogs.

Any Sears home could be built with a masonry exterior, such as block, brick or stone. However, because of the cost to ship masonry, Sears suggested that it should be obtained locally. The majority of Sears homes had traditional wooden sidings, such as clapboard or shingles.

Sears had different grades of housing, but Honor-Bilt was their most heavily promoted and (probably) their best seller. (The great majority of the Sears homes I've identified are Honor-Bilt homes.) Honor-Bilt homes utilized traditional construction standards, such as double headers over the doors and windows, double floors (primary floors over subfloors), exterior sheathing under clapboard or cedar shingles and wall studs on 16-inch centers.

Through the years, they also offered lesser grades, known by different names, such as Standard Built, Econo-Built and Lighter Built. These houses had wall studs on 24-inch centers, single headers, no subfloor and no underlying exterior sheathing.

Simplex Sectional Cottages were at the bottom rung of the construction ladder. These were prefab vacation cottages that could be disassembled and packed away when it was time to go home. They were quite primitive by today's standards.

The 1922 Modern Homes catalog described Simplex Sectional Cottages as, "ideal seashore, lake, winter resort houses and substantial garages." The 1919 catalog stated that they were ideal for summer or winter resorts because, "they can be quickly put up at the beginning of the season and then taken down and moved to a new location."

Walls and gables came in whole sections, with windows and doors pre-hung in their frames. The small homes could be put together with basic tools and their assembly required no sawing or nailing. The houses were held together by strap irons, screws, metal clips and bolts. Two men could assemble the house in eight hours, according to the 1923 catalog.

Honor-Bilt homes, with their "Already cut and fitted" (precut) lumber offered many benefits to the homeowner, but were equally advantageous for Sears. *Catalogs and Counters* states that precutting the lumber lowered shipping charges for Sears, since wastage was removed before shipping. Secondly, Sears could now buy lumber in economical lengths, resulting in additional savings. And perhaps best of all, "…the company was also thus able to use second-grade lumber, converting it into first-grade by cutting out the knotted parts" (ibid, p. 227). The left-over lengths of lumber would be utilized *somewhere* amidst those 30,000 pieces.

Stumbling about with my flashlight in the dimly-lit basement of countless Honor-Bilt homes throughout the country, I'm always dazzled by the *quality* of the lumber. Sears lumber was first growth lumber. ("First

Honor Bilt Construction

"Honor Bilt" Is the Better Home.

Here Are the Reasons:

An "HONOR BILT" home means a home of guaranteed quality. It means the best in quality of workmanship and in quality of material — also architectural and free plan service (see page 3). Judge for yourself by examining the two illustrations on this page. See the difference between ordinary lighter construction and "HONOR BILT" construction.

Have you been in homes that were hard to heat? Where drafts of cold came in through the floors and around the doors and windows? Invariably, the cause is due to faulty and light construction. (None of this in "Honor Bilt" Homes.)

Naturally, a Lighter Built house will cost less than an "HONOR BILT" house of the same size. For instance, the Arcadia "HONOR BILT" Modern Home described on page 90, is $909.00. If furnished in Lighter Built construction, the price would be $704.00, or $205.00 less. But the thirteen reasons clearly explain why the "HONOR BILT" is well worth the low price we charge.

"Honor Bilt" Construction Illustrated Below.

1. Rafters, 2x6 or 2x4 inches, (larger where needed), 14⅜ INCHES APART.
2. DOUBLE PLATES over doors and windows.
3. DOUBLE STUDDINGS at sides of doors and windows.
4. THREE STUDS at corners.
5. Outside casing, 1⅛ INCHES THICK.
6. High grade WOOD SHEATHING, 1³⁄₁₆ inch thick.
7. All glass 24x28 inches and larger is HIGH QUALITY DOUBLE STRENGTH.

8-9. DOUBLE FLOORS WITH HEAVY BUILDING PAPER between the subfloor and finished floor.

    10. 2x8-inch joists, or 2x10 where needed, 14⅜ INCHES APART.

    11. Studdings, 2x4 inches, 14⅜ INCHES APART.

    12. Best Grade of clear Cedar Shingles, Oriental Asphalt Shingles or Fire-Chief Shingle Roll Roofing, guaranteed for seventeen years, as specified.

    13. All outside paint, three coats of guaranteed paint, shingle stain (when shingles are used as siding), two brush coats.

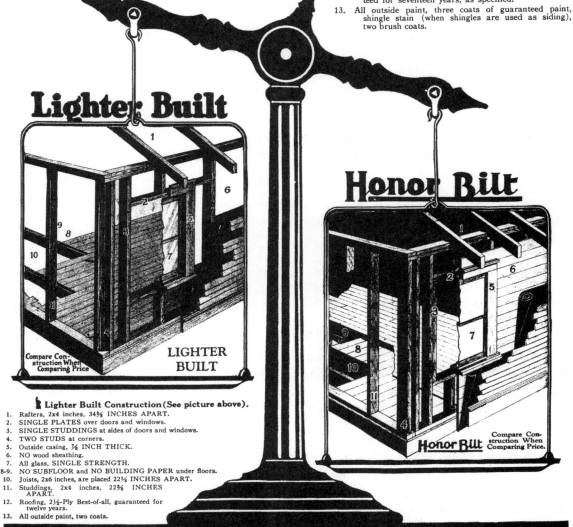

⚖ Lighter Built Construction (See picture above).

1. Rafters, 2x4 inches, 34⅜ INCHES APART.
2. SINGLE PLATES over doors and windows.
3. SINGLE STUDDINGS at sides of doors and windows.
4. TWO STUDS at corners.
5. Outside casing, ⅞ INCH THICK.
6. NO wood sheathing.
7. All glass, SINGLE STRENGTH.

8-9. NO SUBFLOOR and NO BUILDING PAPER under floors.

10. Joists, 2x6 inches, are placed 22⅜ INCHES APART.
11. Studdings, 2x4 inches, 22⅜ INCHES APART.
12. Roofing, 2½-Ply Best-of-all, guaranteed for twelve years.
13. All outside paint, two coats.

Honor-Bilt homes utilized traditional construction standards, such as double headers over the doors and windows, double floors, exterior sheathing under clapboard and wall studs on 16-inch centers. (1924 catalog)

growth lumber" is the name given to wood which grew slowly in natural forests. The slower wood grows, the denser the grain. The denser the grain, the stronger the wood. The stronger the wood, the more resistant it is to decay and rot and the longer it will endure.)

In *American Carpenter and Builder Magazine* (August 1913), Sears had a two page ad with this pitch: "Any shrewd lumber buyer can easily understand why we are in a position to undersell anyone else on lumber and millwork. We buy raw lumber direct from the greatest timber tracts in America. Second, our mills are located right in the heart of the yellow pine districts."

The yellow pine framing members that support these old Sears homes, now nearing the century mark, are harder and denser than most of today's [so-called] *hardwoods*. Some of these houses have had only minimal maintenance, yet all these years later, they're still as square and true and solid as the day they were built.

Sears earned a well-deserved reputation for providing the best quality lumber for both framing and millwork and they were proud of their reputation. In the 1922 Sears Modern Homes catalog, this notice appeared under the heading, "Important."

We do not handle hemlock, spruce or inferior types of lumber. The lumber we furnish is fine, dry yellow pine, the strongest lumber for framing. Cypress for outside finish, [cypress] the wood that lasts for centuries; oak, birch or yellow pine, as specified for interior finish.

Through the years, Sears offered exterior sidings in red cedar, redwood or cypress. Most frequently, exterior sidings were cypress, and exterior trim pieces (corner boards, door and window trim, eaves, etc.) were also cypress.

In the late 1920s, Sears issued a sales brochure promoting cypress lumber. The text was an interesting discourse on the value of cypress. The title was, "Outside finish and trim of Honor-Bilt homes made of cypress. The wood that lasts thru the ages."

The brochure went on to say:

The history of cypress, the wood eternal, runs back through the ages – back to the days of Noah's ark. Cypress was the wood most used among the ancient nations of the world. They made use of cypress for practically everything for which wood was needed - musical instruments, furniture, wine presses, boats and ships, palaces and temples. The ancients engraved their laws on cypress boards, carved images of their gods out of cypress logs, buried their kings and queens in mummy cases made of cypress.

The lasting quality of cypress is conclusively proven in the old Louisiana home of Joseph Jefferson, built of cypress almost 100 years ago and still well preserved. Honor-Bilt homes have only honest materials in them; materials that we know to be the highest grade that is possible to put into a home. That is why we use cypress, *the wood eternal*, to protect all parts exposed to weather.

[I have two questions. Who is Joseph Jefferson and what does *dishonest* lumber look like?]

Interior floors on average-priced Sears homes were typically oak on the first floor; maple in the kitchen and bath; yellow pine on the second floor. In less expensive homes, yellow pine was standard fare throughout the house for trim moldings, floors and doors. However, you could always upgrade.

The Osborn was a mid-range Honor-Bilt home. Through the 1920s, it was offered for $2700, plus or

The OSBORN $2,192⁰⁰
No. 2050 "Already Cut" and Fitted. Honor Bilt

1919 Sears

Modern Homes

Catalog

1. A perfect Osborn in Ohio

2. A mostly-original Osborn in Kentucky

3. An altered Osborne in Illinois

minus a few hundred dollars. It was described as a California bungalow and was a fine looking home with many nice features. Maple floors for the kitchen and bath were standard; the other rooms had oak floors. For an additional $148, you could upgrade to oak trim for the living room and dining room. An extra $15 bought you a ceramic tile bathroom floor, laid in cement of course, instead of a maple floor.

In the 1920s, wooden shingles were commonplace, but for $56, you could upgrade to "Oriental Asphalt Shingles" which were guaranteed for 17 years. As an added bonus, they were fireproof. (This was a big plus, because of the prevalence of coal-fired furnaces. It was not uncommon for hot coals or embers to fly out of the chimney, land on the wooden roof and start a house fire.) If you wanted storm doors and windows for your Osborn, you'd need to send in an extra $81; window screens were an additional $60.

A new way to build houses

In 1928, a quiet little notice appeared in the catalog, indicating that Sears had started building houses a new way.

Initially, it was heralded as "Air-Sealed-Wall Construction in Every 'Honor-Bilt' Home," but to those in the construction industry, it was known as platform construction. Prior to this, Sears homes were built using balloon construction. This was the industry standard for many decades, but in the 1920s, platform construction quickly gained favor and was soon recognized as superior in several ways.

Balloon construction originated in Chicago in the 1830s and replaced mortise and tenon construction (also known as timber framing). Timber framing required cumbersome overbuilding with massive hand-hewn timbers, which were notched into place and held together by wooden pegs. Balloon construction was easier, simpler and required far less skill and smaller framing members – less lumber. It also allowed for infinitely more variety and freedom in design.

In Thomas J. Schlereth's book, "*Victorian America, Transformations in Everyday Life*," he explains the origins of the term "balloon construction." "Naysayers gave the method its derisive name because it seemed so ridiculously light that it would surely blow away" (p. 99).

In balloon construction, one-piece vertical framing members were used from the basement to the roofline. This type of construction presented a serious fire hazard. Fires, hidden in the vertical wall voids, could easily spread from the first floor to the attic. In fact, the natural drafts present in these wall voids could whip hot embers into big fires. In platform construction, each floor is built independently, one platform, or level, at a time. This creates firestops between each floor. A fire within the first floor walls would not be able to crawl up to the second floor, without burning through a layer of wood.

A once-grand three-story home (circa 1885), in my hometown of Portsmouth, Virginia, offers a painful example of what's wrong with balloon construction. In the mid-1980s, a gas line broke under the house and natural gas silently filled those vertical wall voids, from basement to attic. When the refrigerator compressor clicked on, that tiny spark was enough to ignite the gas that filled the home's walls. The house exploded into thousands of wood splinters. Thankfully, no one was seriously injured, but the house and everything inside was completely destroyed.

In a 1928 sales brochure entitled, "Air-Sealed-Wall Construction," Sears was pushing the insulation qualities of platform construction hard and heavy. The two page brochure spoke at length about the cost of heating a home, the expense of hard coal (heating fuel) and the benefits of their "air-sealed-walls."

Open Flues Between Studs Carry Off Heat. The ordinary construction [balloon framing] is customary in most parts of the United States. It costs less because it requires less lumber to build. Its outside walls settle but little, due to using long studs and fewer sills and plates, whereas the partition walls on the inside, necessarily of different construction, will shrink more than the outside walls, causing the floors to settle, doors to sag and windows to stick. Besides, the "open flues" between studs carry off the heat through the attic to the skies, resulting in a big waste of fuel – at least from one-third to one half – a cold and uncomfortable abode during the winter and a very warm house in the summer.

What the brochure did *not* mention is that Sears (just like everyone else in the industry) had built their houses this way (with those "open flues") since 1908, when they abruptly switched from balloon to platform construction. By 1928, Sears had 42,000 homes that were prone to [in their own words], "settling floors, sagging windows and sticking doors, carrying off heat from the attic to the skies."

In the 1930 edition of the Sears Modern Home catalog, platform construction was listed under the heading of "*Our Broad Guarantee Protects You.*" (Sounds like a guarantee that you'll get a good dame.) The text went on to say, "Honor-Bilt homes meet with the codes of the Bureau of Standards, U. S. Government, and the approved details of the modern platform construction which was recommended by Herbert Hoover." (For the historically challenged, Hoover served as Secretary of Commerce from 1921-1928, before being elected President in 1928.)

Details on the building of The Bandon - A Sears Modern Home

Whilst researching the old Sears lumber mill in Cairo, Illinois, I found an incredible document in the vertical files at the Cairo Public Library. The document showed, in detail, the cost of building Sears Modern Home, The Bandon.

The house was built in 1921 in Southern Illinois. According to this document, the lumber for this kit home was shipped from the Sears mill in Cairo.

Cost of The Bandon	$2794.00
Plaster (extra)	133.00
Material to finish attic rooms	241.00
Complete hot water heating system	403.66
Wire and light fixtures	133.66
Labor for carpenter (including masonry work)	1600.00
Total	$5305.32

In 1924, a Sears Cyclone Barn (shipped from Cairo, IL) was built on the property. The kit barn cost $943.00.

Stucco warts, bumps, and swellings which infest the land

In the 1908 general merchandise catalog, in the very first ad where Sears invited interested customers to write and request that very first Sears Modern Homes catalog, Sears lobbed a bit of a verbal grenade at professional architects.

Page 594 of Sears' 1908 general merchandise catalog stated, "This elegant book (the Modern Homes catalog) will convey more ideas to you in five minutes than an architect would in a year."

The 1908 Modern Homes catalog promised, "You will pay from $100 to $200 to any architect for building plans, according to the house you want to build and none of the plans at those prices will go into details as we do. Our specifications are very complete, much more complete than the average architect's specifications."

In the 1909 Modern Homes catalog, the tirade went on.

"Our plans are much more carefully drawn than the plans provided by the average architect, ours being *accurate and correct* in every detail" (emphasis added).

What began as a few lines in the early catalogs had turned into a full-page missive by the mid-1920s. In a snazzy full color ad in the 1920s catalogs, this loaded question launched the diatribe: "Architectural service. What's it worth to you?"

The ad went on to say, "We make no charge for this valuable service when you make your selection from this book. The usual charge is from $100 to $1000 for what we give you free."

Lower on the page, with the heading, "Architect" was this statement.

The scale of prices charged by architectural associations varies according to agreement, but the following is typical: Dwellings costing less than $10,000 – 10%. Dwellings costing more than $10,000, from 6% - 10% on the completed cost.

Architects' fees were *not* quite as high as the catalogs suggested. According to "*The American Family Home, 1800-1960*" by Clifford Edward Clark, Jr., architects' fees typically ran about 5% of construction costs, or about half of what Sears was quoting.

Clark also points out that homeownership was a high brass ring for many lower and middle class families at the end of the 1800s. He tells of two different middle class workers who spent about half their monthly income in housing expenses. He writes, "In both cases, a 5% architectural fee would have consumed close to three months' income" (p. 87).

Architects' fees were not as high as Sears indicated, but they were too pricey for the average person's budget. Americans, it seemed, were far happier perusing free kit home catalogs from Sears, Wards, Aladdin, Lewis-Liberty, Harris Brothers, Sterling, Gordon-Van Tine and others, rather than paying large fees to architects.

The architects didn't like this. They countered by describing the burgeoning sales of mail order homes "a violent architectural epidemic."

My favorite domestic architecture author, Alan Gowans, addressed this issue far better than I could, in his book, *The Comfortable House, North American Suburban Architecture, 1890-1930.*

FIVE REASONS WHY
OUR ARCHITECTURAL SERVICE WILL SERVE YOU BEST

1

SAVES YOU ALL ARCHITECTS' FEES

Good architectural service, when engaged in the customary way, costs from 6 to 10 per cent of the total cost of the house. Manufacturing enormous quantities of material in our own factories, and selling direct to you, lowers our cost of doing business to a point where we can afford to give you this valuable service without an additional charge

2

SAVES YOU FROM EXPERIMENTING WITH UNTRIED PLANS

Of course, you have heard of even the best of architects going wrong—the plans turned out differently than was expected—they were "theoretical" plans, the untried kind. "HONOR BILT" plans are practical, proven so by building each design many times.

3

SAVES YOU FROM BUYING ANY EXTRAS AND SURPLUS MATERIAL

An "HONOR BILT" customer never need worry about the dreaded extras. They know before they start what the cost is going to be. If by chance the material proves insufficient, or of the wrong kind, Sears, Roebuck and Co. pay for the extra material. Did you ever hear of anyone else who did?

4

SAVES YOU FROM POOR WORKMANSHIP AND FAULTY CONSTRUCTION

"HONOR BILT" Ready Cut Houses are cut to a mathematical correctness—every foot of framing material is cut by machine—standardized on the same principle as a good automobile. This prevents "butchered carpentry," and results in a more rigid construction than the ordinary hand framed job.

5

SAVES YOU ON COST OF ERECTION

Many wise contractors prefer "HONOR BILT" Ready Cut Houses in preference to not ready cut. There's a reason. It saves time and money, and makes satisfied customers. No better proof of the Ready Cut system can be found than the recommendation of the man who knows. Don't fail to read all about the 40 per cent saved by "HONOR BILT" Ready Cut system—see pages 8 and 9.

Architects' fees were typically 5% of the total construction costs, which represented a huge sum of money for the average person. Instead of hiring architects, thousands of buyers preferred perusing Sears free catalogs. (1928 Sears Modern Homes catalog)

(The following is reprinted with permission from "*The Comfortable House, North American Suburban Architecture, 1890-1930,*" Alan Gowans, ©1986, MIT Press.)

[From a 1921 pamphlet by the American Steel and Wire Company], "The Function of the Architect, the Material Dealer and the Builder in Constructing a Home:"

> *'The advise of an architect is always advisable when contemplating the building of a home. ...It must not be forgotten that the architect represents the most ancient, scientific and practical of the liberal arts. It is a lifetime study and what has taken him a lifetime to acquire, with the science and teaching of ages back of him, is most useful for the homebuilder to know...'*

But all this sounds a bit pompous, pretentious, hollow and was not an effective response to what many were beginning to consider a crisis. The public should be told directly just what these mail order people produce. Their stuff is vulgar: 'stucco warts, bumps, and swellings which infest the land,' 'small homes of vicious architecture, slapped together by carpetects*,' 'pretentious caricatures...'[1]

A certain professor of architecture at Stanford leaped into the fray with a treatise on Art Principles in House, Furniture, and Village Building, copiously illustrated with his own photographs. He proposed to show the path to enlightenment about bungalow building. My oh my, what wasn't wrong with them!

> *'Monstrosities in their ugliness...freaky details...inconsistent use of materials, overemphatic sloping chimney, exaggerated porch, boastful use of brick, the brackets and vertical lines in the gable are disturbing." His conclusion: "Lack of intelligence is the trouble – the crime of crimes and the breeder of all vulgarity."[2]*

Name calling, was not enough, however. More positive action was needed and in 1919-1920, it was taken by two organizations of architects, the Home Owners Service Institute and the Architects' Small House Service Bureau. ASHSB was founded by a group of Minnesota architects in 1919[3] to meet the competition – no, that's not how it was put – to respond, rather, to the profession's altruistic concern that 'it is the right of every American child to grow up in a real American home.' A real American home, one gathers, could only be one designed by an architect...

ASHSB would protect 'the general public – those who cannot avoid seeing it or else must live in close proximity to it.'

'It' was the 'small house' produced by 'cut-rate draftsmen-designers and stock plan publishers,' whose work represented 'a violent architectural epidemic' that showed signs of spreading rapidly to large homes and buildings, making very definite inroads on the legitimate professional practice of architecture; and that, simply by weight of numbers was 'inevitably going to give the dominant architectural tone to entire neighborhoods and indeed, to the country at large'[4] (pp. 64-65).

All of which goes to say, the architects were not pleased with the tens of thousands of mail order bungalows and foursquares which were popping up all over the American landscape.

Despite harsh words, there was not much the architects could do to stop the trend. Companies like Sears and Aladdin and Gordon-Van Tine were shipping out hundreds of houses each month. It looked like the good times would just get better and better for these mail order companies.

But an economic tsunami was quietly building throughout the 1920s that would soon bring the Sears Modern Homes department to its financial knees. The first wave of economic reversal and hardship would hit America's shores on October 29, 1929. That was Black Tuesday, the opening bell of the Great Depression. By 1941, the Sears Modern Homes department would only be a fond memory, with 75,000 bricks and sticks memorials scattered all over the country.

(These footnotes accompany the above italicized text, from *The Comfortable House, North American Suburban Architecture, 1890-1930,*" Alan Gowans, ©1986, MIT Press.)

[1] *Quoted in Rubin, "Chronology of Architecture in Los Angeles," 528 and 531, from Robert Jones, "The Architects' Small House Service Bureau," Architectural Forum 44, (1926), 208; and Charles Kyson, "Fashions in Architecture," California Southland (August 1928), 30.)*

[2] *Arthur Bridgman Clark, "Some Very Bad Designs," Art Principles in House, Furniture, and Village Building (Stanford: Stanford University Press, 1921), 41-48, and elsewhere through the book.*

[3] *"Architects' Small House Service Bureau of Minnesota, Inc.," Journal of the American Institute of Architects 9 (1921), 134-40; see also Robert Jones, "The Architects' Small House Service Bureau," Architectural Forum 44 (1926), 201-216; Thomas Harvey, "Mail Order Architecture in the Twenties," Landscape 25:3 (1981), 1-9.*

[4] *"Quoted in Rubin, "Chronology of Architecture in Los Angeles," 527 and 528, from Kyson, "Fashions in Architecture," and Leigh French, "The Small House and Candor in Designing," Architectural Forum 44 (1926).*

* Carpetect: In Gowans' text, you may have noticed this interesting word: carpetect. You're not going to find this in any dictionary. I already looked. Carpetect was a denigrating term that architects gave to builders (or more precisely, carpenters) who erroneously presumed to possess the intellectual capacity to design homes. Carpenter + architect: Carpetect. It was quite a slam. Home design, the architects reasoned, was not the purview of the lowly carpenter.

Chapter 5

Milling About Sears Homes:
A Look Inside the Sears Mill at Cairo, Illinois

Almost every single man on the Ready-Cut side (of the Sears Mill) was missing a finger. Some of them were just missing a fingertip, but most of them were missing something.

Morris Morehead
Sears Mill Employee

The 1933 Sears Modern Homes catalog stated, "Sears buys raw materials by shiploads and train-loads. Sears owns and operates its own lumber plants, millwork, building material and paint factories, wallpaper mills and other manufactories covering practically every item that goes into the finished home."

According to this catalog, the Sears mill in Norwood, Ohio (near Cincinnati) covered 17 acres. Their East Coast mill at Newark, New Jersey was eight miles from New York City and sat on 40 acres. The mill in Cairo, Illinois was not mentioned by name in the 1933 catalog, but it was also a massive 40-acre facility.

Wanting to learn more about the mills that supplied lumber for Sears Modern Homes, I visited Cairo, Illinois several times in the Spring and Summer of 2003.

Cairo's location at the confluence of the Ohio and Mississippi Rivers made it a natural for shipping and distribution. At the turn of the last century, Cairo (pronounced "Care-Roe") could boast of having four major rail lines, enabling it to become a centralized shipping point for lumber harvested from the South and sent to the North.

Entirely apart from the history of the Sears mill, Cairo is a fascinating little river town, rich with legends and lore of wild times and rough men and fast women. Established in 1817, Cairo was named after the Egyptian city because of the geographical similarities; specifically its proximity to vital waterways.

The late 1800s and early 1900s were a time of remarkable growth for Cairo, as the downtown area grew and developed and "Millionaire's Row" was created – a residential area filled with ostentatious Victorian mansions.

Industries expanded and commerce grew and the small city flourished. The 1900 census showed that 12,566 people lived in Cairo and by 1910, the population had increased 15% to 14,548. In March 1911, the community's newspaper, *The Cairo Evening Citizen* proudly reported that 100 autos were now registered in the city of Cairo.

The Sears Roebuck Mill, also known as the Illinois Lumber Company, came into being on May 1911, when Sears Roebuck paid $12,500 for a 40-acre tract in North Cairo. *The Cairo Evening Citizen* reported that the property would be developed into a huge lumber mill, eventually employing 1000 men, adding, "Sears Roebuck will immediately begin construction of seven large sheds, each 62 feet by 700 feet to provide storage for 15 million feet of lumber."

On May 21, 1911, The *Chicago Tribune* reported that Sears intended to build a $250,000 plant. A few weeks later, *The Cairo Evening Citizen* had doubled that figure and reported "Half a million to be cost of new Sears Roebuck Plant" (July 29, 1911).

In November 1911, Sears ran a two-page advertisement in *American Carpenter and Builder Magazine* headlined "Great News for Builders." The advertisement said,

> Shipments have begun from our second and newest great lumber plant in Illinois. We can deliver you bright, fresh, clean lumber at manufacturer's prices almost as quickly as you can haul makeshift sizes and weatherworn stock from a high priced neighboring lumber yard. Our mill work is sheltered from rain, sun, soot and wind. Our new Illinois plant is located on two of the largest and fastest railroads in the North with direct connections to over 20 different railroads. (*Weatherworn stock was a reference to the fact that, unlike Sears, many mills did not keep their lumber under roof.*)

Another advertisement in *American Carpenter and Builder* in February 1912 featured a line drawing of the Cairo mill - showing a power plant, six huge warehouses, planing mills, steam dry kilns, log train ramps and log ponds.

In March 1912, F. E. Van Alstine, Superintendent of the Sears mill was quoted in *The Cairo Evening Citizen* as saying that Sears had chosen Cairo because of "their low freight rates, superior shipping facilities and other natural and commercial advantages, (which) made the city more desirable than St. Louis, East St. Louis, Paducah (Kentucky) or Memphis" (Tennessee).

But later that month, the rains came and the floodwaters rose, nearly destroying the brand new mill in Northern Cairo. On April 5th, *The Cairo Evening Citizen* reported that the "main building of the new Sears Roebuck factory was hurled off its foundation and is leaning toward the east. Just what damage was done to these buildings could not be ascertained, as there was no way to reach them except by skiff."

In mid-April, the paper said that all seven lumber sheds had been torn from their foundations and much of the lumber inside the sheds had simply floated away.

By August, *The Cairo Evening Citizen* happily reported that despite the hard times and high waters, Sears Roebuck had decided to remain in Cairo. It also reported that about half the lumber sheds had been rebuilt and some of that floating lumber had been recovered. The same article reported that the folks at Sears corporate headquarters in Chicago were so pleased with Van Alstine's post-flood restoration work that they presented him with a brand new automobile.

A 1914 fire insurance map shows the layout of the mill and scale drawings of the buildings. This map confirms that the four largest lumber sheds were 18 feet tall, 62 feet wide and about 700 feet long. These sheds and other buildings covered about 20 acres of the 40-acre site.

Sadly, there is very little written information about this mill and its day to day operations. However, knowing of my search for information, Richard Kearney, a lifelong resident of Cairo, contacted me and offered to do some digging and see what he could find. One of his best finds was a copy of an extremely rare document: Fred K. Wheeler's unpublished manuscript *"Recollection of 36 Years With a Fascinating Lumber Plant."*

Wheeler was hired at the Cairo mill in January 1920 and in 1925, he was promoted to plant manager. His 20-page typewritten manuscript focuses primarily on the floods of 1927 and 1937 and tells the story of the workers who scrambled to preserve the levees in Northern Cairo that protected the mill. However, it also includes some wonderful details about life at the mill.

The mill produced everything for the Ready-Cut (precut) Sears homes except for millwork. The Sears mill located in Norwood, Ohio, supplied millwork; windows, doors and interior trim and moldings.

According to Wheeler, about 125 houses per month were shipped out of the Cairo mill in the early 1920s and by 1929, that number had doubled to 250. He relates that in May 1926, a record 324 Ready-Cut houses were shipped out. He notes that this number does not include the Simplex Sectional (prefab) homes – only Ready-Cut homes.

There were two sides to the mill; the Ready-Cut homes were produced on one side and Simplex Sectional (portable or prefab) homes were produced on the other side. In the 1920s, about 100 men worked at the mill and about half the workers were men of color. Wheeler relates that race relations between the whites and blacks were remarkably cordial and supportive. *(Remarkable because racial strife and horrific riots would tear Cairo apart in the mid-1960s, causing thousands to flee the city.)*

By the early 1930s, sales of Ready-Cut homes had plummeted and the mill began looking for other ways to generate income. They began building crating material for tractors and other large equipment, including Frigidaire refrigerators and appliances sold by Sears. In the late 30s, the mill produced prefabricated buildings for the camps which housed workers in the Civilian Conservation Corps. Wheeler relates that a typical CCC camp (which included several different buildings) required 400,000 feet of lumber and about 35 of these camps were milled and shipped by the Cairo plant.

In 1940, Sears closed the plant and sold it to the employees. Shortly after the employees purchased the plant, they obtained a contract to build massive crates for shipping B-17 and B-29 bombers overseas for the war effort.

After World War II ended, the former Sears Mill – now called Illinois Lumber Company – drafted and published their own book of house plans and tried to sell Ready-Cut homes again, but without success. *The Cairo Evening Citizen* relates that the plant was liquidated and closed in November 1955. The article adds this interesting aside: "Like several other Cairo lumber industries, it slowly died because the wood articles it manufactured were supplanted by iron and steel."

All that remains today at the site of the Cairo mill are two Sears homes – two Rodessas – which were built as part of an experiment in 1921, to prove the superiority of Ready-Cut homes over traditional stick built homes.

Most of them were missing something

During my visits to Cairo, I talked with several folks in the area, but one of my favorite stories came from Cairo native and resident, Morris Morehead. In the 1930s, he worked at the Cairo mill.

"The men who worked on the Ready-Cut side (where the precut houses were milled) were paid based on what they produced," he recalled. "It was piece work. And almost every man on the Ready-Cut side was missing a finger. Some of them were just missing a fingertip, but most of them were missing something."

He also recalled that they used a massive planer which was more than 20 feet long and five feet wide. "We had to call the Cairo Power Company before turning on that planer and some other equipment," he said with a fond smile. "It was such a massive power draw, they had to fire up more dynamos before we could start up the electrical machinery at the mill."

Huge pieces of redwood, cypress, oak, pine and other lumber – up to 18 inches square – were run through the blades. Kerosene was poured on the massive saw blades to keep them cool.

Through a wonderful set of circumstances, I was introduced to 95-year-old Shelbourne Goode who now lives in Kentucky with his wife Rose. Shelbourne worked at the Sears Mill for several years and was another wonderful resource of information. He worked at the mill with his father and Shelbourne's job was to notch window frames to receive the sash weights.

"It was a big mill," Shelbourne recalled fondly, whilst relaxing one steamy July morning on the screened-in porch of his brick bungalow. "Lumber sheds, one after the other, set on a small hill as far as the eye could see. Those sheds were pretty good size, too. Sears bought only dry lumber and they kept it under roof in those big sheds. Large supplies of lumber were constantly coming in by river and rail. We used so much lumber. I didn't know they could make that much pine!

"On average, we shipped out 10-12 houses a day. The managers and foremen told us several times that if we weren't shipping out at least 11-12 houses, they were losing money. And that doesn't count the 3-4 portable (Simplex Sectional) homes they shipped out each day. If we finished an 8-hour shift and didn't have a house quite ready, we'd stay and work an extra hour of overtime until the house was ready.

"The plants, where the men worked, had a lot of windows in the building. In the winter time, it got awfully cold. During the winter months, the electric heat stayed on. And we had to have electric heat because we couldn't have a fire in there (such as a kerosene or coal-fired space heater) with all that lumber. We couldn't wear gloves because it was just too dangerous (because of the machinery). And the summers were pretty hot, too."

Shelbourne said that the work day began at 7:30 in the morning and there were no breaks until lunch at noon. Most workers brought their lunch in a pale and ate at their work stations. Work ended most days at 5:00 p.m. When the day was over, workers left in a hurry. The plant only had one shift, working eight hours a day.

At its peak, about 80-90 men worked on the Ready-Cut side and about 15-20 worked on the side where Simplex Sectionals (which workers called "portable houses") were milled and shipped.

In 1988, *The Southeast Missourian*, a newspaper in nearby Cape Girardeau, Missouri interviewed Floyd J. Smith who worked at the Sears Mill in 1920. Smith was 90 years old at the time of the interview.

The following contains excerpts from a newspaper article originally published August 14, 1988 in the Southeast Missourian, Cape Girardeau, Missouri and is reprinted with permission.

"It was in 1911," said Floyd J. Smith a Cairo native who remembers the house-building operation well. "Sears located its plant on a 40-acre tract of land, alongside the Illinois Central Railroad's main line."

Smith was only 13 years old at the time, but he recalls the huge red buildings which spread over a 40-acre tract with about half of it under roof. Seven years later, Smith was to become a part of the operation.

"I spent several years at that factory," said Smith, now 90, recently. "I started work there in 1920 and stayed until the plant closed."

Smith, who served as foremen of the prefabricated (portable or Simplex Sectionals) house department, described the plant as a "tremendously large layout, with (four or five) buildings. The manufacturing was in the main big building. We made prefabs on the highway side of the building and they made Ready-Cut jobs on the railroad side of the building."

"Each home shipment included a complete set of blueprints prepared by Sears architects. All you had to supply was some masonry and labor and an empty lot within hauling distance of a railroad siding," said Smith. "Included with each order was a 76-page instruction manual. Every board, every stud, every rafter, every piece of lumber was cut, notched or mitered to fit, and numbered to match the plans. Even the spacing between the nails was listed."

Some closing thoughts on Cairo, Illinois

The first time I visited Cairo, I was stunned. Having traveled to dozens of cities in Illinois, I'd say that Cairo is one the state's most economically depressed communities. Yet there is something about the city that is enchanting and intriguing.

Cairo's downtown area will knock your socks off. When I first discovered it, I stopped my car in the middle of the street and stared in disbelief. The entire business district, which comprised several blocks of brick streets in beautiful condition, was empty – deserted and devoid of all movement. Had it not been for a piece of trash blowing down the middle of the street, the scene could have been a still-frame.

The stillness, the quiet, the absence of any sign of life was fascinating, yet also left me wondering if the next sound I heard would be the theme from The Twilight Zone with a voice-over by Rod Serling.

Looking at the stunning late-1800s commercial architecture – most of which was in original condition and all of which had been abandoned – my intuitive sense told me that folks had left this place in a hurry. And as I began researching the area, I learned my hunch was on mark.

In the mid-1960s, racial unrest and riots were a sad part of the American landscape, but in Cairo, things went especially badly. African-Americans, weary of Jim Crow laws and disparate treatment, threatened to boycott businesses that employed only whites. White business owners responded by closing their stores. Large numbers of families – white and black – left the area and never returned. The population plummeted. Today, downtown Cairo is a ghost town – an incredible time capsule – frozen in the 1960s. The city that once boasted of 14,000 citizens now has about 3000 people living within its borders.

I've returned to Cairo several times since that first visit and each time, I make a point to drive through that incredible downtown area. I park my car and stare. I stare at the old buildings which are in fair to decent condition and still look much like they did when built 100+ years ago. I look at the store fronts whose doorways have not been darkened by a customer in many years. I study the two movie theatres that look much like they did when built in the 1920s and 30s. I take in the long view and look at the streetscapes, devoid of movement or activity.

Just behind those fantastic old commercial buildings lies a seawall and the Ohio River. I do believe that the city could build a fantastic tourism industry off this downtown area alone. I've never seen a sight like it.

Apparently, word is getting out, because on my last visit, I saw two tourists taking a plethora of photos of this eerie but fascinating downtown. However, if you decide to visit – come prepared. Cairo has no public bathrooms, no fast-food joints and no public water fountains. About 15 minutes away, just across the

Ohio River, is Wickliffe, Kentucky – site of the nearest public restroom. The nearest Burger Doodle is 30 miles southwest in Cape Girardeau.

One thing Cairo does have is plenty of vacant lots, such as 1501 Commercial Avenue. This corner lot is a few blocks from the downtown area and according to the 1922 Sears Modern Homes catalog, it <u>was</u> the site of a beautiful "Elsmore" (Honor-Bilt home). The testimonial on page 111 of the catalog reads, "Built by R. P. Fitzjearl, 1501 Commercial Avenue, Cairo, IL. He says, 'Already-cut lumber saves one-third of time. Plans as simple as reading a book.'"

When I drive through Cairo, I look at all those empty lots and try not to think about how many Sears homes have been torn down in the intervening years. Several? Dozens? Or worse?

Thus far, I've identified about 30 Sears homes in Cairo. Many are in poor condition and a few more may be torn down before the city awakens to its architecture treasures. The addresses of these Sears homes are at the Cairo Public Library on Washington Street and make for a fun driving tour.

A final note: Could you do something for me, the ever-so-slightly-obsessed author? When you visit Cairo, enjoy their famous "Magnolia Manor" or even the historic building that houses the library, but please, *let them know that you've come to see <u>the Sears homes</u>*. ☺

Chapter 6

$1 Million Worth of Sears Homes
The Biggest Order In the History of the Sears Modern Homes Department

November 12, 1920

The two hundred (200) houses which you built for us at Carlinville, Wood River and Schoper, Illinois are now completed and are entirely satisfactory in every detail. The workmanship, laying out of streets, sidewalks, sewers, etc., has all been handled in a very satisfactory manner, and the quality of the material is exceptionally good. We are proud of the architectural appearance; also the convenient arrangement of rooms in these houses and we are able to offer these houses to our workmen at a very low price.

This letter, from Standard Oil of Indiana, appeared on the back cover of Sears Modern Home catalogs from 1921 through 1929. Obviously, Sears was quite proud of this letter.

In 1918, Standard Oil of Indiana made mail-order history when they placed a $1 million order with Sears Roebuck & Company for 192 Honor-Bilt homes. It was purported to be the largest order in the history of the Sears Modern Homes department. Standard Oil purchased the houses for their workers in Carlinville, Wood River and Schoper in Southwestern Illinois. Of those 192 houses, 156 went to Carlinville, 12 were built in Schoper and 24 were sent to Wood River. Throughout the 1920s, pictures of these homes were prominently featured in the front pages of the Sears Modern Homes catalogs.

When I first began the research for this book, I had planned to include a short chapter on this large collection of Sears homes. After all, it was *while* researching the homes in Carlinville that I first fell deeply in love with Sears homes.

But while doing that initial research, I discovered the story behind the story - the interesting tale of how a paternalistic corporate giant (Standard Oil), built modern, comfortable homes for the folks on the lowest rungs of the socio-economic ladder - unskilled, often transient immigrant miners, who in many cases, could neither read nor write English. And the story didn't end there. How did the corporate giant respond to its workers and the community when the mines closed? What happened to the houses and the residents when the boom went bust? In each of the three communities – Carlinville, Wood River and Schoper (near Standard City) – this story had an unusual beginning and a surprise ending.

And it's an important thumbnail sketch of not only Sears Modern Homes, but also industrial America, labor relations, corporate giants, mining towns and immigrant workers.

It all began on October 17, 1917, with a small article on the front page of *The Macoupin County Enquirer*. The *Enquirer* reported that a local concern, the Carlinville Coal Company, had sold their mine (comprising several hundred acres and all improvements), to an unknown entity.

The following week the paper revealed that Standard Oil Company of Indiana had been identified as the purchaser of the Carlinville Mine.

The front page article opined, "The Standard Oil Company is a mighty good concern to have with us. It has also been the policy of this company to cater to the general public and to encourage the goodwill of every-one having business with them."

One week later, October 31, the *Enquirer* reported that the Schoper farm, a 500-acre tract of farmland about 8 miles northeast of Carlinville, had been sold. "Herman Schoper of Springfield, who formerly resided here (near Carlinville) sold his big farm in Shaw's Point. It is supposed the property is sold to the Standard Oil Company."

The article continued, "What the purchase means no one knows, but a company like the Standard is not making such investments without developing them."

What folks did *not* know was that Standard Oil had already hired the engineering firm of Robert W. Hunt and Company to drill test holes on the Schoper farm in Macoupin County. These tests discovered a 7-foot vein of coal, which assured engineers that coal would be plentiful.

Standard Oil commissioned Robert W. Hunt Engineering and Company to build two mines at the Schoper farm and to rehab and enlarge the existing mining operation of the former Carlinville Coal Company (at Carlinville's edge).

Standard Oil's decision to buy two coal mines was based on prudence and practicality. In 1917, World War I was in full swing. And there was an enormous demand for gasoline and fuel oil - both at home and on the battlefield. In 1900, there were 8,000 automobiles on the nation's roadways. By the late 1920s, that number surpassed 20 million. The country's need for petroleum increased proportionately.

Standard Oil needed great quantities of coal to fire the stills that would convert crude oil into gasoline. Because of shortages in labor and materials brought on by the war, coal supplies were capricious and expensive. News of coal shortages was a recurring headline and Standard Oil wanted a steady, massive and reliable supply of coal, to ensure the continuous operation of their refineries. Carlinville was an especially attractive location because it was on the *Chicago and Alton* rail line and centrally located between Standard Oil's refineries in Whiting, Indiana (near Chicago), and Wood River, Illinois (near St. Louis).

An interesting aside: According to "A Generation of Industrial Peace: Thirty Years of Labor Relations at Standard Oil Company" by Stuart Chase (1947), the refinery operations in the early days were extremely primitive. "Refining petroleum at first was hardly more exact than making bathtub gin," he states in his book. "You dumped crude oil into a vat or still and built a fire under it." Chase explains that gasoline was the first vapor to rise off the crude, followed by kerosene. Lubricating oils and then heavy oils were the next byproducts of the refining process.

In January 1918, before Standard Oil's two new mines, Berry Mine (in Carlinville) and Schoper Mine (on the old Schoper farm) were operational, an on-going national coal shortage became increasingly severe. A tidbit in *The Alton Evening Telegraph* (a newspaper in nearby Alton, Illinois) said that children at the local orphanage were going to bed each night at sundown, tucked warmly under heavy covers, in hopes of conserving coal. Government officials shut down businesses nationwide for five days and ordered Monday closings thereafter for nine weeks (until Spring) because of the scarcity of coal. To make matters worse, it was the coldest winter of the decade.

Standard Oil was desperate to get their new mines up and running as soon as possible. Finding workers to mine coal 400 feet underground was also challenging. Many able-bodied men were overseas. In the state of Illinois, more than 351,000 men had gone to war. (*Alton Evening Telegraph*, May 10, 1919.) The labor shortage was acute.

In order to attract the highest quality workers, Standard Oil decided to build houses for them. At the time, Carlinville was a farming community of fewer than 4000 people. It didn't have adequate housing or facilities for the 2000 miners, workers and other new residents that would soon arrive.

The Schoper farm had been just that - a farm with one house and a few outbuildings. Within months, about 1000 people would come to live in that area and in 1920, the 500-acre farm, together with an adjoining tract was incorporated as a village and named "Standard City."

On June 12, 1918, *The Macoupin County Enquirer* reported that Standard Oil had entered into a contract to purchase at least 150 houses for Carlinville miners. The article said that the houses would cost $3000 each and would be erected on 216 lots recently acquired on the Burton Tract (in Carlinville).

"On the basis of five to a family, these houses will provide for 750 people. The new homes are to be two story with all modern conveniences [indoor plumbing, electricity and a coal furnace] and will be of different architectural design" (June 12, 1918, *Macoupin County Enquirer*).

The newspaper then launched into another pro-Standard Oil opine, stating, "Do the people of Carlinville realize what it means to have the Standard Oil Company locate here? Property has advanced, new houses are being put up and hundreds of people are trying to locate here." ("Property has advanced" simply meant that real estate prices had increased.)

Reading through *American Builder* magazines from 1918 - 1922, I learned that it was fairly common for large corporations to build housing for their workers. Modern and decent housing attracted a steady, reliable and skilled workforce.

In 1919, Perfection Tire and Rubber Company of Fort Madison, Iowa, built 100 homes for workers and then sold these "modern homes" on easy payment plans. General Motors Company built 950 houses for its workers in Flint, Michigan in 1920. The $3,000 - $7,000 houses were then sold to employees on a "time payment plan," most likely a corporate-held mortgage or contract for deed.

"Auto Company Combats Housing Shortage," told the story of the Studebaker Corporation of South Bend, Indiana. They erected 204 houses for their workers. Once complete, the spacious two-story Dutch Colonials were sold to employees for $7500, with payments amortized for 10 - 14 years at 6% interest.

This article summed up the current corporate philosophy, saying, "Studebaker Corporation recognizes that a good home in pleasing surroundings is absolutely necessary to maintain the high grade of efficient [workers] wanted and to attract the type of men the Studebaker organization desires to employ."

The opening pages of the 1920s Sears Modern Homes catalogs featured a "bird's eye view" of other corporate Sears-built neighborhoods in Akron and Dayton, Ohio and Plymouth Meeting and Chester, Pennsylvania.

Sears realized that good quality housing had the potential to solve labor shortages for industry and promoted a few of their houses with this in mind.

The Madelia, offered in the 1910s and early 1920s, was pitched with this headline: "For Foreman or Manager." The heading over The Windsor (also known as The Carlin) read, "For Better Class Workers."

An interesting aside: The Windsor was renamed The Carlin in honor of Carlinville and the $1 million Standard Oil purchase.

The Sears catalog promoted The Lebanon as a good home "For The Skilled Laborer" and the opening description stated, "This house solves the problem where it is desired to retain skilled labor."

Providing homes was also a way to keep employees devoted to the corporate paterfamilias. Perusing *The Alton Evening Telegraph*, I found frequent headlines telling of explosions, fires, pipe ruptures and other horrible industrial accidents that burned, maimed and killed Wood River's refinery workers. It was shocking to see how often these accidents occurred.

The Macoupin County Enquirer and *The Carlinville Democrat* carried frequent stories of equally horrible accidents down in the mines, resulting in disabilities and fatalities. During this same period of time, the local papers ran an article about a mining accident in Colorado that took the lives of 100 miners. Mining was dirty and dangerous work.

An article in the *Enquirer*, dated September 19, 1923, said 18 miners died that year in Macoupin County, which was in line with the national average of "one [miner] fatality per 279,354 tons of coal produced." Between 1884-1912, 42,898 miners died in this country.

The Story of Macoupin County (published 1979 by the Carlinville and Macoupin County Sesquicentennial, Inc.) states that the miners of Macoupin County were mostly immigrants - Serbians, Bohemians, Hungarians, Polish, Greeks, Italians, and some Scandinavians. The men worked in damp, dirty conditions with only a dim headlamp to guide them, 400-feet deep in Schoper Mine.

A typical miner's lunch consisted of cheese sandwiches and fruit, covered with a generous coating of coal dust. *The Story of Macoupin County* describes it this way: "Miners went below by 7:00 A.M., carried their lunch and drink in a double tin pail and ate at their work spot without any chance to wash the coal dirt from their hands."

One coal miner recalled that he learned how to eat an entire sandwich by pinching it tightly between his thumb and one finger. When he got down to that last bit of blackened bread pinched between his fingers, he threw it to the rats that scampered through the mines.

In these pre-OSHA times, I suspect that these corporations knew that they owed their faithful workers something more enduring and substantial than 60 cents an hour. (In 1919, the *Macoupin County Enquirer*

1919 Sears
Modern Homes
Catalog

A happy Madelia
in Southern
Illinois

An unhappy Madelia -
trapped in a tavern's
body. (Ohio)

stated that coal miners in Macoupin County earned, on average, about $6.00 per 10-hour day. Miners were actually paid by tonnage, not by the hour.)

Standard Oil wanted and needed a lot of houses in a hurry, so they ordered 192 Honor-Bilt, Ready-cut homes from the Sears and Roebuck catalog.

In Carlinville, their 156 houses came in eight different styles: The Carlin, The Madelia, The Warrenton, The Gladstone, The Whitehall, The Lebanon, The Roseberry and The Langston. The homes filled a 77-acre tract near Berry Mine and the neighborhood was named "Standard Addition."

According to the 1919 Sears Modern Homes catalog, the cost of the eight designs that would comprise "Standard Addition" ranged from $1,092 for The Lebanon to $1555 for The Roanoke, but those prices are a little misleading. In the 1922 Sears Modern Homes catalog, the total cost for The Roanoke was estimated to be $4600. This included the kit home, the furnace, electrical, plumbing and all labor expenses. Sears estimated The Lebanon's finished cost would be about $3600.

Each kit also included paint and varnish, wood putty, roofing, windows, doors and trim mouldings. The only lumber that did not arrive precut was interior trim mouldings such as baseboard moulding. Nominal differences in the thickness of plaster walls could alter the dimensions of the rooms.

Note: The Honor-Bilt homes that Standard Oil purchased for miners and refinery workers were precut, but not all Sears homes were precut. Kit homes that required measuring and sawing of the lumber were a little cheaper, but not by much. In the early 1920s, an Honor-Bilt "Arcadia" home, precut and fitted, sold for $911. As a Standard Built home (fewer framing members, no subfloors or exterior sheathing, less sturdy and no precuts), The Arcadia sold for $645.

An article in the *Illinois State Journal* (March 27, 1967) states that a rail line spur – leading directly into Carlinville's newest neighborhood - was built to expedite the unloading the of construction materials from the hundreds of boxcars. Children as young as 12 years old were hired to unload the box cars full of house parts. They worked 10 hours a day and were paid $1.50 for the day's work.

It also records that the basements for the Carlinville homes were dug with slip-shovels and horse-drawn scoops. Contractors were paid $17 to dig out a basement for the five-room (two bedroom) houses and $20 for the six room (three bedroom) houses.

A woman named Mrs. Spaulding supervised the massive building project. "The Lady on Horseback," as she was called, would ride her horse from house to house and keep a close eye on the workmen. She kept the construction workers on their toes. Men she'd hired in the early morning were sometimes fired by noon. (*Illinois State Journal*, "Dear Sirs; Please Send Me 156 Houses.")

On June 12, 1918, when *The Carlinville Democrat* first announced that Standard Oil would soon build 150 houses, it was expected that the homes would be ready for occupancy within six months. On April 23, 1919, a small box ad appeared in *The Carlinville Democrat* which said:

Houses in Standard Addition to Carlinville now ready for occupancy. Prospective purchasers apply to Charles Fitzgerald, Office of Standard Oil Company (Indiana) corner High and Rice Streets.

Construction of the 156 houses took nine months, not six as expected. The reason? A nationwide shortage of wheat. Charles Fitzgerald, spokesman for Standard Oil and Manager of Houses explained to *The Chicago Daily Tribune* (November 3, 1919) what happened.

"The company (Standard Oil) purchased a forty acre wheat field and the government would not permit the destruction of the crop," he said. "On the first home, we were erecting the studding while the harvesters were shocking wheat twenty yards away."

The Chicago Tribune reporter, Oscar Hewitt, took a ten-day tour of mining homes in Illinois and liked Carlinville's homes the best. John Black, an union official for the coal miners went so far as to describe the 1000 - 1200 square foot houses as "mansions."

A patch of 30 homes in the mining town of Greenridge (in nearby Nilwood), was panned by Hewitt as having "the worst looking miners homes" which "…were set out in the field years ago and left to care for themselves."

(An interesting aside: Greenridge, once a thriving community with several hundred residents, dissolved and disappeared when the mines closed in the 1920s. The area formerly known as Greenridge is now a cornfield.)

Hewitt, an investigative reporter for the Tribune, was a native of Plainview, Illinois, a tiny farming community about 10 miles from Carlinville. It's likely that he knew this area of Illinois - Carlinville and Nilwood - like the back of his hand. In 1911, at the age of 33, he went to work for the *Tribune* and became Plainview's most famous son.

Hewitt never said that Carlinville had "the best looking miners' homes," but that sentence, attributed to this Tribune article, has been misquoted repeatedly in subsequent articles and books about Sears homes. While accurate in substance, it is nonetheless a misquote, an extrapolation (apparently) from the caption over a large photo, which states, "Row of Houses at Carlinville That Represent Best Type of Residences for Bituminous Mine Workers."

Hewitt described these houses in detail. He wrote:

Fifty-two are five room houses. 104 have six rooms. Each is on a lot 47 x 144. All of the houses are two story frame with an asphaltic roof, shaped and colored to resemble slate shingles. The roof carries a guarantee of fifteen years. Each house has a front porch and some have rear porches and a few garages. All have city water, electric light, hot air furnace heat, porch light, shades and are plastered. Each has a tiled bathroom, with a skirt bottom tub, medicine case, ornamental washbowl, towel rack and other trimmings.

Some are of a semi-bungalow type and others are house shaped. The floors are stained and varnished yellow pine, the kitchen floor looks like maple. Each has a cement basement, a pantry and a clothes closet for each sleeping room. All will have gas as soon as the local utility company will extend its mains.

Cement walks have been laid and the sewers are in and attached. In the spring, the streets will be paved with the oil asphalt with which many Chicago streets have been surfaced. Trees and shrubs have been planted on each lot. The prices for the houses range from $3370 to $4060. The purchaser pays one percent a month and in addition, taxes, fire insurance and six percent on the unpaid portion of the cost. The one per cent is reckoned this way: A house that sells for $3500 will require $35 a month until paid for.

The accompanying photo shows "A Typical Family" in the foreground and a street view of Carlinville's new Sears homes in the background. This family is identified as Mr. and Mrs. Arthur Karr and their children, James, Arthur, Jr., baby Michael, Pratt, Florence and Josephine. The Karrs were living in a five (or six) room house with less than 1100 square feet, with six children. Arthur, Jr., the oldest, appears to be about 12-years-old.

The Karrs were far surpassing the *Macoupin County Enquirer's* estimation of "five people to a house." Regrettably, I can't reproduce the article or photo here. The quality of microfiche is extremely poor. However, I can say that Mrs. Karr looks plum tuckered out. She is an extremely thin woman, with a drawn face and sad eyes, sunk deep into their sockets. Her thick black hair is pulled back in a tight bun and baby Michael is sitting contently in her lap. Mr. Karr looks quite dapper, bright-eyed, relaxed and well-built. The family is dressed in their Sunday best, which includes a simple white cotton dress for Mama and a suit and tie for Papa. Two of the boys are wearing overalls, with button-down collared shirts underneath.

*The Tribun*e article said that Fitzgerald had already sold 24 of the houses and expected they would all be sold by Christmas, adding, "We are offering them for $1000 less than the present cost of reproduction."

Under this plan (which was a "contract for deed"), the miners would own their homes at the end of ten years.

For the next few years, the community flourished. In June 1921, the *Stanolind Record* (a monthly employee magazine) reported that the Standard Addition would soon "come out of the mud." This was a 1920s colloquialism meaning that hard (concrete or asphalt) streets, curbs and gutters would soon be installed.

Reading old newspapers and magazines, you get the feeling that there was tremendous camaraderie among the residents of Standard Addition. *The Illinois State Journal* (March 27, 1967) says that rows and rows of sheets fluttered to and fro on backyard clotheslines while women talked to one another in this neighborhood full of immigrant miners and their typically large families. The men would gather on their Honor-Bilt front porches at the end of the day and holler back and forth at each another.

Times were good. In the early 1920s, miners at Berry and Schoper worked about 298 days per year, while (nationwide) most miners were working about 200 days per year.

The coal was shipped via Chicago & Alton Railroad, but since the C&A Railroad was bankrupt, Standard Oil had to buy 500 coal cars and ten 800-series steam locomotives for the coal's transport. Each of the 500 cars bore the company's imprint: "Standard Oil of Indiana, Mining Department." The 800-series steam locomotives were massive engines - weighing 292,000 pounds - for a massive operation.

Schoper was the largest coal mine in the state of Illinois, employing 650 men and hoisting (mining and removing to the surface) up to 4,000 tons of coal each day (at their peak). About 450 men worked at Berry Mine, which hoisted half as much coal as Schoper.

But the good times came to an end. As it turned out, none of the Carlinville miners paid off their homes under Standard Oil's generous installment plan.

By the mid-1920s, Carlinville's boom had busted. World War I had ended seven years earlier. The unpleasant memories of the coal shortages had faded and it seemed as though the miners were either striking or threatening to strike. Standard Oil was tired of the labor woes and they were, after all, in the petroleum business – not in the mining business.

(An unpublished coal miner's reminiscence, written in 1960, stated that one strike was proposed because the miners didn't like the interior temperature of the "Schoper Special," the railway car that carried them to work each morning. Considering the working conditions these early miners endured, it's hard to believe they'd threaten to strike because their tootsies were cold.)

The price of coal had dropped repeatedly after World War I. Standard Oil could now buy coal from non-union Kentucky mines (and other areas) cheaper than they could mine it in Macoupin County.

They took out the mules.

When the mules came out of their stables at the bottom of the mines, it was a sign that the mines were being closed for weeks or months. A sighting of mule-removal was a cause for much consternation in this community where mining was the heart and soul of the local economy. (Berry and Schoper Mines were highly mechanized and mules were used only for hauling explosives and a few other chores.)

On November 21, 1923, the mules were brought back to the surface. *Macoupin County Enquirer* sadly reported that Standard Oil would close both Berry and Schoper Mines, adding, "The action of the company in closing the mines is reported to be due to the condition of the coal markets. Just how long the shutdown will [last] is not known. By the end of the week, both mines will cease operations."

The final paragraph in the November article said, "The shutting down of the two mines employing a large number of men will make quite a difference in Carlinville and vicinity as the company paid out a large sum of money (employees' wages) every two weeks." In subsequent months, Schoper Mine (larger than Berry Mine) would open and shut several times.

Several years down the road, these mines would open and close again under new management, but for now, Standard Oil was out of the mining business. Approximately 1100 miners and workers in Schoper and Carlinville faced one of two choices: Change careers or move. Many miners moved 60 miles south for the industries of St. Louis.

Some of the miners remained in Carlinville and searched for new work.

Standard Oil Company, Oil Pioneer of the Midwest (Paul H. Giddens) offers a fascinating detail about what came next for these unemployed miners. In Standard Addition (with 156 Sears homes near Berry Mine) and Standard City (with 12 Sears homes near Schoper Mine) the mine workers were *not evicted from their homes* when they fell behind on their "mortgage" (contract for deed) payments to Standard Oil. They were allowed to remain in their homes without making any additional payments. Some families remained in the houses up to *three years* after the mines closed.

By 1935, the houses of Standard Addition had fallen into terrible disrepair and Standard Addition was given the denigrating title of "Substandard Addition" and "The Phantom City." All but five of the homes sat vacant.

It was the bottom of the Great Depression. Times were bad. Standard Oil was going to give the folks of Carlinville one more golden opportunity.

In August 29, 1935, a small four paragraph article appeared in both *The Carlinville Democrat* and *Macoupin County Enquirer*. It said that Standard Oil had put about 150 houses in Standard Addition up for sale. (Three had burned to the ground in the last 15 years and one had been moved.)

The five and six-room houses, formerly occupied by Standard Oil employees, would now be sold for $350 and $500. Even in the midst of the Great Depression, this was a tremendous value; houses selling for about a tenth of their original value ($3300 - $4000 in 1919).

An interesting aside: I don't know Thomas W. Paul, but my heart sure goes out to him. On July 11, 1929, Mr. Thomas Paul paid $3,938 for a fine little house in Standard Addition. Six years later, 150 identical houses would sell for $350 - $500.

Long time residents of the area recalled that these old Sears homes were in terrible condition when Standard Oil finally sold them in 1935. Students from Blackburn College (whose campus adjoins Standard Addition) would come into the desolate houses and have parties, build bonfires in the living room (sans fireplace), conduct séances and worse. Vandals, foolish students, severe weather and ten years of abandonment had wreaked havoc. Windows were shattered, doors had disappeared and roofs leaked. There comes a point when it's not economically feasible to rehab a house. These houses teetered on that precipice.

However, for $350 and $500, most of the houses were (probably) still a good value. They were quickly snapped up by bargain hunters. Some folks bought several of the small homes as investments and some people just wanted a home of their own. Four different members of the "Dunn" family bought one house each.

Another interesting aside: Perusing the warranty deeds, recording the sale of these 152 Sears homes, I found an interesting pattern - many of these homes were sold to unmarried women. Tallying 115 of the deeds, I found that 22% of the houses were sold "femme sole." In Depression-era times, a $350 or $500 house must have seemed like a golden opportunity for single women.

A week after the initial offering, both newspapers reported that interest in the houses had been great. More than 100 sold in seven days. The *Carlinville Democrat* reported with joy that Standard Addition, which had been abandoned for years, was now coming back to life. In late September, names of the new homeowners were published and a warm welcome was extended by the newspaper.

On November 27, 1935, the last warranty deed for a Standard Addition home was recorded in Macoupin County. Within three months, Standard Oil had sold *and* closed about 150 houses.

The warranty deeds show that the houses were sold with a restrictive covenant: Standard Oil retained all coal and mineral rights underlying said properties. This seems quite odd, because Standard Addition had already been undermined by Standard Oil during the 1920s, so mineral rights were a de facto issue. Perhaps

"The Company" was covering their backside, by inserting this restrictive clause into Standard Addition's warranty deeds.

Through the ensuing decades, Standard Addition had its ups and downs. Too many landlords took a toll on the neighborhood in the 60s and 70s. But in the 1980s, interest in Sears homes surged and Standard Addition bounced back, one more time.

During the 1980s and 90s, writers and reporters representing an impressive array of national periodicals came to see these Sears homes. The neighborhood was featured, photographed and esteemed in newsprint and on the glossy pages of leading magazines. New folks moved into Standard Addition. Things got better.

In 1987, the Carlinville Chamber of Commerce scheduled its first historic homes tour through Standard Addition. Folks in Carlinville expected moderate interest in these houses, but to everyone's surprise, visitors and tourists came by the hundreds. The Sears homes were a hit. Despite recent challenges from other Illinois' cities, Carlinville still holds title to a very special (though not *the* largest) collection of Sears catalog homes.

An aside: Carlinville has more Sears homes than they realize. In addition to these 152 homes, there are many other Sears homes within Carlinville that I discovered while casually driving through the city. (Okay, I was lost.)

Carlinville's House Tour is now an annual event and the tourism dollars it generates for the community are not insignificant.

An interesting aside: There's been loose talk of taking one home in Standard Addition and creating a museum for the community, but that's not happened yet. It'd be a wonderful idea and using a 1920s Sears Modern Homes catalog, it would be fairly easy to faithfully restore one old Sears house to its original condition - inside and out.

Today, one of the biggest problems facing these 80-year old houses is settling problems and cracks along basement walls and floors. Residents believe these problems are a legacy of the coal mines. Coal mine maps from the Illinois State Geological Survey show that the whole area under Standard Addition was undermined. The neighborhood was built close to Berry Mine for the convenience of the miners. Close enough to walk; close enough to undermine.

The 12 Sears homes in Schoper and the community of Standard City

Standard City, population 100, is a tiny little town about eight miles northeast of Carlinville. Standard City adjoins Schoper Mine, the site of 12 Sears houses that Standard Oil purchased in 1918 for their employees (as part of this $1 million order).

In October 1917, Herman Schoper sold his 500-acre farm to Standard Oil of Indiana. In addition to Schoper's farm, Standard Oil purchased 20 acres of timber (lumber on the hoof) which adjoined Schoper's 500 acres.

After purchasing Herman Schoper's farm, Standard Oil acted quickly and spared no expense in creating a first-class, progressive mining operation at the site. Two material shafts - where men and materials ascended and descended - were dug about ¼ mile apart. Each material shaft also had a ventilation shaft directly beside it, with an 8-foot tall squirrel cage fan, which forced fresh air into the mines. The ventilation shafts had steel steps which provided a secondary escape route in case of accident.

A three-story Federalist-styled solid concrete office building and powerhouse was built to provide electricity for the machinery in the mine. A creek that ran through a small valley beside the powerhouse was damned to create a seven acre, 40-foot deep man-made lake (which became known as Schoper Lake).

Underground pipes drafted water from the lake to the powerhouse for the steam engines. It was claimed that the powerhouse's six dynamos had the potential to create enough electricity to power the entire state of Illinois. The local papers claimed that it was the most powerful steam-driven power plant in the world. The smokestack was 213 feet tall and was the second highest peak in Macoupin County, only a little shorter than the spire atop the Macoupin County Courthouse in Carlinville.

When completed in mid-1919, the powerhouse also brought electricity to those twelve Sears houses, just across the street. They were the only "electrified" houses in Schoper or Standard City. The rest of the community would not know the joys of electric lights until power lines from Carlinville made their way to Standard City in the 1930s.

Schoper Mine and its buildings stretched out for more than 1.5 miles east and west of what is now known as "Mine Road." The deepest part of the mine was 440-feet deep and in the early 1920s, it was the largest colliery (coal mining operation) in Illinois.

In 1921, a letter to the editor of the *Macoupin County Enquirer* (reprinted in the August 1921 *Stanolind Record*), stated that Standard Oil had invested $1 million in Schoper Mine. A promotional ad in the *Macoupin County Enquirer* said the powerhouse *alone* cost $2 million. The truth is probably somewhere in-between.

Regardless of the precise dollar amount, one fact was clear: Schoper Mine was a first class operation, built by visionary, progressive men who had very deep pockets.

Railroad tracks were laid parallel to Mine Road and led to the mine's two material shafts. Another railroad siding ran within a few yards of the future site of the Sears homes, so that unloading those 360,000 pieces (12 houses worth) of building materials would be easier.

The Sears homes and one long 12-bay garage were built for the superintendents and foremen. Several large bunkhouses, located behind the powerhouse and beside Schoper Lake, housed miners and other workers.

About 1000 people (which included miners and their families) came to the site to work and live and love and raise children. Little houses sprung up, a school was built, stores popped up and a post office subleased space in the back of a store. A seven-room hotel was built in town, as well as a dance hall, two boarding houses, a bakery, a shoe store, a meat market and a theater.

This center of activity now needed an identity.

"Let's call it Standard City," someone may have suggested. "After all," (I can imagine them saying) "we wouldn't have a city out here, were it not for Standard Oil." Or perhaps Standard Oil made the pronouncement.

On June 1920, Standard City was incorporated as a village and on June 16th, the new village held their first election for a board of trustees. (Lest you get confused, Standard Addition was the name of the neighborhood located in Carlinville, where the 156 Sears homes were built. Standard City was the Schoper farm-turned-village, eight miles northeast of Carlinville. Standard Row was the name given to Ninth Street in Wood River, where 24 Sears homes were built by Standard Oil.)

Sears put Schoper on the map by featuring it in their Modern Homes catalogs. From 1919-1925, a photograph (presuming to be) "12 Sears homes in Schopper [sic], Illinois" appeared in the front pages of the Sears Modern Homes catalogs.

And throughout the 1920s, Sears printed Standard Oil's thank-you note (that opens this chapter) on the back cover of their Modern Homes catalogs. (Fortunately, Standard Oil spelled Schoper *correctly* in their thank-you note.) In the second half of the 1920s, Sears catalogs no longer offered the letter's date. It had disappeared from view.

Having spent months researching this chapter, visiting the area, talking to residents and even looking at old plats (which is not something I'm very good at), I have to make a confession. I'm not sure where Schoper begins and where Standard City ends. The line that distinguishes Schoper from Standard City is fuzzy. Residents within Standard City tell me that Schoper was the name of the mine and consequently, the entire region around the mine became known as Schoper. Schoper was a community *within the borders* of Standard City.

Regardless, one of the most frequently perpetuated mistakes in books and articles on Schoper's Sears homes is this: Schoper was renamed Standard City in 1985. This is not true.

Schoper has always been known as Schoper (since Herman Schoper sold his farm to Standard Oil) and Standard City has always been known as Standard City (since incorporation in 1920). These areas were not renamed in 1985.

It's fun to try and imagine life in this sleepy, rural community 80 years ago. According to all accounts, it was a bustling mining town with busy streets filled with busy people. Interesting sounds filled the air, from the screech of tipples (tipping over carts of coal) to the shrill whistle of an 800-series steam locomotive dragging a long stretch of coal cars on to the refineries in Wood River.

There is very little written history about the 12 Sears Modern Homes of Schoper. Even the captioned photo that appears in the front pages of several 1920s Sears Modern Homes catalogs is in error. The caption reads, "Sears, Roebuck and Company houses at Schopper [sic], Illinois, sold to the Standard Oil Company."

But the photo is a street view of the Sears homes in *Wood River*, not Schoper.

With my Sears Modern Homes catalog in hand, I recently walked along Ninth Street in Wood River, noting that the houses captioned "Schopper" [sic] matched the houses lining Ninth Street. And then another interesting detail about that photo caught my eye, giving me one of those "ah-ha" moments. The homes pictured in the Sears Modern Homes catalog are in a residential area, with curbs and sidewalks. The 12 Sears homes by Schoper Mine had a cornfield on one side and a massive power house on the other. The houses in Schoper never had curbing.

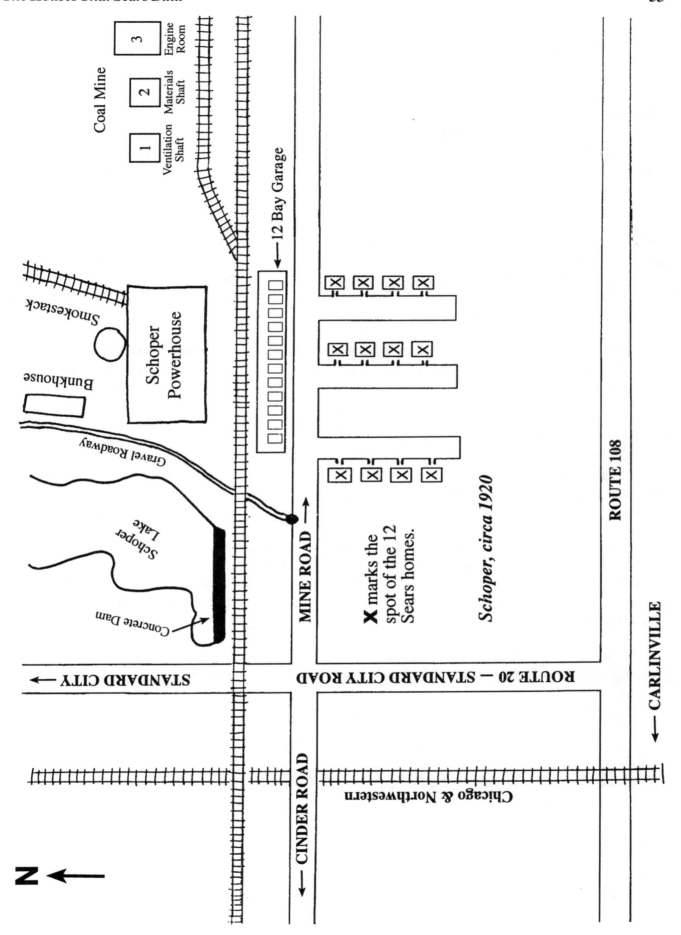

Coal Mine

1 — Ventilation Shaft
2 — Materials Shaft
3 — Engine Room

Smokestack

Bunkhouse

Schoper Powerhouse

Gravel Roadway

12 Bay Garage

Schoper Lake

Concrete Dam

MINE ROAD

STANDARD CITY

ROUTE 20 — STANDARD CITY ROAD

CINDER ROAD

Chicago & Northwestern

CARLINVILLE

ROUTE 108

X marks the spot of the 12 Sears homes.

Schoper, circa 1920

N

The boom goes bust.

1920 - 1924 were the boom years for Standard City. But when Schoper Mine started shutting down for longer and longer periods in the mid-1920s, the economy of Standard City suffered – and so did the real estate. The houses in Standard City began to spontaneously combust. House fires became a regular part of the village's evening routine. *The Story of Macoupin County* records that a house burned almost every night after the mine closed. Because houses burned so frequently and so thoroughly, area insurance companies canceled the villagers' fire insurance policies and the mass exodus of Standard City began.

And what happened to those 12 Sears homes across from the mine?

According to long-time residents, about nine of the Sears homes left the same way they came in: In pieces and loaded on a boxcar. A few years after Schoper Mine closed, nine of the Sears houses were disassembled and shipped by train to destinations unknown. Two of the Sears houses were moved, intact. They didn't get too far from their original site; one was moved to Route 108 and another house was moved to Atwater Road, both of which are just outside Standard City.

For many years, that last remaining Sears house stood alone on a plot that was rapidly reverting to its primitive status as farmland. The Gladstone, the last survivor of its 11 siblings was still occupied by former mine superintendent, John McMillan, and his wife. The house and the powerhouse were in a showdown now, to see who would last the longest; which structure would be the lone survivor of a once bustling and massive colliery?

After the mines closed, McMillan became the mine's caretaker. It was his job to descend into the deserted coal mine several times a week, grease the water pumps and turn them on. Ground water, which seeped into the mine, had to be pumped out frequently. He was also responsible for turning on the powerful ventilating fans to remove any build-up of firedamp - highly explosive methane gas - which accumulates in coal mines.

Sometime in the 1940s, Standard Oil sold the mine. New owners opened the mine again for two or three years, but it was a small operation employing 95 men at its peak. In May 1947, *The Carlinville Democrat* reported that Schoper Mine was closed (again) for an indefinite time. The same article reported that the mine's owners, "Standard Coal Mining & Converters Corporation," based in Chicago (not affiliated with Standard Oil) had declared bankruptcy.

In June 1952, the water pumps were removed from the bottom of the mine and the ventilation shafts and material shafts were sealed with massive slabs of concrete, measuring 25 x 45 feet.

John McMillan remained in his Gladstone for many more years. Of the 152 Sears houses in Standard Addition and the twelve in Schoper, McMillan was the *only Standard Oil employee* who remained in his Sears home (until 1935 or later). Residents recall that his home was always one of the nicest houses in Standard City.

After John and his wife passed on, their heirs rented out the 1918 Honor-Bilt Sears house. Sometime in 1996 or 1997, the house caught fire and burned to the ground.

In Summer 2002, the Schoper powerhouse – the last structural remnant of the Standard Oil Coal Mine – was finally demolished. According to the *Macoupin County Enquirer*, the 213-foot tall smoke stack was brought down August 27th at 10:19 a.m. with carefully placed explosives.

An interesting aside: The contemporary newspaper articles about the demolition of the power-house stirred some memories. On September 5, 2002, the Macoupin County Enquirer ran an article about the Sears home that was moved from Schoper Mine to Route 108. It said the Armour family purchased The Gladstone (another Gladstone; not the McMillans') in 1938 for $250 and moved it to their farm (about two miles from its original site at the mine).

Today, the only reminder of the 12 Sears homes is a little bit of gravel that cuts into an open field, where one of three short side streets existed years ago. A subtle depression on the terrain marks the area where the basement of The Gladstone was carved out by a pair of ornery mules, dragging a weighted scoop across the old Schoper farm.

Lush green crops now carpet the land that was once filled with sidewalks and short streets and houses and back porches and clothes lines and kids and toys. Eighty years ago, Flivvers, Kissels, Overlands and Studebaker Sixes lined the busy streets. There was so much life lived here.

In doing the research for this book, I read and studied old stories and articles and interviews until I found myself living in the 1920s and thinking and pondering and wondering about these people and their lives.

In August 1925, the last Carlinville/Schoper column appeared in the *Stanolind Record*. I *loved* reading these columns, because they were a little gossipy and full of interesting details about life in Schoper. They contained precious information about these Sears homes and their occupants that would otherwise have been lost to history.

That last issue in August 1925 reported that Top Boss John Dunn couldn't decide if he should name his new baby boy "Pat" or "Mike" and that Willard Clark was working at the mine during his college break. It also said the flume at the power house was drained recently and as the water became low, miners jumped in and started swimming and came out with "wriggling victims [frogs, snakes, etc.] in their hip pockets," adding, "there was a grand scramble for awhile."

And without a summary or closing chapter, that's the end. We're left hanging. It's like having your favorite soap opera switched off in the very middle or having a compelling book snatched from your hands. How did these stories end?

Did Mr. and Mrs. Wylder ever recover from the loss of little Ethel May, their baby daughter? Did Veva Fuller and daughter Gwendolyn eventually find peace, after husband and father Louis died when part of the mine's roof collapsed? What became of widower Frank Rodgers' three children, who became orphans when their father died in Schoper Mine on May 30th?

Did John McMillan's boy, Paul, ever go to college and get his law degree, as he'd hoped to do when he left his night watchman's job at Schoper Mine in 1925? And what about his sister Peggy, who was born in the McMillan's Gladstone on October 1921?

Did John Estes ever find out which practical joker covered his seat at the rotary dump (a piece of coal loading equipment) with oil? Did Don March and John Dunn settle their disagreement, after Don loudly pro-claimed that with "Dunnie" as a boss, Noah could have built the ark in 30 days? How did life turn out for 14-

SIX ROOMS
AND BIG
PORCH

**1924 Sears
Modern Homes
Catalog**

**Gladstone
in Illinois
with partially
enclosed porch**

**Gladstone
in Washington
D.C. area**

year old miner Allan Pierce, son of miner William Pierce, who became all-star quarterback on the high school's football team, center on the basketball team and a member of the Glee Club?

For those interested in visiting Standard City, I'd say, it's worth the trip. There's something about this place that is compelling, even haunting. Driving into Standard City, you can turn on "Mine Road" to go to the old mine or turn left for "Cinder Road" (a road originally paved in the 1920s with coal cinders). A residential street - "Pershing Avenue" was undoubtedly named after General John "Black Jack" Pershing, World War I hero and commander of the American Expeditionary Force. Another street is "Rice Street," probably named for the man who handled real estate acquisitions for Standard Oil.

It is a place that exudes a feeling of a palpable history.

Standing on the plat of land once occupied by the massive powerhouse, gazing out at Schoper Lake, you can close your eyes and almost hear the steam whistle signaling the end of a shift. Listen, *really listen* - and maybe you'll hear the metal cables of the hoist groan and creak as a steel cage raises three dozen coal-blackened miners from 440 feet below grade. Let go of the present for a second and maybe you can hear the snatching and clunking of the couplings on 150 fully loaded coal cars, as they pull out for the Wood River refinery.

Here, at the old mine site, it feels like the thin veil of time that is the lone separator between the lush, green farmland of 2001 and the busy workplace of the 1920s, could probably be pierced or parted for an instant, if you could just focus a little harder, concentrate a little better and listen more intently.

Einstein said, "To those of us who are committed physicists, the past, present and future are only illusion, however persistent."

Nowhere in my experience have I intuitively felt that this illusion of time is more fragile and ethereal, than at the site of Schoper Mine. And if you're not a romantic/tangential/historical/ fanatic dreamer (as I am), but just someone who enjoys visiting towns that boomed and busted, it's still worth the trip.

Just don't speed and don't litter and don't tromp on the crops and don't trespass. Watch out for the many potholes and if it's wet, drive extra slow so that you don't splash mud on people or pets or crops. Standard City is still home to about a hundred folks and they (rightfully so) love their community.

Wood River

In the late 1800s, Wood River was the horseradish capital of the world. It was also a watermelon patch. The sandy soil, a left over from the ice age, lent itself well to watermelons and horseradishes. The ubiquitous sand burs were known as "Wood River Roses." They were the primary vegetation that thrived in the soil that was once the Mississippi's river bottom.

In 1910, Wood River's population was 84. But the times were changing. In 1908, Henry Ford introduced a new and improved automobile, which superseded the prior automobile, known simply as "Model N." The new car would be called "Model T." It would accomplish his stated goal of providing "a car for the masses." Ford sold 19,000 cars that first year. In 1910, there were 450,000 Fords and Chevrolets and other automobiles on the road. Three years later, that number jumped to 1.2 million.

Standard Oil Company of Indiana opened a refinery in Wood River (about 30 miles from Carlinville and across the Mississippi River from St. Louis), in January 1908. The refinery was an enormous operation. By 1919, the *Stanolind Record* reported that the refinery covered 630 sandy acres and contained 207 stills and could process 16,000 barrels of crude each day. Standard Oil recruited and hired hundreds of workers to fill the expanding work force. But housing in Wood River was woefully inadequate.

In 1920, the census showed that the population of Wood River had increased more than 4000% (to 3,476), making it the fastest growing city in the *country* and earning it a place in national headlines. In December 1920, *American Carpenter and Builder Magazine* dubbed Wood River "The Miracle City."

Twenty-four houses from Standard Oil's $1 million order landed in Wood River. The homes were built in a row on Ninth Street. On February 1920, the *Stanolind Record* printed a photo of the newly built houses in Wood River captioned: "These houses were built by the Standard Oil Company (Indiana) and sold to employees on the same plan that was used in disposing of miners' homes in Carlinville."

The *Stanolind Record* had about a five week lead time between event and publication date. The houses in Carlinville were finished by April 1919, but the majority of the 24 houses in Wood River weren't ready for occupancy until eight months later.

On April 26, 1919, the *Alton Evening Telegraph* reported that Standard Oil had just started construction on the first of the houses on Ninth Avenue. About two weeks later, on May 5th, the *Telegraph* reported that the 24 houses now had roofs.

"Frank Gainor of the Standard Oil office has completed a new home in Standard Row (Ninth Street), and the Gainor family will move in this week," reported the *Telegraph* on July 8, 1919.

The Gainor's home was "The Fullerton" and it was the largest and fanciest house in that $1 million order. It was also the *only* Fullerton in the order.

Frank Gainor was Assistant General Superintendent at the refinery and had come to the Wood River refinery in 1907, when it was still under construction. John Gainor, a retired attorney who now lives in nearby Godfrey, Illinois, was Frank's son. John was 5 or 6 years old when the house was built in 1919 and he remembers his parents discussing the house.

"That house has a few little extras, like that entry foyer and the good-morning stairs," Gainor told me in a phone interview. "This house wasn't for the run of the mill employee. That's the way Mother and Dad ordered the house built. There are probably several things in the home that were built to Mother's request. In Dad's case (because he held a prestigious position at the refinery), he had some discretion in wanting certain things."

The rest of the Sears houses along Ninth Street (Standard Row) were quite plain, built without the extras and options found in The Fullerton. Because of Frank Gainor's position with Standard Oil, it is probable that the family was offered the option of picking out a nicer home with a few amenities. John Gainor recalls that his parents paid the mortgage off a few years later and lived there until they passed on. The Fullerton, now covered in pink aluminum siding, sold most recently in the mid-1990s, for less than $65,000.

It seems very likely that The Fullerton was one the first Sears houses completed along "Standard Row."

The other 23 were apparently not finished for several more months.

In January 1920, the *Stanolind Record* reported that C. M. Smith and his family had just moved into their new home on Ninth Street in Wood River.

Most likely, the construction crew that erected these homes started in Carlinville and Schoper and then came to Wood River in late April (1919), when the houses in Carlinville and Schoper were complete.

In Carlinville's Standard Addition and also in Wood River, the Sears homes were built for the miners and the working class. The houses across from Schoper Mine were for the foremen and bosses. The miners at Schoper lived in huge bunkhouses behind the mine.

Wood River today

Decades later, in the 1970s, Wood River's industrial landscape was changing. Standard Oil, turned American Oil, turned Amoco, was shutting down their refinery in Wood River a little bit at a time. By the mid-1990s, BP Amoco (now BP) had completely pulled out of Wood River, leaving behind the typical environmental nightmares, some old buildings, a few tank farms and dozens and dozens of Sears Modern Homes.

Today, Wood River has about 11,500 residents and their biggest employer is the local Wal-Mart. The second biggest employer *was* Wood River Township Hospital, but they recently closed their doors. It's a city that's still staggering from the loss of its industries.

Unfortunately, there are no other records about the acquisition or construction of Wood River's many Sears homes. When the Wood River Public Library burned to the ground in 1929, many historical documents and records were lost. And most of the people who might remember the details about the Sears homes are no longer with us. Neither Standard Oil nor Sears Roebuck & Company preserved records about the purchase or building of these homes.

As of this writing, the Sears homes in Wood River sell for $40,000 - $85,000. A home that's been extensively remodeled and modernized (in other words - uglified) brings $85,000. For the most part, the historical significance of Wood River's Sears homes is not yet understood, appreciated or valued. Decimating, detail-destroying remodeling - that effaces and erases all evidence of the homes' historical significance - continues.

There are eight different designs of Sears homes on Wood River's Standard Row on 9th Street. They are: *The Roanoke, The Carlin, The Elsmore, The Argyle, The Whitehall, The Fullerton, The Madelia, The Gladstone.* One of the Sears homes was torn down several years ago, to make way for a street widening.

Conclusion

This was the largest order in the history of the Sears Modern Homes department. One corporation (Standard Oil) purchased three sets of houses for three different communities that went in three different directions. Carlinville stumbled a bit after losing Standard Oil, but eventually, they found their feet again and had a full and impressive economic recovery, coming back stronger than ever. Standard City's population went from 1000 to 100 and nearly reverted back to its original state as a cornfield. Wood River - home of the Standard Oil Refinery - didn't lose Standard Oil until the 1970s, but between the late 1930s - 1970s, they didn't really boom or bust.

**1919 Sears
Modern Homes
Catalog**

MANY ATTRACTIVE FEATURES

The ROANOKE   Honor Bilt $1,555.00
No. 226 *Not Cut or Fitted.*

**One of the
Roanokes built by
Standard Oil in 1919**

**Picture from 1919
Stanolind Record of Wood
River's "Standard Row"**

COMPANY BUILT HOUSES, WOOD RIVER

These houses were built by the Standard Oil Company (Indiana) and sold to employees on the same plan as that used in disposing of miners' homes at Carlinville.

The 12 Sears homes adjoining the Schoper mine have all been moved or destroyed. Carlinville still has 152 of their original 156 homes and they've developed a large-scale tourism event, centered around these houses. And Wood River has 50+ Sears homes (there are others in the city, in addition to the 23 on Ninth Street), but they've never done anything (yet) to capitalize on and promote this impressive collection.

These three cities' stories are a perfect example of what has become of this country's 75,000 Sears homes. Some burned down, some were burned down, some were torn down, some were moved, a few were disassembled, some were remuddled and some are now being beautifully and thoughtfully restored and cherished. Some communities aren't interested in doing anything to preserve and promote their Sears homes and some communities are striving to locate and preserve their collection of Sears homes.

Some closing thoughts about Standard Oil and Sears homes

As I started learning about Standard Oil, labor relations and life as a Standard Oil coal miner or refinery worker in the 1920s, my opinion of "The Company" sank lower and lower.

In order to write this chapter on Carlinville, Standard City and Wood River, I did some research on early 1900s coal mines in other parts of Illinois, as well as West Virginia, Pennsylvania, Colorado, Alabama, Tennessee and Kentucky. Through this study, my eyes were opened to some sad facts.

I'd been using my own paradigm - the (ex)wife of a blue-collar worker in today's post-OSHA, safety-is-king-America as a gage - when I looked backwards through the prism of time at a miner's life. That was a skewed view. When I learned more about the 1920s and the typical miner's work experience, I recognized that Standard Oil was quite progressive for its day.

In 1919, Standard Oil was developing innovative and proactive safety policies that became benchmarks for other industrial giants. (Source: *Standard Oil Company (Indiana), Oil Pioneer of the Midwest* and *Stanolind Records*, 1919-1927.)

Scanning the papers of the day, it appears that there were fewer deaths at Berry and Schoper Mines than other coal mines of that period. Studying photographs of other mining towns, I understood why *The Chicago Tribune* (Nov. 3, 1919) described the modest frame houses in Carlinville as "mansions."

Miners in other areas often lived in squalid shanties. When the miner's employer was finished with the miner's pay - deducting debts to the company store, the company doctor and other inflated expenses - the miner was often left with nothing but a few pennies in his pay envelope.

Conditions in the mine were hellish. Men sometimes spent their entire 12-hour shift on their knees or ankle deep in bone-chilling, foul water. Company doctors frequently lied to the miners about the severity of black lung disease and sent them back into the mines when they were ill. Miner's wives sometimes died of black lung, just from washing their husband's clothes.

When miners died, the mine records sometimes listed them only by nationality, neglecting to even record their name, as in "Italian #14." (Source: *Index of Fatalities in West Virginia Coal Mines, 1883-1925*, Helen S. Stinson, 1985.)

Oscar Hewitt's article in the *Tribune* was accurate: Standard Oil *was* different. By today's standards, their workplace practices and policies left room for improvement, but they did give their mine workers an incredible opportunity to become homeowners. Even if the miners ultimately lost those houses after the mines closed, that new view and that feeling of owning a fine modern home must have shaped and changed their life in profound ways. Or maybe if gave the immigrants' children a keyhole peak at what life in America could mean. That memory of a fine home in a nice neighborhood must have made a powerful and lasting impression on the children and their parents.

Letters sent from immigrant miners to their relatives in the homeland might have inspired more Serbs or Italians or Poles or Slavics to make the (emotionally and physically) difficult trip to America and seize a tiny bit of that dream for themselves. Who knows how much good came to these families (and conversely, how much good these new people brought to their surrounding communities and even the country), as a direct result of those 192 houses in Carlinville, Schoper and Wood River?

In erecting these homes, Standard Oil offered a bit of the American dream to their workers. I commend Standard Oil for that. While other mining communities look back at their history and miners' squalid living conditions with white-hot shame and embarrassment, Carlinville and Standard City can hold their head high. They can point with pride to the 1920s pictures of their *rows and rows of the prettiest little houses that you ever did see.*

It's a legacy to be proud of, and Standard Oil gave them that legacy.

Chapter 7

The Houses that Sears Sold and Repossessed: Sears Modern Homes, Sears Mortgages and the Great Depression

Never before in all the history of the industry has such a revolutionary, outstanding (financing) plan been offered to the public! Never before has anyone dared to propose such a liberal, low cost finance plan. Because only Sears Roebuck and Co., with its immense cash resources, could afford to finance (your home) at such a low cost. The liberality of our plan will appeal to the thousands who have experienced the usual difficulty in financing a home. It is really very simple – as you'll readily see! The easiest of any (plan) we ever saw!

1929 Sears Modern Homes catalog

Contemporary magazine and newspaper articles frequently report that Sears sold more than 100,000 homes during their 32 years in the housing business. That's not an accurate figure. In fact, I suspect that it's part of the misinformation that has swirled around Sears homes for many years now.

Here are the facts as taken from the front pages of the Sears Modern Homes catalogs.

In 1918, the Sears Modern Homes catalog stated: "*You have the satisfaction of knowing that you are not facing an experiment because over 25,000 people have built houses according to our plans and with our materials.*" In 1924, a large headline on pages four and five stated: "*Over 30,000 houses sold. Every customer satisfied.*" In 1926, Sears proclaimed they had sold 34,000 homes; in 1930 – 48,000. The 1931 "Homes of Today" catalog stated "*57,000 Sears houses have been built.*"

The years and the numbers:

1909 – "hundreds"	1924 – 30,000
1911 – 1,000*	1925 – 30,000
1914 – 4,000°	1926 – 34,000
1916 – 16,000	1928 – 42,700
1918 – 25,000	1929 – 44,200
1922 – 25,000	1930 – 48,000
1923 – 25,000	1931 – 57,000

* Source: February 1911 *American Carpenter and Builder Magazine* (Sears ad)
° Source: 1914 Sears Building Materials Catalog

In January 22, 1932, *The Wall Street Journal* reported, "Sears…expects to build its 100,000[th] home during 1932." A statement on pages 44 and 45 of the 1933 Sears Modern Homes catalog echoed this news. It said, "More than 100,000 homes have been built this Sears Way." By 1934, the back page of the Sears Modern Homes catalogs said, "Over 100,000 homes built and backed by this guarantee."

Obviously, Sears did not sell 43,000 homes between 1931 and 1932 (the date of the *Wall Street Journal* article) or 1933 (the date of the first catalog with the "100,000 homes sold" pronouncement). "Black Tuesday," October 29, 1929 was the official start of the Great Depression. Reviewing sales numbers for Sears Modern Homes, it seems *very unlikely* that Sears could have sold 43,000 homes during the first years of a contracting economy.

Like most writers, the copy writers (folks who write copy for ads) at Sears were pretty shrewd wordsmiths. The 100,000 number was qualified with this statement, "…built and backed by this guarantee." In 1931, the Sears Modern Homes department was regrouped and reorganized under the name "Home Construction Division." The Home Construction Division did home improvements, house designing and house building. It seems likely that Sears was including home improvement projects from their Home Construction Division to boost this number.

If you hired Sears Home Construction Division in 1931 to put a new roof on your 1902-built home, then technically, the house would have been "backed by Sears guarantee." Homes that were built with a large number of items ordered from Sears Building Materials catalogs could also have been included as being "built and backed by this guarantee."

Sears was still selling mail order homes in the early 1930s, but their best sellers were the itty-bitty homes - the $1,000 homes. The magical jump from 57,000 to 100,000 in one year could only have come about from a new way of doing the math. Adding in those "improved" houses that were "backed by Sears guarantee" is the only logical explanation for this huge jump.

The Depression hits home(s)

An article in the *Chicago Tribune*, dated January 22, 1931, said that housing starts for the year (1930) were down 53%. The same article indicated that despite this, sales of Sears homes had shown a "substantial increase" from 1929. Most likely, this vague language ("substantial increase") indicates that even though actual sales income had *decreased* (as is reflected by sales figures quoted below), the *number of homes sold* through Sears Modern Homes department may have *increased*.

An article in April 1933's *Fortune* magazine found all this house-selling in the midst of a depression pretty fantastic. The article reported that despite the Depression, sales of Sears smallest homes were rolling right along.

Fortune reported that in 1927, 3,303 Sears "stock houses" (small houses with minimal customization) priced between $5,500 - $6,000 (completed costs) were built that year. In 1930, Sears sold 2,191 of these small kit homes and in 1931, that number was 1,765.

"The Crafton" (also known as #3318) was one of the best-selling Sears home during these early years of the Great Depression. It was a very modest 600-800 square foot frame home, offered in four different floor

THE CRAFTON ..
▲ FOUR, FIVE AND SIX ROOMS WITH BATH

No. 3318A
ALREADY CUT
AND FITTED
PRICE $1,021⁰⁰

No. 3318C
ALREADY CUT
AND FITTED
PRICE $1,170⁰⁰

No. 3318D
ALREADY CUT
AND FITTED
PRICE $1,330⁰⁰

JUST before this catalog went to press, we counted the number of home builders who have been made happy by building one of these attractive low cost American type bungalows. When over a thousand vote these plans their choice, there can be only one answer—they meet the requirements where four, five or six rooms are needed, at a minimum cost. No "gingerbread"—just attractive, livable space.

You have your choice of three plans. No. 3318A size 22 ft. wide by 30 ft. deep contains four rooms and bath. Plan No. 3318C size 24 ft. by 34 ft. 6 in. contains five rooms and bath, and plan No. 3318D size 26 ft. by 38 ft. contains six rooms and bath. All rooms well proportioned with good wall space and plenty of large windows.

Each plan has a large porch with baluster railing. The exterior walls are planned to be covered with No. 1 24-inch Cedar shingles, finished with one dip coat and one brush coat of super quality shingle stain.

At the price quoted, we guarantee to furnish all necessary material according to specifications, plans and instructions for erection, to complete this home. All framing material cut to fit, reducing cost.

Fill out attached form for complete delivered price and details about optional equipment.

PLAN No. 3318X

Plan No. 3318X is the same as No. 3318D, but roof is raised and attic stairs are furnished over cellar stairs. This will make ideal storage. Write for details about this plan.

FLOOR PLAN 3318A

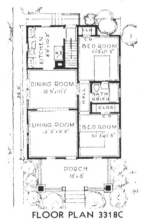

FLOOR PLAN 3318C

FLOOR PLAN 3318D

Sears, Roebuck and Co.   642   ▶ Page 25 ◀

Figure 24 - The Crafton was one of Sears best selling homes during the Great Depression. It was offered in four models, 3318A, C, D or X. The floor plan for model 3318X was identical to 3318D, but "X" had a raised roof and stairway to the attic. (1934 catalog)

plans (A, C, D or X). The price of The Crafton in the 1933 catalog was $911, $1013 and $1165, for the four room, five room or six room model. (Note: This price did not include plumbing, electrical or heating equipment, and also did not include lot costs, excavation, masonry work, construction expense, etc. A $1013 Crafton could easily have cost $5000+ [inclusive of lot] when completed.)

Even so, considering that the economy was in the early years of a major contraction, the fact that Sears was still selling houses – even Craftons - by the *hundreds* was nothing short of astounding.

According to *Catalogs and Counters, A History of Sears, Roebuck and Company*, Sears hit their peak – dollar-wise - in 1929. That year, Sears sold $12 million in houses and originated nearly $6 million in mortgage loans.

That was also the year that the Modern Homes catalog featured a lengthy "article" on Frank W. Kushel, general manger of the Sears Modern Homes department. In that piece, Frank was asked, "Why are you (Sears, presumably) in the home building business?"

Kushel responded, "Because, it was an obligation that our organization could not overlook. It was – and is – a service that we must perform regardless of *whether or not there is any profit in the business"* (italics added).

That was a pretty noble sentiment, but as things turned out, not even Sears could afford to offer this "service" when their profits took a nose dive and annual losses were in the millions.

According to *Catalogs and Counters,* sales volume dropped to $10.6 million in 1930, with $6.8 million of that amount tied up in Sears mortgages. Still, these sales numbers were not too shabby, considering what was happening with the rest of the economy. The article in *Fortune* states, "In ultra-depressed 1932, some 1300 (modest Sears homes) were constructed."

In January 1930, a short piece appeared in *Business Week*, announcing and praising Sears' new and improved and even-more-generous mortgage policies and programs. The upbeat piece said that Sears would "…be in friendly and constant touch with their [mortgage] customers."

By the end of 1932, the Great Depression had caught up with Sears - with a vengeance -and trustees from Sears would soon be in "friendly and constant touch" with thousands of those mortgage customers.

Fortune stated that the sales of Sears homes decreased 40% in 1932 and the Modern Homes department had taken a loss of $1.15 million for the year.

"Defaulted mortgages were the trouble," *Fortune* reported. "Sears reacquired 1,081 properties with unpaid balances of $4,370,642." The article went on to say 219 of these homes had been sold, which left "…Sears holding 862 [homes] with $3,539,721 [in defaulted mortgages] unpaid."

Those 1,081 foreclosures - houses which had housed formerly-loyal Sears customers - were undoubtedly a public relations nightmare for the giant mail-order company. Many of these Sears homeowners had built these homes *with their own hands*. Foreclosure is a hard experience to pass through (I speak from personal experience), but to lose a home that you *built*, must make it doubly so.

In happier, pre-Depression days, these people – the 1,081 former Sears homeowners – had pored over the pictures in their Sears Modern Homes catalog, hoping, looking, figuring, thinking, studying, dreaming, wondering, pondering and thinking some more. Several of my Sears house catalogs have scribblings in the corner or at the side of the page. Columns of numbers were ciphered in pencil to determine the final price. How much would the total package cost? Could they afford the Hercules Steam Heat outfit or would they have to settle for the cheaper hot air "pipeless" furnace? Or did they, like one family I know, buy the house first and then save their coins and buy the furnace later?

But then one day, the house they've waited for and dreamt about finally arrived and the family got right to work, even calling in a few markers from friends and neighbors to get those 30,000 pieces nailed together before winter. Maybe they wrote a letter back to Mama in the old country and reported, "You won't believe this, but we are building a modern home! Our very own home! Bathrooms inside! Electric lights too, and a furnace!"

One day, the last nail goes in and the family invites everyone over to their sweet home for the "grand event" – moving day.

And then comes the day when Sears forecloses on them.

It must have been horrible. Horrible for everyone – from the sheriff who served the warrant – to the housewife who struggled to hide her tears from the children as she told them they'd soon be moving to a new place. Horrible for the husband too, as he looked at the scar on his right hand – a remnant from the time the door moulding fell down on his thumb while he was building the back bedroom - and wondered if they'd ever own a nice house again.

"We are moving out," the wife tells the neighbors who have noticed the wooden moving crates in the front yard. Bending over to shove a book into a small crate, the wife adds, "Sears, Roebuck and Company has evicted us from our *home*."

According to *Catalogs and Counters,* 219 of the foreclosed homes resold in a fairly short time for about 85% of their original value. During these hard, lean and deflationary times, Sears houses, coupled with some unknown family's back-breaking labor and sweat-equity, still retained a surprising amount of their value.

It was under much better circumstances that some Sears copy writer penned this paragraph for the 1922 Sears Modern Homes catalog:

We need your good will. When you purchase a house from us, we have not only your best interests in mind, but our own reputation. We want the house we sell you to be so good that you will be a friend and customer of ours forever afterward. We want to supply the furnishings for this new home of yours when you build it; we want to sell you clothing, groceries, musical instruments, shoes and books. Don't you see that [this transaction] is as much to our interests as it is to yours?

And this, from the 1929 catalog: "We don't want to sell a home and lose a friend." (Quoting Frank W. Kushel, general manager of the Modern Homes department.)

How many of those 1,081 homeowners (and that was just in 1932) continued to be Sears' "friends" after these foreclosures. Did the very name Sears make them cringe? Was every catalog a reminder?

After the first edition of *"The Houses That Sears Built"* was published, I received hundreds of letters from readers, including two letters from people who remember hearing an elder relative talk about their Sears mortgage and the Great Depression. In one case, the family lost their beloved Sears home to foreclosure when they could not make the payments on the Sears mortgage. Two generations later, that family still refuses to patronize Sears Roebuck and Company. One can only imagine the depth of feeling and contempt that this family felt toward Sears during the time of the eviction.

Another letter came from a man whose father wrote to Sears and explained that he was out of work, but would catch up on the mortgage payments as soon as he had a job. Sears responded by saying, "do the best you can" and *did not pursue foreclosure proceedings.* A short time later, the Sears homeowner found gainful employment and was able to make up back payments. Although I don't know the details, I suspect the second instance happened later in the 30s, when the Depression was further along and Sears had taken in as many houses as they cared to.

Those were tough times, but the people who made those decisions for Sears were in a terrible spot. Homeowners and renters were evicted from their homes all across the country. People who lived through the Depression have told me, "We lost our home, but so did everyone else. That's just the way things were back then."

Homes of Today

By 1931, the Sears Modern Homes department was changing. First, they changed the look of their catalog. The traditional and time-proven Sears Modern Homes catalog had been replaced with a modernistic, art deco flavored catalog titled, Homes of Today.

The catalogs from the 1920s contained line-drawings of houses, which listed (and puffed) their features, extolled their virtues and plainly stated the price. The 1931 Homes of Today catalog had good quality photos and featured primarily high-dollar, custom built homes.

The new catalog featured a reproduction of George Washington's home, "Mount Vernon," which had been built in Paris, for the Exposition Coloniale Internationale De Paris. The full size Mount Vernon replica had been designed and built by the Home Construction Division of Sears. The catalog also had full-page spreads with interior and exterior shots of the Sears-built "Red Shield Lodge" in Palatine, Illinois, with its massive 60-foot living room (big enough to hold two Craftons!), oversized stone fireplace, vaulted ceiling and oak beams.

There were also photos of "The Boat House," built for a physician in New Jersey. It was another magnificent house, built by the Home Construction Division of Sears' Philadelphia Office. The house featured "an original 16th century stained glass window" which, according to the 1931 catalog, cost the homebuilder "considerably more than…an average eight-room home."

In the very back of the catalog, a scant two pages featured twelve pictures of "smaller homes of charm and beauty, attractively planned at modest prices." These houses, now pitiably relegated to the back pages, were Sears' old bread and butter: The Winona, Lynnhaven, Collingwood, Starlight, Gladstone, Cedars, Mitchell and more.

But was the new catalog a success? Was Sears leaving the little people in the dust, to go into the business of high-dollar architectural design and manse building? In January 1932, *The Wall Street Journal* reported that the Home Construction Division built 450 homes costing more than $15,000 (in 1931). This was an *enormous* price for a house in 1931.

In the early 1930s, the average factory worker earned less than $20 a week. Today, he earns about $450 - $500 a week. Roughly speaking, Sears was building houses that would be valued at more than $375,000 today, not counting the lot.

In what sounds like terrible English, Sears was still pushing hard on their mortgage plans.

Substantial. Beautiful, Efficient and Modern! Perfect proof that Sears are [sic] indeed the World's Largest Builder of Fine Homes. But Sears go even further! Only 176 equal monthly payments as low or lower than rent…And Sears do still more! Sears even lend you the money! …How do Sears do it?

(By firing all their copy editors would be my first guess.)

In 1933, Sears got out of the mortgage business once and for all. The 1933 Modern Homes catalog (probably printed before this decision was made) was still pushing easy financing, but the mortgage department at Sears was now officially closed. The 1933 annual report for Sears stockholders said that foreclosures had slowed significantly.

There were those who thought that these mortgage troubles were Sears' own fault. Their mortgage policies had become more and more lax throughout the 1920s, culminating in January 1930, when Sears announced they'd offer their customers 75% mortgage loans. Prior to 1930, Sears offered homeowners a maximum loan-to-value ratio of 60% on their mortgages.

In March 1930, Wardway Homes (which were primarily Gordon-Van Tine houses sold through Montgomery Ward) offered their homebuyers the same generous 75% financing. (source: *Business Week*). *Fortune* took note of this and reported: "Montgomery Ward tried to follow suit, but Sears was on the job first and took the *cream* of the business" (April 1933).

With cream like that, who needs soured dough?

Sears stopped offering mortgages in 1933, but Montgomery Ward had already decided it was time to get out of the game. In 1932, they threw in the towel and stopped selling Wardway Homes.

In 1933, Sears abandoned the slick and snazzy "Homes of Today" quasi-catalog/promotional book, featuring grandiose mini-castles and high-class mansions and returned to their tried and true sales techniques with a smaller catalog titled simply, "Homes." The red booklet measured 4 x 6 inches and had 94 pages, containing text, floor plans and sketches of their best-selling, low-priced homes.

By 1934, the catalogs went back to full size (roughly 8.5x 11 inches) and the words "Modern Homes" reappeared on the front cover of the catalog. The pages of the 1934 catalog were once again filled with the perennial favorites, including The Crafton, Gladstone, Vallonia, Winona, Dover and more; a total of 48 house designs. The 65-page catalog was less than half the size of the 140+ page catalogs of the roaring 20s.

But old mortgage problems continued to haunt the Modern Homes department. Things would get worse before they got better. According to *Catalogs and Counters*, Sears liquidated more than $11 million in mortgages in 1934. Sadly, the foreclosures and repossessions were still coming in. Sears would have a few more houses to take in; a few more homeowners to put out. It was in 1934 that Sears officially closed the Modern Homes department. Time to cut and run.

On August 31, 1935, *Business Week* reported that Sears was "getting ready to re-enter the housing market." The news must have come as a shock to everyone in the industry who knew the background of the Modern Home's department. But there was also good news: Sears would not be financing the houses and secondly, Sears was considering a probationary partnership with General Houses, Inc.

A little background: In the early 1930s, magazines and newspapers of the day loudly proclaimed that steel prefabricated homes, which could be easily assembled and disassembled, were the wave of the future. This idea of a "packing up a house and taking it with you" may seem a little far-fetched today, but at the time, experts thought that modern housing was about to undergo a major and radical shift.

In a *New York Times* article, the Chairman of the Architectural Commission of the 1933 Chicago World's Fair, Harvey Corbett, was quoted as saying, "With modern machine transportation we are again becoming nomadic. Hence the...space in which we live must be constructed in a way that it too can move" ("New Industry Foreseen: [Architect] Sees Future Homes Bought Like Autos," *New York Times*, May 25, 1932).

Another article in the *New York Times* predicted that the new prefabricated homes could be traded in for newer models and could be "set up or taken down in four days" (June 23, 1932).

The 1933 Chicago Century of Progress Exposition featured several steel houses, including one sponsored by *Good Housekeeping* magazine and another by "General Houses, Inc." of Chicago. Steel houses were starting to edge their way into the mainstream.

In the many different articles about the new prefab houses that would certainly be part of our American future, there was one company name that appeared repeatedly: General Houses, Inc. In 1932, the *New York Times* reported that this revolutionary company was just getting started, but their designs and the low prices looked very promising.

The homes offered by General Houses had steel frames on 3-foot centers, flat steel roofs, steel windows and were "100% prefabricated." (Sources: *A History of Prefabrication* and *Business Week*.) The article in *Business Week* explained, "erection will involve only a simple assembling process."

Doors and windows and walls were all interchangeable units, enabling the homeowner to make any changes their little heart desired. Floor plans could be reversed, if the view on the south side of the house was better than a northern exposure. Windows could be placed where doors had been and vice versa.

The houses designed and built by General Houses, Inc. for Sears would be one story homes made of pressed steel, with a selling price of $2900 to $3500. The houses could be assembled with relative ease in a few days. It was expected that larger, two-story homes would be available in the near-future. (The "near future" never happened for General Houses.)

Because FHA financing was now available, 70% financing could be obtained. Figuring a $1000, fully paid-for lot, the houses required $350 cash down. Payments on a $3500 loan would be $28 a month (*Business Week*, August 31, 1935).

While several 1930s-era newspapers and magazines reported on this possible partnership, I have never found a Sears catalog that offered these unusual houses. On September 2, 1939, *Business Week* reported that Sears had ended their partnership with General Houses on a sour note, "over too close a relation between exterior and interior temperatures in their pre-fabricated structures."

This whole partnership between Sears and General Houses, Inc. is quite puzzling. In May 1936, *Business Week* reported that industry insiders were aware "…that Sears and General Houses were hatching something new. However…Sears is *not going to sell these new houses*." The article goes on to say that Sears was gearing up to sell a whole line of special fixtures and accessories, specifically for these prefabricated, steel houses and that this special marketing was the full extent of Sears partnership with General Houses, Inc.

The details regarding the Sears/General House partnership are unclear, but by the late 1930s, one thing was clear: Sears had returned to selling modestly priced, conventional frame homes for the average family. And their primary problem – providing easy terms and affordable mortgages - had been solved by the introduction of the Federal Housing Administration in 1934.

In 1936, Sears abandoned the whole idea of steel houses with a degree of ferocity. The 1936 Sears Modern Homes catalog devoted the full inside page of the front cover to an essay titled, "Homes of Wood, Built to Last…And Built to Be Beautiful." This essay described wood as "the friendly material," and said that "wooden walls can shut out…the troubles of the world."

"The Wooden Home," it stated, "is still the most economical and satisfactory home a man can build." Toward the end, the article said that, "Hundreds of years from now, America may have to…adopt stone, adobe or other materials…[for homes], but that time is far in the future."

In other words, no matter how desperate mankind becomes for housing, steel ain't never ever never gonna be an option for building a home. (That may have been true for Sears, but after World War II ended, Lustrons and other prefab steel homes made a brief appearance on the architectural scene.)

In late-1938, it looked like Sears might be gearing up to revitalize their Modern Homes department. That year, they introduced nine new house styles, even sticking a 3-page supplement into the 1938 Sears Modern Homes catalog with the note:

Nine new Sears Modern Homes, too late for publication in the catalog are shown in this enclosure. Since they represent the latest thought in architectural design and planning, we think you'll find them especially interesting.

The nine houses were The Colebrook, The Malden, The Yates, The Branford, The Lynn, The Fulton, The Nantucket, The Medford and The Warren. All but two of the houses were Cape Cods. And all nine were very traditional. And they were all made of wood. (These homes appeared in a catalog dated 1938, but this 3-page supplement was dated January 1939.)

The enclosure that offered these nine new houses also promised that all of Sears Modern Homes met FHA requirements and Sears even offered to assist homebuyers with the loan application process.

In September 2, 1939, an article in *Business Week* said that there were 19 sales offices for the Modern Homes department, now all located "east of the Mississippi and north of the Ohio."

The article stated that the fresh blood at Sears wanted to give the Modern Homes department another go, but that upper management wouldn't hear of it. *Business Week* stated "Upper management all sweated buckets bailing the company out of the big-scale housing catastrophe that followed the slap-happy 20s. [They] would cheerfully get out of the whole department if they only knew how to get their money out."

The money they hoped to get out included the millions of dollars Sears had invested in their lumber mills, such as the $3.5 million recently invested in Norwood, Ohio and Port Newark, New Jersey.

In 1940, the Modern Homes department closed once and for all.

A few months after the last catalog was issued in 1940, America stopped building houses and started building bombers. When World War II ended, a new architectural phenomena emerged when former Navy Seabee Bill Levitt turned a 1000-acre potato field in New York state into a neighborhood full of 750-square foot houses which sold for $8,000. Assembly-line house construction enabled Levitt to erect the houses at the rate of 30 per day, a volume unimaginable to the 1900s builder who might spend months building a single, ostentatious Queen Anne home.

Levitt was able to accomplish and maintain the fast pace by assigning one man to one task – day in and day out. One man painted window sills. One man bolted washing machines to the floor. It was the Model-T of house building.

Sears provided an important link in the evolution of American construction techniques. They had *mass produced the parts* (lumber for Sears homes was precut at central factories in an quasi-assembly-line production), but Levitt took it a step further and put the houses *together* in an assembly-line fashion.

In the early 1900s, precut and prefabricated houses were a radical departure from typical construction techniques of the day, when Sears first entered the scene with their precut Modern Homes and their Simplex Sectionals (prefab homes). Sears was not the first nor the last company to sell kit houses by mail, but they *may* have been the biggest. Sears and Aladdin Homes (Bay City, Michigan) were pretty close in sales numbers; both selling about 75,000 homes.

Because people trusted the Sears name, they were willing to give this new idea of precut, ordered-by-mail, shipped-by-rail, do-it-yourself home-building a try. Faster and cheaper *could* mean better. Measuring and sawing lumber at a central factory, rather than on-site, *was* radical, but people gave the new concept a fair hearing and a fair trial. And because of Sears well-known name, people bravely put their life savings in a small brown envelope, together with a carefully filled-out order form for "The Walton" or "The Starlight" and sent it on to "Sears Roebuck & Company, Chicago, Illinois."

There's no doubt about it – Sears was one of the pioneers in home-building and they were instrumental in changing the way that America thought about housing. And because of Sears, this country now has about 75,000 of the prettiest little mail-order houses that you ever did see.

Sales Numbers (in dollars):

1929 - $12,050,000   *Catalogs and Counters*
1930 - $10,658,000   *Catalogs and Counters*
1931 - $8,442,000   *Catalogs and Counters*
1932 - $6,324,000   *Catalogs and Counters*
1933 - $3,670,000   *Catalogs and Counters*
1936 - $2,000,000   *Business Week*
1937 - $3,500,000   *Business Week*
1938 - $2,750,000   *Business Week*
Note: Sales information for 1934-35 and 1939-40 was not found.

Sears mortgages: The swingin' deal that Sears offered their homebuyers

In the early 1900s, conventional wisdom suggested that young and old alike should work tirelessly to avoid debt. And Sears penned these words (below) specifically to assuage people's natural aversion to debt. The following is one of my favorite "it's okay to be in debt" advertisements from the 1916 Modern Homes catalog. It states,

Stop and think. About 75% of all the houses built in this country are put up by means of borrowed money. The most prudent and keenest business men borrow money for building purposes. Any bank or building and loan association will gladly make you a loan if you own a lot and can pay for the labor to put up your house. You simply pay them interest for the use of the money, just as a bank would do for the use of *your* money. (Payments can be) …paid at the rate of about $15 a month for five years. Isn't this easy?

In the 1918 Modern Homes catalog, a new promotion for Sears' "easy payment" mortgages appeared on page one. A version of this same advertisement appeared on either the inside cover or page one of each subsequent catalog until 1929. The 1918 advertisement stated,

Build on Easy Payments. Rent Receipts or a home of your own? Your rent money will now buy an "Honor Bilt" Modern Home. You can pay for your home in small monthly or half yearly payments, just as you would pay rent. We want you to be a home owner and we know that our trust in you as such will not be misplaced.

Occasionally, bankers or real estate agents attending my lecture will ask about the specific terms of a Sears mortgage. Their terms changed through the years, but here are the broad strokes.

In the 1916 Modern Homes catalog, Sears promised that their kit homes could be ordered and built within a 90-day period. Their mortgage documents *required* that the homeowner "completely finish (the house) in good workmanlike manner and be ready for occupancy within four months (after receiving the materials)."

A 1926 Sears mortgage document on file in Madison County showed that a Sears homebuyer and borrower paid about $2800 for the kit home. The kit home arrived on site in July and the first payment was due November. The annual interest rate was 6% and monthly payments were made to "The First National Bank of Chicago." The agreement also stated "said dwelling after being completed to cost not less than $5000." (Presumably, upon completion, the home should appraise for $5000.)

In general, Sears offered a wide variety of mortgages and terms, with annual interest rates ranging from 6-7% and up to 15 years to repay.

In the late 1920s, Sears mortgages peaked out at a 75% loan to value ratio, but that 75% is not a "hard" number. The LTV (loan-to-value) ratio included the value of the lot. If the homebuyer owned a lot (without debt), Sears would count that lot as his 25% down payment. If the owner was willing to do some or all of the construction work, that could also be counted toward his down payment. Monthly payments did not begin until four months after the house had been shipped, allowing the owner time to build and move into his new home.

An interesting aside: According to the 1933 Sears Homes catalog, the 15-year repayment plan was not an option if your home was built with a crawlspace. Homes had to be built over basements to qualify for these 15-year mortgages.

By anyone's accounting, their financing was very generous and a radical departure from the typical mortgages of the era. During the 1920s and 30s, mortgage brokers and bankers were pushing some pretty sketchy home financing deals, including second mortgages with brutal repayment terms and/or massive prepayment penalties and/or renewal fees. Renewal fees were especially treacherous, because each year (or every three years or whatever), the mortgage had to be "renewed" (renegotiated) and homeowners often ended up in foreclosure after their "renewal."

The 1931 Sears "Homes of Today" catalog stated,

To make it easier for the average family to own a home, President Hoover called a special White House conference. High charges attending second mortgages with their extra commissions, "service" discounts and other charges prove the greatest problem. This burdensome system has done much to stifle home building activities and has proved a leading source of unemployment in building trades. Our equal (fully amortized) payments are as low or lower than rent and the home is yours. And only a single interest charge of 6%. No commissions for renewals. That's our challenge to the dangerous second mortgage deplored by President Hoover.

Sears mortgages *were* straightforward and simple: There were no confusing rules or sneaky tricks, no renewal fees, no high interest second mortgages and no exorbitant financing fees. Their repayment terms were clear (one mortgage, no renewals) and affordable (15-year amortization) and the 25% down payment was very low, compared to other conventional lenders.

In fact, Sears may have been a little *too* lenient. Their mortgage application contained only one financial question: *What is your vocation?* Sears probably theorized that if someone built their own home, they'd go through hell and high water to keep it. No one knew that hell and high water was on its way in the form of the

Great Depression.

On the plus side, this easy financing enabled countless immigrants, single women, African-Americans and other "undesirables" to obtain mortgages and homes when conventional lenders turned them down flat.

This testimonial, which appeared in the 1929 Modern Homes catalog, was probably quite accurate. It stated, "Your method of financing is the best that I have heard of and makes possible the purchase of a home by people who might not otherwise feel able to undertake it."

A bit of additional information on Sears Modern Homes sales offices.

Catalogs and Counters stated that Sears opened their first Modern Homes sales office in Akron, Ohio in 1919, to accommodate that city's housing boom. That may have been the first sales office *outside* of the Chicago area, but as early as 1908, the Sears Modern Homes catalog was already promoting an impressive building materials showroom in Chicago (Sears' headquarters).

This interesting pitch from the 1908 catalog accompanied the photo of their building materials showroom:

If you intend to build…and have not seen or used any of our goods within the past six months, you have no idea of the great improvement we have made in our line and how much we have bettered its quality. Please understand it is not necessary to come to Chicago to select your material. Nine hundred and ninety-nine customers out of every thousand make up their orders from the illustrations and descriptions shown in our catalog.

Sears concluded with this statement: (Caution - read the last line very slowly. It's a good example of Victorian verbosity.)

If you do not feel perfectly at ease in sending us your order without first inspecting our goods, we by all means recommend that…you come to Chicago and see our line, as we guarantee that the saving we will make you will repay you many times the amount you will pay out for the railroad fare.

One of the persistent rumors about Sears Modern Homes sales offices is that they were all located east of the Mississippi. *This is not true.* From 1929 - 1934, Sears had a Modern Homes sales office in St. Louis, Missouri. (For the geographically challenged, St. Louis is *west* of the Muddy Miss.) Another sales office opened (and closed) in Kansas City, Missouri around 1927.

As the sales of Sears homes waxed and waned, the number of sales offices increased and decreased. In 1930, there were 48 Sears Modern Homes sales offices in the country. That year, Sears had sales offices in Connecticut, Illinois, Indiana, Maryland, Michigan, Missouri, New Jersey, New York, Ohio, Pennsylvania, Wisconsin and the District of Columbia. But that peak (and many of those sales offices) came and went pretty fast.

Next year, in 1931, they were down to 27 offices and by 1933, they had only 13 sales offices and two of *those* were actually the Sears mills in Norwood, Ohio and Newark, New Jersey.

By 1939, there were 19 sales offices for the Modern Homes department, all of which were located "east of the Mississippi and north of the Ohio." These "stores" probably occupied a small office next door to a Sears storefront or may have been a small space <u>within</u> the main store and their closing in 1940 may have gone largely unnoticed. It's also likely that these old Modern Homes departments were transmogrified into hardware sections or building materials departments. *(I've spent a significant portion of my life looking for a way to use that word – transmogrified.)*

Cities which had a Sears Modern Homes Sales Office

Connecticut
New Haven

Illinois
Aurora
Calumet City
Chicago
Elgin
Joliet
Peoria
Rockford
Waukegan

Indiana
Fort Wayne
Gary
Hammond
Indianapolis
South Bend

Massachusetts
Boston

Michigan
Ann Arbor
Detroit
Flint
Jackson
Kalamazoo
Pontiac
Port Huron
Saginaw

Missouri
Kansas City
St. Louis

New Jersey
Camden
Elizabeth
Hackensack
Long Branch
Newark
Paterson
Plainfield

New York
Albany
Buffalo
Long Island
Mt. Vernon
New Rochelle
New York
Peeksville
Rochester
Schenectady
Syracuse
White Plains

Ohio
Akron
Cincinnati
Cleveland
Columbus
Dayton
Lorain
Mansfield
Marion
Norwood
Portsmouth
Toledo
Youngstown
Warren
Zanesville

Pennsylvania
Greensburg
New Castle
Philadelphia
Pittsburgh
Rochester
Scranton

Washington DC
(Three locations)

West Virginia
Wheeling

Wisconsin
Milwaukee

SIX ROOMS AND BATH

The AMERICUS Honor Bilt $2,050.00
No. 13063 "Already Cut" and Fitted.

Americus in Ohio

MAKES ITS OWNERS PROUD

The ARGYLE Honor Bilt $1,479.00
No. 2018 "Already Cut" and Fitted.

Argyle in Illinois

SIX ROOMS, BATH AND PORCH

Honor Bilt
The Puritan
No. 3190 "Already Cut" and Fitted.
$2,098.00

Puritan in Washington D.C.

Honor Bilt
The Lewiston
No. 3237 "Already Cut" and Fitted
For Complete Delivered Price
Fill Out Information Block
Pages 379-150

FIVE OR SEVEN ROOMS
Monthly Payments as Low as
$45 to $60
Built Complete on Your Lot

Lewiston in Indiana

Lynnhaven in Virginia

Mitchell in Indiana

Kilborne in Illinois

Bandon in Illinois

Chapter 8

The Other Sears Homes: Homart Homes

Remember that Sears has drawn on over 40 years of experience in the housing field to bring you these fine quality Homart Houses. We have utilized the tremendous economies of factory production – parts are standardized and partially assembled at the factory in a fraction of the time with a minimum of waste. This allow [sic] us to pass on to you the economies of factory fabrication over conventional site assembly.

1951 Homart Homes Catalog

A few minutes after I gave a lecture in the St. Louis area, an older gentleman and his wife approached the podium.

"We built a Sears home in 1952," he said, with a broad smile on his face. "I brought some pictures to show you."

I never know what to say in these situations. Sears closed their Modern Homes department in 1940, so I knew something wasn't right about his statement. I figured he'd probably purchased an Aladdin kit home, since they were sold until 1981. Folks frequently confuse the different mail order companies.

But then he added, "The house came in on a truck in sections. We bolted the sections together. It was a prefab house from Sears."

An aside: Many people confuse prefab and precut. Sears Modern Homes are often described as "prefab homes" but they were NOT prefab – they were precut or "Already cut and fitted" as Sears liked to say. This meant that the lumber had been sawn to the correct length; ready to be nailed into place. "Prefab" – short for prefabricated - means the house was partially assembled at a factory and arrived at the building site in <u>sections</u>, which were then fastened together at the site.

Only a few weeks before I met this man, I'd learned that Sears sold prefab homes for a short time after World War II. From about 1948 to 1952, Sears issued a thin 24 –26 page catalog of 10-12 prefab houses. These houses were extremely modest and simple. The smallest home was 24-feet square and the largest was 24 feet by 40 feet and they all looked the same: Little boxy homes with the same covered stoop (not even a proper front porch!) and the same basic floorplan and a low roofline. Prices were not listed in the catalogs, but there was a coupon on the back page for requesting a price quotation.

The houses were called "Homart Homes."

Under the heading "Build a Homart Home Yourself" appeared this statement in the 1951 Homart Homes catalog:

You need not be a skilled carpenter to build these homes. In fact, many Homart Home Builders are clerks, farmers, factory workers and professional men – anybody who can use a hammer and saw. When you receive your Homart House, you will find each section, piece or bundle of materials plainly marked for quick, easy identification.

Each of the houses in this catalog is semi-factory built, in ready-to-join sections and in precut lumber. This eliminates most of the work of cutting and fitting materials when the house is being erected. To erect a Homart Home you merely have to put the sections together and nail or bolt them in place.

Even a beginner can follow the step-by-step erection method. See how the precut joists fit in place. Notice how easy it is to erect the wall panels some of which have doors and windows already hung in place.

Getting your Homart House under roof is not a long, time-consuming job – many of our customers report they have assembled the floor structure, erected the walls and roof section in three days or less!

George Nuernberger, the man who spoke with me after the lecture, built his Homart Home in 1952. I found his story fascinating. It's another chapter (albeit a short one) in the history of Sears homes. George related the following:

I worked at a Sears retail store in St. Louis. One day I was having coffee at the counter (inside the Sears store) and I was talking with the guy who worked in the farming supplies department. He told me that they had these do-it-yourself houses in the catalog.

A short time later, when I was ready to buy a house, I went to the farming supplies department – which is where they sold these houses – and they showed me some catalog pictures of the different houses they offered. A salesmen who worked at Sears had built one of these houses in Bellefontaine Neighbors (a St. Louis suburb). I went out there and looked at the house and I thought it looked pretty good.

The house I chose cost about $3000 and was 24 by 40 feet. Because I worked for Sears, I got a 10% discount on the house and wrote them a check for about $2800. It took about one month for the house to arrive. It came in on one truck but it was a big truck and was packed from top to bottom. It took us all day to unload that truck. My wife's grandfather had a big garage near the lot, so we put a lot of the building materials in there.

The sections of exterior wall were 8 feet tall and came in lengths of 2 feet, 4 feet, 6 feet and 8 feet. The windows and exterior doors were already hung within those wall sections. The pre-built walls were framed with 2 x 4 studs on 16-inch centers. The exterior sheathing - 1 x 8-inch planks – were already nailed to the framing. The sections were bolted together and made for a very strong wall.

The roof was made up of trusses on 24-inch centers with 2 x 4 blocks inserted, to create 16-inch centers for nailing up the sheetrock. The inside walls got sheetrock and the outside walls were covered in asbestos siding. The house had double floors and the primary floor was oak. The lumber throughout was top-notch and everything was the best quality - no junk. It came with blueprints and plans and the average guy could learn to assemble a house like this real quick.

Building this little house taught me how to do carpentry work. It was pretty interesting. It took me seven months to build the house and that was doing it on Thursdays and Sundays (my days off).

We lived in it for 23 years and sold it in 1974. It was a wonderful house for our family.

Unfortunately, I have no idea how many of these homes were sold, however, the 1949 Homart Homes catalog lists specific addresses.

According to those lists, Homart Homes were built in Nevada, Iowa; Tiffin, Ohio; Dubuque, Iowa; New Glarus and Madison, Wisconsin; LaSalle, Cerro Gordon, Pekin and Monmouth, Illinois. After these homes are covered in vinyl siding and the front porches get changed, they are nearly impossible to differentiate from any other simple little home.

Chapter 9

Is it Really a Sears Home?
How to Identify Sears Homes From The Curb, The Kitchen or The Courthouse

When I ordered Sears Modern Home #34, I had you send studding two feet longer so my house is two feet higher on the second floor. I also added windows to the side rooms, giving the house a better appearance and more light.

Testimonial by Patrick McNamara
"Successful Building"
(1912 Sears Homes Promotional Booklet)

It's impossible to know how many Sears homebuyers, like Patrick McNamara, "tweaked" the building plans and made changes to their kit house. And it's impossible to know how many Sears homebuyers custom-ordered and/or built a home that was *radically different* from the known Sears house designs.

One day while traveling through Southwestern Illinois, I met a man who shared a remarkable story about the Sears home his mother built many years ago.

"My mother was looking through the Modern Homes catalog," he recalled, "and she couldn't decide between two different houses. She liked the top half (roof lines) of one house and the bottom of another house. She cut these two pictures out of the catalog and taped them together. She really liked the looks of her 'modi-fied' house. She sent this taped creation to Sears - with a note asking if they could send her *this* house with *that* roof line - and they said, 'We sure can!'"

Imagine trying to identify *that* as a Sears house, 80 years later!

These Sears house hybrids are not that uncommon. I've seen an Alhambra (a Spanish-flavored four-square) crossed with the Fullerton and an Ardara with the front porch of a Crescent. Fellow kit house historian Rebecca Hunter found a Sears house that had the distinctive architectural features, porches and columns of the Osborn but the floorplan of the Walton. (Does that make it a Wal-born?)

Sears architects designed many different houses in many different styles and offered a wide variety of options. Want two dormers instead of one? Want a big dormer or an itty-bitty one? Switch from a gable roof to a hip roof? Would you rather have brick in place of clapboard? Take out a window? Add two windows? Reverse the floorplan? Try a different front porch? No problem!

Sears encouraged homeowners to customize these houses to suit individual needs.

In the 1930 Sears Modern Homes catalog, under the heading "Complete Architectural Service" is this statement:

If you wish any changes in the design or have any special plan that you would like to have us figure, we can give you the best advice and technical help. Our engineers will be glad to help you build your home as you want it (p. 3).

A few pages later in the catalog was this: "Prepare a rough outline [of the house you want], showing the approximate size, number of rooms desired and style of exterior preferred. Our staff of architects are at your disposal to prepare these special plans for you" (p. 10).

In this 1930 Sears Modern Homes catalog are photos of two "special" houses. One is a Special Berwyn, which, according to the caption, has been "increased in size." The other house is a Special Claremont, a modest neo-tudor. The caption reads, "Several changes have been made in the above house, which materially increased the cost. The roof was raised and two rooms were added on the second floor."

Sears advertised a variety of upgrades and options throughout their catalogs, such as different entry-ways, sun-porches, second floor sleeping porches, alternate front porches, side porches and more. While these add-ons could spruce up an otherwise plain looking home, they also make it incredibly challenging to identify specific models 80 years later.

Modernization and the passage of time creates yet another challenge: Most of these houses have been altered and remodeled to meet current needs. Many Sears homes were modest and small when originally built. Bedrooms were often eight or nine feet by ten or eleven feet; tiny by today's standards. As housing needs evolved and families needed more space, the houses were changed and expanded.

In the 1930s, substitute-siding salesmen began promising homeowners that their product could put an end to the chore of painting. First came asbestos siding, then asphalt siding, then aluminum and eventually vinyl. Distinctive architectural features were hacked off when substitute siding was installed. Old windows were tossed aside for vinyl thermopane windows. Front porches were glassed in and sleeping porches were enclosed and turned into bedrooms.

Siding salesmen, violent storms, floods, termites, ill-informed remuddlers and people who think wallpaper borders with dancing geese belong in an old house can cause extensive damage to a historical home. (I think of remuddling as "Friendly Fire." It's a terrible mistake, but the hapless victim still dies.)

Yet Sears homes are just that: *Homes.* They are lived in, loved in and they evolve through the decades. After 80 years, there are inevitably many changes.

Puffed houses

An elderly man called me at home one night to tell me about a Sears home in his neighborhood. He'd lived in the same house for several decades and was certain that the house next door was a Sears home.

"How do you know it's a Sears home?" I asked, hoping for an answer that was credible. The neighborhood he lived in was full of 1950s frame houses. I wondered how there could be a Sears home in *that* area. (Sears homes were sold from 1908-1940.)

"It was moved here from another location," he told me, "and I knew the man who built it." The next morning, I drove to the house. It was "The Roseberry" - a one-and-a-half story home with one broad, oversized gable dormer. A cute house but certainly unique.

Staring at this Roseberry, I was puzzled. It was definitely a Roseberry, but it was several feet too wide. An extra-chubby Roseberry. Further investigation revealed it was a *customized* Sears home. A puffed Roseberry.

And then there are mistakes.

In "*The Comfortable House*," Alan Gowans tells the story of a West Virginia family that purchased, "The Argyle," a small, attractive and popular Honor-Bilt home. The family hired carpenters to build the house, but they put it together *backwards*, reversing the floor plan. As soon as the error was discovered, the carpenters were fired and the house was disassembled. This time, the family did their own carpentry, while closely studying that 75-page instruction book. When the house was nearly finished, they realized they'd mixed-up the living room and dining room windows. Their Argyle, Gowans relates, still has those two transposed windows on the front of the house.

Sadly, when the Sears Modern Homes department closed in 1940, the sales records and promotional materials were destroyed. Now, it's up to individual communities and homeowners to seek out and find the Sears homes in their locales.

"Lady, are you crazy? This ain't no Sears home."

This chapter on identifying Sears homes comes from *personal experienc*e.

I've nearly been arrested twice (who knew they really *meant* "no trespassing" at that abandoned Sears house with the open back door?), and I've had lots of folks question me (some happy, some not) as to why I'm staring at their house. One fellow slammed the door in my face after I told him he lived in a Sears home. Another man swore at me and *then* slammed the door. Ah well. Two angry men out of hundreds of homeowners isn't bad. The occasional homeowner does make a passing reference to my sanity.

I've also had the blessing of spending time with friends and fellow-kit-house-historians Rebecca Hunter (Elgin, Illinois) and Dale Patrick Wolicki (Architectural Historian, Bay County Historical Society in Michigan).

In the last two years, I have visited Missouri, Illinois, Indiana, Kansas, Kentucky, Ohio, Maryland, Washington, DC and Virginia for the purpose of identifying and studying Sears homes.

So, how *do you* identify a Sears home?

First, begin by eliminating the obvious. Sears sold these homes between 1908-1940. If your home was built outside of that time frame, it can *not* be a Sears catalog home. Period. Exclamation mark!

The List of Nine Signs

1) Look for stamped lumber in the basement or attic
2) Look for shipping labels
3) Check house design using a field guide such as "*Houses by Mail*" or original catalogs.
4) Look in the attic and basement for any paperwork that might reveal that you have a Sears home
5) Courthouse records
6) Hardware fixtures
7) Goodwall sheet plaster
8) Unique column arrangement on front porch and five-piece eave brackets
9) Original building permits

1) Look for stamped lumber in the basement or attic. Sears Modern Homes were kit homes and the framing members were stamped with a letter and a number. When the lumber arrived on site, that number, along with a 75-page instruction book, told you how all those pieces went together. This stamp will be located in two places on each piece of lumber. It will be at the butt end and also on the face of the lumber. Typically, the stamp on the face of the lumber can be found two to ten inches from the end of the framing member.

On a 2 x 8 floor joist, the mark will be on the 8-inch side. Often you can find these stamps in the center of the basement, where the butt ends of the floor joists overlap and rest on a center beam. To find this mark, you'll need a very bright flashlight.

These stamps were in blue, black or red ink and were a little less than an inch in height. If you don't have a basement or don't wish to crawl through the attic, you can also take a peak in the plumbing access door behind the bathtub.

Not all Sears homes have stamped lumber. Most Sears homes built before 1920 do not have a stamp on framing members and a few built after that date have no marks on the lumber. By 1920, Sears had sold 25,000 houses, so <u>at least</u> one-third do not have stamped lumber. However, if you suspect you have a Sears home but don't see any stamped lumber, there are some other things you can do.

The stamped lumber is the "low hanging fruit." It's a fast and easy way to authenticate Sears homes, but its absence does not mean you <u>do not have a Sears home</u>.

2) Look for shipping labels. Shipping labels can often be found on the back of millwork (baseboard molding, door and window trim, etc) or in the basement, sometimes around or under the basement staircase. The words Sears, Roebuck and Company will appear on the label or you might see a return address of *925 Homan Ave, Chicago* (Sears Headquarters – in the early years of the 1900s). Also look around for stamps on millwork or other labels showing that the lumber was shipped from Norwood Sash and Door. Norwood Sash and Door in Ohio supplied millwork for Sears homes. If you find that your home contains millwork from Norwood, that doesn't absolutely prove it's a Sears home but it's a good clue that says, look closer.

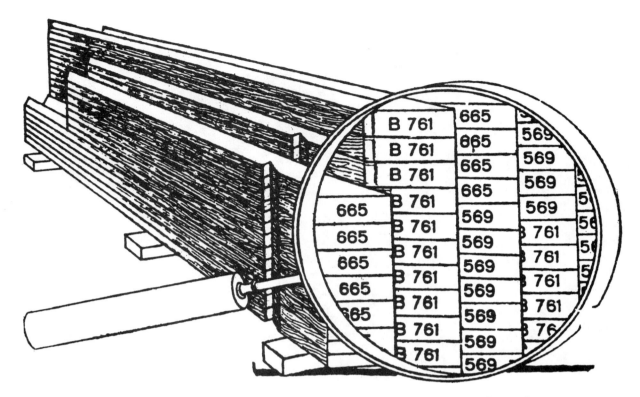

Pieces numbered to correspond with the numbers on the plans.

Top graphic - This drawing appeared in Sears Modern Homes catalogs for many years. Sears lumber was stamped with a letter and a number (note: B761 in drawing). These numbers, coupled with that 75-page instruction book, enabled novice homebuilders to assemble those 30,000 pieces of house. Today, these numbers provide a fast and easy way to identify a property as a Sears home.

Lower graphic - Actual stamped lumber in a 1930 Sears home.

The Vallonia has interesting features on the front porch that are often spared the fate of being "aluminized" (covered in aluminum siding).

1) Look at the stick work on the porch columns. About two dozen Sears homes [designs] have these distinctive features on the front porch columns.

2) The Vallonia has the center block on the underside of the front porch roof.

3) The tapered columns and 2nd floor side windows are two features that were altered in different model years. In other words, some Vallonias have tapered porch columns and some don't. Some have two side windows on the 2nd floor and some have one window and some Vallonias have one sash (a single hinged window, similar to a basement window).

4) Note the chimney placement. Chimney's don't move, regardless of how much remodeling a home has endured.

(The Vallonia was one of Sears best selling homes.) 1924 Sears Modern Homes catalog

The Sunbeam

This Sunbeam offers a few hints on how to identify a Sears home.

1) Look at the center blocks on the front and side of the Sunbeam's porch. These blocks were not unique to Sears, but they *are* fairly unusual.

2) See the five-piece eave brackets? They're another sign that suggests that this *may* be a mail order home, or even a Sears home.

3) The front edge of the main roof drops down much further than the rear edge. This is not unique to Sears homes, but it's an architectural nuance to look at when comparing housing styles.

4) Also note how the fireplace chimney passes *through* the roof. This does not make it a Sears home, but it's another unusual architectural feature.

5) The flower box in the fireplace chimney is a wild card. Don't rule out a perfectly good Sunbeam (or other Sears house) if it does *not* have a flowerbox in the chimney. (1924 Sears Modern Homes catalog)

Learn how to examine and study these odd little details. When you discover your *first* Sears home "in person," stare at it, study it, think about it and above all, note the address so that you can return to it later. I keep a small notebook in my car, just for this purpose.

The Fullerton in Wood River, Illinois still has an original shipping label (C&A, Chicago and Alton Railroad) on the backside of the basement stairs. (Thus, my title for this chapter: Identifying a Sears home from the basement stairs is like identifying a Sears home from the kitchen, isn't it?)

3) *Houses by Mail* by Katherine Cole Stevenson and H. Ward Jhandl is a wonderful field guide. It lists the hundreds of different designs of homes that Sears offered from 1908-1940. The houses in this book are categorized by roof style. Start with the footprint – or the exterior dimension of the house. And then compare the position of the windows, chimney placement, floorplan, room size, etc.

Room size and floor plan can be a key in authenticating Sears homes. If you have a purported Sears house but can't find stamped lumber, look at the room size. It should be a *spot-on match* to the room sizes listed in *Houses by Mail*. The fraternal twins - houses that *look like* Sears homes but are *not* Sears homes - usually do not have identical exterior dimensions and the sizes of the rooms are tweaked a little bit. An example is the Sears Mitchell, the Aladdin University and the Gordon-Van Tine Patrician. From the exterior, these three houses appear *identical*, but the exterior dimensions and room sizes were ever-so-slightly different.

Pay special attention to the placement of the furnace chimney. Chimney location is something that (usually) won't be altered even by aggressive remodeling. Fireplaces are a little different. Fireplaces were optional.

These houses were offered in reverse floor plans, so don't be thrown if the house shown in *Houses by Mail* is a mirror image of your home.

4) Ephemera and paperwork – Look in the attic and basement for any paperwork that might reveal that you have a Sears home. A Sears homeowner in Alton, Illinois found a complete set of Sears blueprints tucked away in the eaves of her attic, with the words Sears Roebuck stamped on the corner of each page. Also look under the bottom shelf of bookcases and any other nooks and crannies.

5) Courthouse records – From 1911 to 1933, Sears offered home mortgages. Using grantor records, you may find a few Sears mortgages and thus, a few Sears homes. Here's how: Look at grantor records from 1915 through 1940. Sears stopped offering mortgages in 1933, but when a mortgage was paid in full, the mortgage release was recorded, so you're going to be looking for that document, as well.

You may find a few Sears mortgages by looking under the name Sears or Sears, Roebuck, but you'll probably find more mortgages by looking under the names Walker O. Lewis and Nicholas Wieland. Both of these men served as trustees for Sears. Walker O. Lewis served as trustee until 1930, when Wieland took over. When you find the names of Lewis or Wieland, you'll probably find the notation "tr" which is an abbreviation for Trustee. More information on this topic is offered at the end of this chapter. (Thanks to Dale Patrick Wolicki for the trustee information.)

6) Hardware fixtures. Plumbing, electrical and heating equipment was not included in the basic kit but could be purchased separately. These fixtures were pictured in the back pages of the Sears Modern Homes catalogs and were offered in different grades – good, better and best. This enabled customers to save a little money on their plumbing, heating and lighting fixtures.

Dover Publishing sells a reprint of the 1926 Modern Homes catalog and Schiffer Publishing sells a reprint of the 1912 Modern Homes catalog, which show the type of fixtures that Sears offered. You can also pick up original Modern Homes catalogs from on-line auction sites, antique stores and flea markets.

Even if the plumbing and electrical equipment in your house has been replaced, you'll often find that the old fixtures have migrated to the basement. Compare these old fixtures to the catalog pictures. Also check the plumbing, electrical and hardware fixtures and see if they bear the initials "SR." Sears homes built during the 1930s often have a small circled "SR" cast into the bathtub in the lower corner (furthest from the tub spout and near the floor) and on the underside of the kitchen or bathroom sink.

7) Goodwall Sheet Plaster - Another clue that you have a Sears home is the presence of Goodwall plaster. In the 1910s, Sears began offering a new product called "sheet plaster" (sheetrock). The Sears product was known as Goodwall Sheet Plaster and each 4 x 4 sheet bore the stamp "Goodwall" on the backside. If during remodeling, you discover this sheet plaster, that suggests that you may have a Sears home.

Goodwall Sheet Plaster was also offered in their building materials catalog, so it's not absolute conclusive proof that you have a Sears home, but it sure makes for a strong case! But if your home does NOT have Goodwall Sheet Plaster, that doesn't mean it's not a Sears home. Most houses of this era had plaster walls, with lath and plaster.

8) Clues outdoors. About two dozen of Sears most popular house designs had a unique column arrangement on the front porch. This was distinctive to Sears and is an easy way to spot Sears homes from the street. Note the interconnecting stick work and the flared blocks at the top of the columns. If you spot a house with this design, it is most likely a Sears home.

Five-piece eave brackets (the diagonal supportive brace between the roof line and the exterior wall) are also a sign that you may have a Sears home. Most eave brackets are comprised of *three pieces*. The five piece bracket is unusual. The five piece eave bracket is *not* proof that you have a Sears home or even a kit home, but it's another sign that says, slow down; take another look.

9) Building permits. In Washington, DC, Mary Rowse (President of "Historic Washington Architecture") discovered that Sears Roebuck was occasionally listed as the *architect* on original building permits. It will be interesting to find out if this technique works in other cities, as well. In one county in Illinois, the words "House supplied by Sears Roebuck" appeared on an old city plat.

Some additional notes on identifying Sears homes

In 1895, Sears began selling lumber, construction supplies, building materials and hardware. Some home builders used Sears lumber, hardware and fixtures, which might make it difficult to distinguish a true catalog home from a home built with Sears building materials.

A 1912 promotional booklet (titled *"Successful Building: A Book Written By Our Customers"*) has a testimonial from a builder that states, "I build suburban residences and two years ago, I commenced using Sears Roebuck and Co.'s building materials, millwork, hardware, mantels, furnaces, ranges, etc."

Is it a Sears house if it is made entirely of materials from Sears? In my estimation, NO! In my round little world, it is a Sears home *if* it was built from plans and blueprints offered in the Sears Modern Homes catalog *and if* the building materials were part of a kit home package offered by Sears.

The look-a-likes

Whilst doing the research for this revision, I decided to read 32 years of *American Carpenter and Builder Magazine*, a well-known trade journal for the building industry. I read issues dating from 1908 – 1940; the years that Sears sold their Modern Homes. (By the way – that's 384 issues. I loved the process but was often distracted by the great ads. How could you not read a full page ad for a folding bathtub?) I knew this magazine would contain useful bits of information about Sears houses and the kit home business in general that would never be referenced in any reader's guides. And I was right. I found a plethora of fascinating trivia within its pages.

One of the most interesting finds was the Blue Ribbon Homes. These were home designs that had won *American Carpenter and Builder's* Blue Ribbon Award for being innovative, attractive, affordable, practical and artistic.

Sears obtained their house designs from a wide variety of sources, such as architectural magazines, individual architects (not employed by Sears), plan and pattern books and more. And this was in addition to the designs created by Sears' own staff architects. It seems likely that the majority of those 370 different house designs came from the hearts and minds of the architectural staff at the Modern Homes department.

But the Sears Del Rey (a small L-shaped cottage) probably was not an original Sears design. I found the Del Rey look-a-like in the January 1922 issue of *American Carpenter and Builder*. It was heralded as a "dignified, homey bungalow with a Colonial doorway and French windows, with well dimensioned bedrooms and ample closet space."

In some cases, the Blue Ribbon winners were a spot-on match to the Sears design, but more frequently, Sears made minor alterations to the floor plan or changed the exterior dimensions of the house by a couple feet. The Sears version – the Del Rey – was 38 x 40 feet. The Blue Ribbon Home was offered in different sizes but the model *closest* to the Sears Del Rey was 39 x 44 feet. Trying to distinguish a "Blue Ribbon Home" from the Del Rey (sans tape measure) based on exterior appearances alone would be impossible.

But the coup de grace was a short letter to the editor that I found in a subsequent issue of *American Carpenter and Builder*. The writer was Burton Palmer of San Jose, California. It read,

The enclosed photo shows one of your Blue Ribbon homes which was featured in the January 1922 number of the Builder. I am a student at Sanford University; thought you might be interested to know that I erected and completed this charming little residence with the assistance of one carpenter during my summer vacation. It was sold as soon as finished. I will build more during the coming year.

In other words, some early 1920s college student spent his summer vacation building the Del Rey's clone in the San Jose area. (Sing with me: "Do you know the 'Rey in San Jose?")

FIVE ROOMS AND SLEEPING PORCH

Honor Bilt
The Del Rey
No. 13065 "Already Cut" and Fitted.
$2,146.00

**1922
Sears Modern Homes
Catalog**

BLUE RIBBON HOMES

PRACTICAL & ARTISTIC

**January
1922
American
Carpenter
& Builder
Magazine
"Blue Ribbon"
Winning Design**

**A Sears Del Rey
in
Northern
Illinois**

Somewhere in California, some architectural historian is getting all excited because he found one or 51 (who knows how many were built) Del Rey clones, not realizing they're "Blue Ribbon Homes" built 80 years ago by a college student financing his tuition.

Another case in point: There is a lovely Sears Avondale in Springfield, Illinois. This spacious bungalow with its two bay windows and large front porch was one of Sears' best selling homes. The interior of the Sears Avondale is unusually roomy and thoughtfully-designed. This Avondale, located in an older section of the city is in wonderful condition. However, there's a catch. According to local historians, this Avondale is not really an *Avondale*. Sometime in the 1910s, the home's original owner saw a genuine Sears Avondale in another city. He was so smitten with the design that he contracted with a local builder to *re-create* this bungalow. That builder did a good job – it is <u>identical</u> to a Sears Avondale – but it is not a Sears home!

Authenticate, authenticate, authenticate

The above examples show why you *must* authenticate suspected Sears homes. I've found near-perfect matches to Sears designs in both national and regional kit home catalogs. The 1919 Pacific Homes catalog (a regional kit home company based in Los Angeles) offered several house designs identical to Sears designs, as did Aladdin, Gordon Van Tine, Lewis Homes and Sterling Homes. Plan books (which sold blueprints and plans – very popular in the 1920s) such as Home Builder's Catalog have several Sears clones, too. Everyone was copying everyone else and altering the designs a wee bit to make it all legal.

Very few people can eyeball a Del Rey or any other house and say, "Yup, that house is 38 feet wide, not 39. Must be a Sears model."

Whilst lecturing and traveling in 2003, I visited a community in Virginia that laid claim to an impressive collection of Sears homes. I was given a lovely tour of the town, including the neighborhood with all the "Sears houses."

As my tour guide drove to the first purported Sears home, I sat in silence and stared in disbelief. The house before me bore little resemblance to any Sears house I'd ever seen. I didn't know what to say, so I gave my stock reply to the folks in the car.

"This is not a Sears home design that I recognize," I said, trying to blend gentle words, grace and poise with authority and expertise. "It's possible it is a Sears home that was extensively customized when built, but it does not match any of the houses offered in the Sears Modern Homes catalogs.

We went to the next house and the next and the next. All in all, I disallowed the majority of their Sears homes. Over the course of several weeks, it turned into quite a brouhaha in the local papers, but my primary question – "Has anyone been inside these homes to look for stamped lumber?" – was never addressed or answered.

Thanks to the persistence of reporters, I was able to get into six of the houses. The three I had identified from the curb as being Sears homes *had* stamped lumber. The three I had ruled out did *not* have stamped lumber. (The neighborhood was built in the late 1920s, so I knew their Sears homes should have telltale stamps on the framing members.)

It was a messy situation and cost me quite a bit of time, trouble and heartache and even a few tears. Several articles in the local papers questioned my credibility, my motives and intentions and even my professionalism.

Again, this is so important: You *must* authenticate purported Sears homes.

Old houses and big changes

Learning how to identify Sears homes is a lot like bird-watching, but (in my humble O) *infinitely* more enjoyable. One slight difference is, you'll never see a yellow-bellied sap sucker covered in aluminum siding. Whether you're looking for a Sears house or a Tufted Titmouse (bird), you'll need to study and memorize the different styles and then *start looking*!

In my community – Southwestern Illinois – fewer than 5% of the Sears homes retain their original siding. You must train your eyes and mind to look *beyond* the contemporary siding materials and "unsee" the changes a home may have endured in the last several decades.

Porches get closed in and new porches are added. Roofs get raised. Houses get additions. Windows disappear. Yet observing window and door placement is a key element in identifying a potential Sears home. While you're comparing a 1923 foursquare in Jerseyville, Illinois to The Gladstone, pause and think about the evolution of windows in a typical 80-year old house.

When bathtubs are converted into shower enclosures, bathroom windows get covered up. Many Sears homes had closet windows. (Remember, electricity was in its infancy at the turn of the 20th Century and closet windows were a big plus in an otherwise dark closet.) These small closet windows are usually the first casualties of substitute sidings.

Sears offered bathroom-less houses from 1908 through the 1930s. Bathrooms (fortunately) are added to these old houses in later years. Windows are added to new bathrooms.

Attic windows get covered by vinyl siding or replaced with louvered vents. Kitchens get enlarged. Pantries (and their windows) disappear. Kitchens and baths endure the most remodeling through the years and their windows are frequently altered. Big windows get converted into bay or bow windows and those new windows might not bear the slightest resemblance to the old windows. And that glorious vinyl-siding covers it all.

First Starlight I see tonight

While driving through Wood River, Illinois one afternoon, I found three Starlights (Sears homes) in a row. Whipping out *"Houses by Mail,"* I was saddened to learn that the Starlight pictured in that book had a clipped-gable dormer. The Starlight-look-a-likes in Wood River had small shed dormers.

"Oh well," I thought. "I'm learning by my mistakes."

A few weeks later, I purchased a 1919 Sears Modern Homes catalog. On page 30, I found a caption that read, "Eight of Nearly 200 Starlights Now Built." The picture showed several different Starlights in different sections of the county. Some had big shed dormers, some had little shed dormers. Some had gabled dormers,

INTERIORS – *The* STARLIGHT

**The Living Room
and
Dining Room**

A LOW priced bungalow can be made attractive, inviting and comfortable in its interior. Our Starlight Modern Home, the living room and dining room of which we illustrate on this page, makes a little home of which, with the correct treatment, any family can justly be proud.

PEOPLE who have built our houses express themselves as being amazed not only at their low cost but also at the ease and small expense of furnishing them. Our part in enriching the interior of this bungalow consists in furnishing high grade flooring, casing and moldings. The owner and the housewife can do their part in the remainder of the furnishing, consisting of the lighting, decorating and furniture. To produce proper satisfactory results, a modest sum only is required. Our co-operation is yours for the asking.

Eight of Nearly Two Hundred "Starlights" Now Built

Built at La Crosse, Wis.

Built at Castalia, Ohio.

Built at Stithton, Ky..

Built at Nilwood, Ill.

*Every Builder
Is Pleased*

Built at Niagara Falls, N.Y.

Built at Painesville, Ohio.

Built at Boone, Iowa.

Built at Detroit, Mich.

SEARS, ROEBUCK AND CO. CHICAGO

The Starlight was one of Sears best selling houses. Note the different dormers featured on these eight models. These many different options are part of what makes identification so challenging! (1919 catalog)

others had hipped dormers. Starlight dormers, I learned, came in every shape and size. In subsequent catalogs, I've discovered that dormers were offered in a wide variety of styles on Sears homes.

Blocks of cinder

This next item is a curious tidbit, but it works in my section of Southwestern Illinois. Limestone quarries and brick yards were a large part of our local history. The majority of homes in this area were built with limestone or brick foundations. Brick masonry and stonemasonry was a demanding skill and not something the average homeowner would even attempt. Building a stone foundation (or wall) was akin to putting together a three-dimensional jigsaw puzzle with 80-pound puzzle pieces.

Most of the kit homes in our community are on cinder block foundations or basements. Hiring a workman to lay square blocks would be far cheaper than hiring a stone mason to lay a limestone foundation. And a capable homeowner *could* lay his own cinderblock wall. Again, not every house on a block foundation is a kit home, but it's another clue, that tells you, "slow down, look closer."

Additional info on finding Sears homes through grantor records

In the 1920s, about half of all Sears homes were financed through Sears "easy payment plans" - Sears mortgages. These mortgages (a legal document secured by real estate) were recorded at the county courthouse. In *theory*, if your community has 100 Sears homes, you'll find 50 Sears mortgage documents on file in the local recorder's office.

Let's take the Madison County Courthouse in Edwardsville, Illinois as an example. Madison County is a rectangular chunk of Southwestern Illinois which adjoins the Mississippi River on its western border (next door to St. Louis, Missouri) and covers 725 square miles with a population of 258,941 people.

The Recorder's Office at the courthouse has several computers and microfiche readers scattered about, but the older records and documents (pre-1980) haven't made it into the database.

A large part of the Recorder's Office is filled with endless rows of cloth-bound books which rest inside the waist-high metal bookcases. Want to research an old mortgage from the 1920s? Get ready to do some serious lifting and hauling. The old books that contain these records weigh 15 pounds *or more*. You'll need to reserve a crane if you want to pull out a plat book. Those books weigh a little less than my car. And the research is pretty intense. Studying pages and pages filled with tiny, faded, handwritten script is wearying. I've done a lot of time at the Madison County Courthouse, studying those old books. As singer/songwriter Harry Chapin once said, "I spent a week there one afternoon."

During my search, I found ten Sears mortgages, which was a bit disappointing. After all, Madison County (probably) has hundreds of Sears homes.

But I didn't even find *those* ten names until I knew how to look.

[The following information came from Dale Patrick Wolicki, an architectural historian with Bay County

(Michigan) Historical Society.]

As was stated in the beginning of this chapter, start by looking at grantor records from 1915 through the early 1940s. Sears stopped offering mortgages in 1933, but when a mortgage was paid in full, the mortgage *release* was recorded, so you're going to be looking for that document, as well. The grantor records are categorized by date and loosely alphabetized.

Look for these names in grantor records: Walker O. Lewis and Nicholas Wieland (sometimes misspelled as Weiland). Both of these men served as trustees for Sears. Walker O. Lewis served as trustee for Sears until January 1930 and that's when Wieland took over.

The front of the grantor record will be indexed by last name. As an example, the index may direct you to look on pages 72-78 for the name "Lewis." Finding those pages can be tricky. Many of the records at Madison County have been re-numbered two or three times, so you'll be looking at two or three sets of numbers, often scribbled on the upper right hand corner of the page. Sometimes, these numbers are in error, so you'll have to thumb through dozens or *hundreds* of pages, looking for that elusive name. (Been there, done that, too.)

Once you find the pages with the last name "Lewis," start looking for the first name, "Walker." When you find "Walker O. Lewis," you may see "Trustee" or "tr."

Further to the right of that *same line,* you'll find the homeowner's name and then "book #339, page 198." This means the mortgage document can be found on page 198 of book #339. (You may have to hunt around for a few minutes to find book #339 and gain an understanding of how these different books are categorized.) When you turn to page 198 of book #339, you'll see the grantor's name (Lewis, Trustee for Sears) and the grantee's name, "Mr. Hap E. Cottedge."

In a perfect world, the document will state that "Mr. Hap E. Cottedge" lives at 29 West Beautiful Street in Troy, Illinois. But that perfect world does not exist at Madison County Courthouse. In that world, I found something more like this: "Lot 12 and part of lot 13, block 3, Miller's Addition, Madison County."

Sometimes, the mortgage document will include a plat number and sometimes not. If it *does* include a plat number, you can look at the plat and get an idea of the home's location. However, Madison County covers 725 square miles. There were many times I looked at plats and could find no mention of a city. In this case, I took the legal description (Lot 12 and part of lot 13…) to the Office of Maps and Plats (which is usually near the Recorder's Office) and asked *them* to look it up. In Madison County, it took the clerk about 3 minutes to find each location and the clerk was never happy to see me. After looking up the third legal description in 30 minutes, she cut me off.

A few days later, I went hunting for Sears homes, using these new addresses I'd found at the courthouse. The first house on the list was on "I Street" in a tiny city in Illinois. Unfortunately, there was no "I Street" on any map of this area of Madison County.

Eventually, I found a cluster of older folks working in their yard on this nice September afternoon. Older folks, I reasoned, would remember the names of old streets. Neither she, nor her gardening buddies had ever heard of "I Street."

Now I was in trouble. I stopped in at the Fire Department and asked a fireman for help. He knew exactly where "I Street" was. ("Was" being the operative word.)

"I Street was renamed many years ago," he replied. "And you're one block away from it."

Back in the car, I made a couple turns and found my Sears home. It was not the fancy, fine home I'd hoped for. Instead, it was the most non-descript 600 square-foot house I'd ever seen. I couldn't have picked it out as a Sears house in a million years. I thought about knocking on the door, but decided against it. The house was too boring and I was too disheartened. I snapped a picture of the plain little house and returned home.

Next weekend, I went out to another section of Madison County and went looking for another few houses. Those results were also pretty uneventful.

One of the addresses was an empty lot with a driveway and sidewalk, which lead to a house-shaped patch of dirt. Obviously, a house had occupied that spot at some point. This Sears house had burned down or was demolished. Bottom line, it was gone.

Another address was a Sears home that had been extensively customized. It was an amalgamation of several different styles. And it was in a terrible section of town and in poor condition.

I tried to visit a fourth Sears house only to find that the streets had been renamed and the fire department had no idea where the old street could be. That was disappointing, too.

In summary, my experience in finding Sears homes through the courthouse has been interesting, but not overwhelming with fruitage. Information from the 1920s and 1930s is not always accurate, because street names and even house numbers are sometimes changed. Communities evolve and redistricting occurs and homes burn down or are torn down. A lot can happen in 75+ years. Conversely, my friend Dale has found hundreds of Sears homes using this technique.

Conclusion

If you want to get serious about finding Sears homes, here are some tips.

Keep a copy of "*Houses By Mail*" in your car. Learn to look at your community with "new" eyes.

Visit an area with a large collection of Sears homes, such as Carlinville, Wood River or Elgin, Illinois and you'll learn a lot about Sears homes in a hurry. Seeing these houses "in person" will teach you a great deal about Sears homes.

Try studying the bigger, fancier homes, first. The little houses, like The Winona and The Grant and The Clyde are ubiquitous and frustrating to differentiate! There is little to distinguish them from the thousands of small, plain homes that line every modest street in America.

Publicity (newspaper stories and local radio shows) can teach people how to search their homes for stamped lumber, blueprints in the attic, shipping labels on lumber, etc. Such publicity can spark personal reminiscences, which can help find Sears and other mail order homes.

And visit Rebecca Hunter and Jim Chapa's website at www.searskithouse.com to learn more about the new field guide to Sears Homes that should soon be available.

Important note from the author: (Well, it's not that important, but here goes.)

If you've skipped to the end of this chapter because this all sounds like too much work or if you don't want to follow my footsteps and devote your entire life to Sears homes; and/or you don't wish to memorize each of the 370 different designs of Sears homes; and/or you wish to stay married; and/or you don't want your face to appear on a milk carton because your family has now officially listed you as a missing person; there is another way to find Sears homes. Hire the Sears Queen (as I'm fond of calling myself) to come to your town and find the Sears homes. A fun time is always had by all. ☺ For Rose's contact information, turn to the back pages of this book.

Chapter 10

A House For the Little Woman and The Kiddies
A Fascinating Look Inside the Sears Modern Homes Catalogs

It takes a woman to appreciate the attractive features of Honor-Bilt Modern Homes. Men are concerned with ruggedness of construction, with excellence of material, with the plan of financing a home. And women are, too. But women are interested in other things as well. With beauty and with style. They are concerned with the convenience of room arrangement; with the features that add to the appearance of the interior and exterior; with the many modern-day improvements which help to lighten the task of home-keeping.

1929 Modern Homes Catalog

If you love Sears homes, you'll probably love the Sears Modern Homes *catalogs*, too. This entire chapter is devoted to the interesting tidbits that are scattered throughout the pages of these catalogs.

1908 Book of Modern Homes and Building Plans

My favorite tidbit begins with the cover page of Sears' first catalog. Look at the foursquare house on the cover with the two-story porch and chamfered third-floor dormer. Sears *never offered this particular house* in any of their Modern Homes catalogs at any time in their 32-year history. They just thought it was a good looking house so they put it on the cover.

Next, look at the man walking on the sidewalk. He's being chased by a Sheltie. (Sears never offered Shelties in any Modern Homes catalogs either.) But this man is carrying two buckets away from his modern house. Hopefully, he's carrying two buckets *full of water* to his barn. Let's hope his new *modern home* does not lack indoor plumbing and running water. Let's hope he's not going out to fetch a pail of water.

The fact is, bathrooms were *optional* in about half of the house designs offered in this 1908 catalog. However, you could always buy a fine looking outhouse. In this 1908 catalog, Sears promised that their kit homes would save the homeowner $500 - $1000. That was a pretty bold promise, considering that house prices started at $495.

The first page also made this promise: "Our plans are more complete and simple than you can get from ordinary architects. We go much further into details...so that you can not make a mistake."

On pages 28-32, Sears included a detailed building plan of Modern Home #102, later known as The Hamilton. This house was offered by Bachman as an HO model home kit, for model train enthusiasts. The Hamilton was probably selected because detailed drawings of the front, rear and side elevations were included in this catalog.

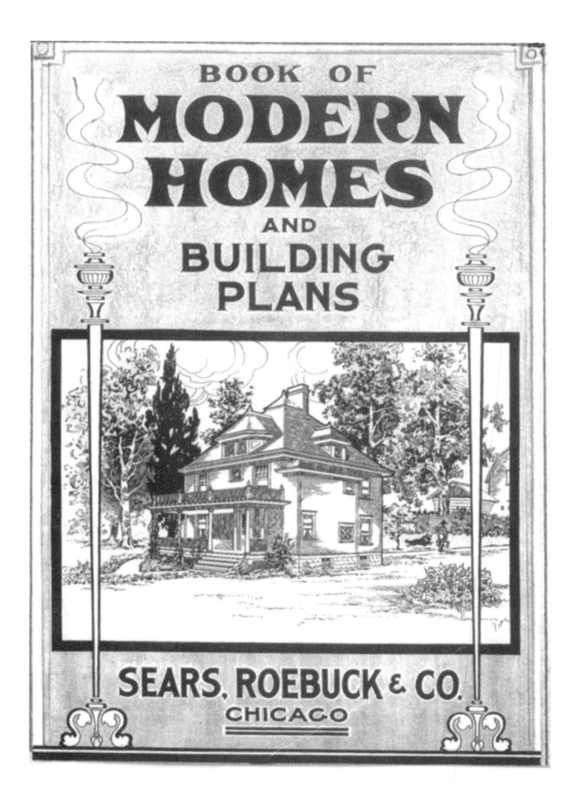

Sears never offered the house pictured on the cover of this 1908 Modern Homes catalog. Note the art deco lamps in the foreground.

There were at least seven editions of this first-year 1908 Modern Homes catalog. One of the earliest editions contained this statement (which was removed from later editions):

We cannot make changes on the plans for the Modern Homes illustrated and described in this book. Blue prints or plans are made from pen and ink silk tracing sheets drawn by our architect, which cost from $65 to $125 for tracing for one building, and if we attempted to make changes it would render these valuable tracing sheets worthless. Therefore, we will make no changes on our plans.

A few years later, Sears was *encouraging* people to customize their "Modern Homes."

1909 Book of Modern Homes

In the 1909 catalog this statement appeared: "Hundreds of our customers during the past year selected homes from former editions of this book. Every builder of any of our modern homes is a satisfied customer because he saves all we claim. We can save him from $150 to $1500 or more on a building."

The 1909 catalog had 73 house designs. Two 1908 houses - models #128 and #138 - were dropped from the 1909 (and subsequent) catalogs. Model #303 was offered *only* in the 1909 catalog. Testimonial letters appearing in this catalog told of saving up to $1000 by purchasing and building a Sears Modern Home.

An announcement appeared at the bottom of page one of the 1909 catalog stating, "Our architects are now preparing plans for several designs of good substantial up-to-date barns for which we will be able to furnish plans about July 1, 1910."

1911 Book of Modern Homes

The 1911 Modern Homes catalog stated, "Our plans [have been] drawn by licensed architects of wide experience, embodying all the very newest ideas in convenient and artistic arrangement." An insert stuck between the bound pages of the 1911 catalog announced the opening of the Sears Mill in Cairo.

1912 Book of Modern Homes

The first page of this catalog boldly states, "This book has solved the home building problem for thousands of people." Further down the page it continues, "Stop paying rent. Quit building castles in the air. Build a real castle – A home of your own."

This catalog shows the layout of the buildings at the Sears Mill in Cairo, Illinois and also shows several kit barns and garages.

The 1912 Modern Homes catalog was reprinted by Schiffer Publishing (*"Homes in a Box; Modern Homes From Sears Roebuck"* copyright 1998) and makes a great addition to the Sears House Aficionado's collection.

1915 Book of Modern Homes

By 1914, Sears was offering precut houses. In the 1915 catalog, Sears stated that lumber orders would be filled and shipped quickly. The catalog promised: "We have been able to give good service as far west as Colorado and as far east as Connecticut." (I guess they could give lousy service to points further west and east.)

In 1915, Sears was promoting their "Goodwall Sheet Plaster," which was plaster encased in layers of heavy cardboard. Sears promised that this sheet plaster was superior to lath and plaster for many reasons, including its fire resistant qualities.

1916 Book of Modern Homes

On the opening page of this catalog, Sears stated, "There are 420 of our Modern Homes in New York, 448 in Illinois, 354 in Ohio, 401 in Indiana, 219 in Iowa and 134 in New Jersey." Now that's the kind of trivia that makes a history nut's heart go pitter-pat.

On page one, the "big" sales pitch continued:

Thousands of people have built houses according to our plans and with our materials. Why not send for your plans today? Select your Modern Home from the big collection of designs shown in this book and let us tell you all about it without the least obligation on your part. We have a big force of architects, draftsmen, building experts, women advisers and home decorators to help you in building your home. This big organization will solve your problems and best of all, *the service is free.*

1918 Book of Modern Homes

In the 1918 Modern Homes Catalog, Sears houses were no longer known by numbers, but were given names.

The Magnolia, Sears finest home, was the "cover girl" of the 1918 Modern Homes catalog. This 2900 square foot, 10-room home was little more than a puffed-up American Foursquare with illusions of grandeur. The house had some snazzy features, such as the Ionic columns supporting the two-story front porch; a single balustrade railing at the tippy-top of the hipped roof and a pedimented dormer; and a small balcony off the master bedroom on the second floor.

In the 1918 catalog, the Magnolia's price was $7,960, but that was because of the inflated price of building materials caused by the Great War (World War I). In *Modern Carpentry: A Practical Manual* (a 300-page builder's tome published for Sears Roebuck in 1918), an ad for the Magnolia appeared in the back pages of the book. It seems likely that this book was written in late 1917, as it identified the Magnolia by *number* (Modern Home #2089) at a price of $4,485. Rebecca Hunter of Elgin, Illinois discovered a price sheet from a 1920 Sears Modern Homes catalog that showed the price of the Magnolia had jumped to $9,900! (This was due to post-war hyper-inflation.) By 1922, building prices had stabilized and the Magnolia's price dropped to $5,849.

The opening pages of the 1918 catalog said:

No matter where you live – along the Pacific Coast, in the Central West, in the New England States or in Dixieland – this book will enable you to pick out a house that will be entirely at home in your surroundings.

This last comment was added specifically to counter architects' complaints that kit homes were inherently flawed because regional climates and different locales demanded differing architectural designs. How dare anyone suggest that one type of house could be appropriate for different parts of the country! A house "at home

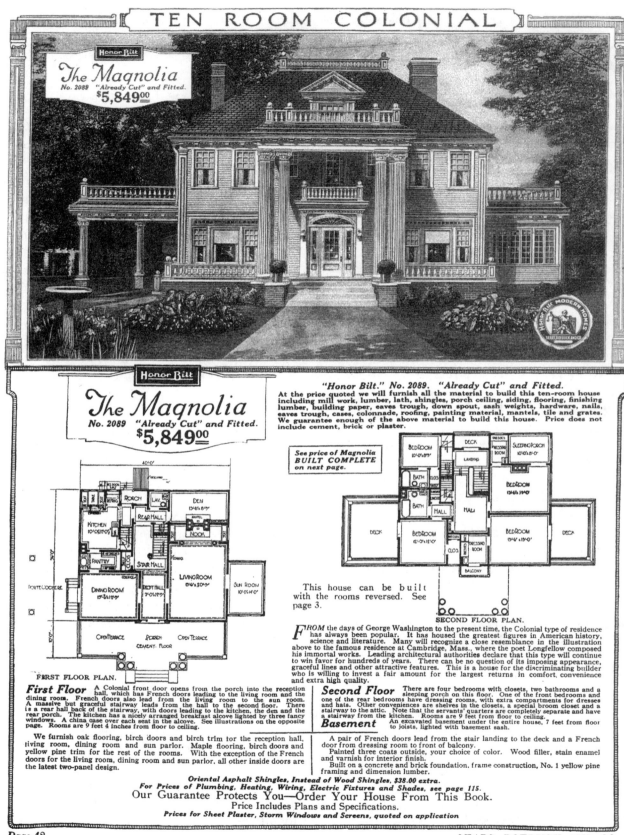

Sears offered The Magnolia from 1918-1922.

in your surroundings" in Dallas, Texas would surely not be suitable for Northern Wisconsin – or so the nay sayers claimed.

1919 Book of Modern Homes

The 1919 catalog showed pictures of Carlinville's Standard Addition under construction. On the same page, Sears proclaimed, "Over Six Million Customers." Upon reading the smaller print, you'd learn that "six million customers" referred to their general merchandise customers.

Sears praised their modern homes, saying, "Every architectural error or discrepancy has been overcome. Over 25,000 persons have built houses according to our plans and with our materials. We can refer you to satisfied customers in every state in the Union." It appears that Sears had mastered the shipping of building materials *beyond* the Rockies.

On page nine, Sears delineated the differences between their Honor-Bilt houses and Standard Built homes, adding this caveat: "We recommend and guarantee our Honor-Bilt Modern Homes because they are better in every way for the man who wants a *permanent* and *high class home*." I guess the man who wants a low class home needs to stick with Standard Built?

But even their Standard Built homes were "permanent." I've found a few Standard Built homes in Southwest Illinois that are more than 75 years old and they're in remarkably good condition.

1922 Book of Modern Homes

Headlines in the front pages of this catalog promised, "Easy Payments! Special Inducement to Build Now!" and then promised, "The greatest building proposition ever offered."

In 1922, there were three levels of quality - Honor-Bilt, Econo Built and Lighter Built. Lighter Built was what we'd (today) describe as a hunting shack, best suited for areas with warm weather, calm winds and serene wildlife. One angry moose could do a lot of damage to your "Lighter Built" shack/house.

Honor-Bilt homes, as discussed in Chapter Three, utilized traditional construction standards, such as double headers over the doors and windows, double floors (primary floors over subfloors), exterior sheathing under clapboard or cedar shingles and wall studs on 16-inch centers. In later years, Econo Built and Lighter Built would be renamed and known as "Standard Built," but it appears the *cheapest grade* of Sears homes (known as "Lighter Built" in 1922) was eventually dropped.

1923 Book of Modern Homes

On the back pages of this catalog, Sears offered their plumbing supplies (in two grades).

The higher-priced "Chippendale Bathroom Outfit" had a pedestal tub, pedestal sink and modern potty. An elegant woman dressed in a fashionable kimono is flashing a bit of leg as she prepares to bathe in her snazzy "Chippendale" tub.

The cheaper "Fairview Bathroom Outfit" sports an old fashioned "pregnant toilet" (so named because of the protrusion at the front of the stool), a claw foot tub and a wall-hung, half round sink. In this drawing, a pitiful-looking child is standing in the tub, tightly clutching the shower curtains to cover his nakedness. The look on his face pleads, "This is a miserable bathroom outfit. Go for the Chippendale!"

1924 Book of Modern Homes

This book is nearly identical to the 1923 Modern Homes Catalog. Simplex sectional cottages (temporary houses) are still promoted in the back of the catalog, as they have been for about 15 years. And that poor kid is still standing in the Fairview tub.

1925 Book of Modern Homes

In 1925, Sears began offering a greater variety of electrical fixtures for the home. Electricity was becoming more affordable, reliable and widely available.

Good thing, too. In June 1923, *American Carpenter and Builder* ran a story about the importance of adequate electrical fixtures to the harried housewife. Presented as a housewife's narrative, the article stated,

> If I do not have this (a home adequately wired for electrical appliances) I may go on for years trying to do without the help I could so easily have had. I may lose all zest for living and for loving husband and family and people and culture and nature in the treadmill of hard work.

> I may forget my sense of proportion, grow ragged of nerves, keyed to tears over trifles. I may begin whining over the ceaselessness and the exhaustiveness and the monotony of my job – and in the hysteria of dissatisfaction and fatigue, I may make shipwreck of that which was launched with such high hopes! You architects can help me to make a success of my life and to make most of my wishes come true!

1926 Book of Modern Homes

This catalog was reprinted by Dover Publications, Inc. (copyright 1991). A preface in this book (which Dover added) states that Sears began selling precut homes in 1916, but I disagree. A 1914 Sears building materials catalog contains an ad offering The Gladstone (foursquare) as a *precut* house.

1929 Book of Modern Homes

The 1929 catalog was full of prose and interesting articles, such as the two page spread on Elmer M. Blume, described as "a well known contractor of Des Plaines, IL" (near Chicago). According to the accompanying story, Elmer and his brother Oscar began building Sears homes in the early 1920s and felt they were dandy little houses.

"…I said to my brother, Oscar, this is the method for us. He agreed. …In little less than six years, we have erected 104 homes - and every one of them by Sears Roebuck."

The 1929 catalog is also the source of much information about Miss. E. L. Mayer. She was on the architectural staff at Sears, but not as an architect. She was an interior decorator who reviewed the blueprints and plans before they were given final approval.

Sears offered the Fairview and the Chippendale Bathroom outfit in the 1924 (and other) Sears Modern Homes catalogs. The Chippendale is definitely a better value. The Fairview doesn't have any toilet paper.

As page 20 of the catalog stated:

Miss E. L. Mayer, recognized throughout the world as one of the greatest feminine home authorities, is constantly endeavoring to equip "Honor-Bilt" homes with the necessities and comforts that mean so much to every woman. Every floor plan and interior decorating sketch must bear her approval before it is adopted. She must see that provision is made in the plan for pianos, davenports, radios, beds and dressers and that all conveniences appealing to the housewife are not overlooked. She selects kitchen cupboards, the built-in ironing boards, telephone stands and other contrivances so important in home comfort and assists the "Honor-Bilt" home builder in the selection of draperies, rugs and other furnishings. She also suggests the most effective way of landscaping the various houses to bring out their individual charm and beauty.

(Author's Note: Who was the greatest masculine home authority at this time?)

There is a story that Sears had a woman architect on staff – something virtually unheard of in the 1920s. I've not been able to confirm or disprove this, but would love to track down the source.

October 1925, *American Carpenter and Builder* reported that New Jersey had *three* licensed women architects in the *state*. One was employed by a magazine and one worked in "an advisory capacity." *(Author's note: Does that mean they wouldn't let her have her own drafting table and a pencil?)* As of 1925, Mrs. Trimble of Westfield, New Jersey was the only licensed woman architect in New Jersey who was "actively engaged in the practice."

After reading this, I began to question this story that Sears had a woman architect. Was Miss Mayer's position as interior designer the basis of this legend about a "woman architect"?

It was also in the 1929 catalog that this comment appeared: "The kitchen…the room where most women spend practically two-thirds of every day should be strictly modern in every aspect." *(Author's note: Gasp.)*

1930 Book of Modern Homes

Easy payment mortgage plans were still being heavily promoted in 1930. Amortization tables compared the cost of mortgage payments to the cost of rent. Sears promised, "Honor-Bilt homes can be bought to fit any pocketbook, from the smallest bungalow to the $25,000 residence."

Lest you be tempted to think $25,000 is modest, keep in mind - most of these homes sold for $1500 - $3500. A 1930s $25,000 house would have been an extraordinarily expensive home.

1931 Homes of Today

In 1931 (and 1932), Sears tried something new. Their 1931 catalog had a new look with a decided art deco flair. Customized homes were promoted on most of the 28 pages.

1933 America's New Low Cost Homes

Still searching for that right look, Sears tried something new (again) in 1933. They also issued a sales booklet, which was a petite 4 x 6 inches and was titled "Homes." Inside the front cover, the first page read,

"America's New Low Cost Homes." The 94-page booklet was offered by the Sears Home Construction Division and contained 109 house designs. The accompanying text was in diminutive font. Apparently, part of the "low cost" was the tiny little catalog with its tiny little pictures.

The little pamphlet was awash with promises of low down payments, easy terms and affordable monthly payments. On page 92, the catalog promised, "The easiest, most convenient homeowning plan ever devised."

Under "small payments," the catalog went on to say, "Monthly payments like rent. No payments for first 4 months. Small cash down payment, if you own or can buy, a well located lot. No renewing of mortgages, no unexpected costs."

1934 Modern Homes

In 1934, Sears no longer printed the small catalog and offered only the full size catalogs, which offered basic houses for basic prices. The 64-page catalog featured 48 houses. The 1936 catalog bore a striking resemblance to the 1934 catalog.

1938 Modern Homes

The 1938 catalog looked like the 1934 and 1936 catalogs. However, in 1938, Sears was pushing FHA mortgages with a vengeance.

"Modern Home Specifications meet FHA requirements," the catalog stated on its front pages. "To protect you as the owner," it continued, "and themselves as insurers of the loan, the Federal Housing Administration has laid down rigid standards of materials and construction. All Sears Modern Homes are guaranteed to conform with these requirements. This fact is your best assurance of dependable quality, long-life and the utmost in value."

1940 Modern Homes

This was the final catalog for the Sears Modern Homes department. Between 1908-1940, Sears sold (*approximately*) 70,000 - 75,000 homes in about 370 different styles*. When Sears closed the Modern Homes department in 1940, their sales records, promotional information, catalogs and other paperwork associated with the modern homes department were destroyed.

1941 Sears Modern Homes

Recently, my friend Dale Patrick Wolicki called to share some information. He'd recently found and purchased 15 line drawings of "Sears Modern Homes."

The 15 drawings – each on separate pieces of 8 x 11-inch paper - may or may not have been part of a catalog. Their source is unknown. However, at the bottom of each page, it states, "*Sears Modern Home - Copyright 1941; Sears Roebuck & Co.*" Unlike other Sears homes designs, these designs list an architect's name: *Randolph Evans, AIA*.

Dale shared these 15 drawings with me and all I can say about them is — they are house designs I've never seen before. Perhaps by the time this book is in its third revision, I'll know more about this new mystery that Dale has uncovered. (*Author's note: <u>Third</u> revision? Did I say that out loud? Eeh gads. The first book took two years to write; this revision took more than a year. Gasp.*)

* Sears offered 370 different designs, but I've only found about 150 of these designs in the field. And that's with a lot of driving and traveling! I'd suspect that many of the house designs that Sears offered were *never actually constructed*. And Sears had their "best-sellers"; I see the same 65 house designs again and again and again, city after city.

Chapter 11

Those Dandy Houses:
Testimonials, Trivia and Reminiscences of Building a Sears Home

I have the Sears Modern Home No. 167 finished and as everybody says, it is a <u>dandy</u>.
You will have many inquiries in regard to this house.

Testimonial from D. A. Fish
"Successful Building"
(*1912 Sears Homes Promotional Booklet*)

One of my favorite parts of the old Sears Modern Homes catalogs are the testimonials. I love old things and old houses and even old language. And I love the natural, simple way these letter-writers expressed themselves. A common theme throughout all these testimonials is the sheer joy and delight expressed by these new homeowners. The pride of ownership shines through their words.

My Honor-Bilt home (The Crescent) is an ornament to the street on which it is located. (A. A. McCrone, Pennsylvania)

My house is beyond my wildest hopes. You have in me one of your ardent boosters. (D. Curran, Ohio)

I am exceedingly pleased with my new home, The Woodland. The built-in ironing board and the table with an electric light socket has already proved to be worth its weight in gold. (W. W. Shaw, Jr., Illinois)

The Sears Home we built is a constant source of joy and inspiration. Our daughter, who lives in the house, is one of the happiest housewives in the country. (Robert Stansfield, New Jersey)

Everyone says I have the best and nicest house in town. Men from the local lumber mill say they cannot get such lumber anywhere. (John Bone, Kentucky)

My (Sears) home is admired by everyone who sees it. (S. R. Wantz, Maryland)

We are very proud of our Sears Home and cannot speak too highly of it. There is not a thing that we can find fault with, for everything is perfect. (W. E. Somerville, Ohio)

Words cannot express how pleased I am with my home. (Leslie Hill, New Jersey)

We think our Alhambra is the best looking house on Lexington Avenue. (J. W. Shippers, Ohio)

We are now living in our new (Sears) home and I cannot find words to tell you how much we are pleased with it and to thank you for the honest way you treated us. We are complimented on having the nicest home in Monongahela for the price. (E. F. Addison, Pennsylvania)

The best way to find out how I feel about my Vallonia Home would be to talk to me personally, as it is no easy matter to express how deeply I feel in a letter. (Isaac Sechler, no city mentioned)

As these testimonials truly show, Sears empowered and enabled potential homebuyers to get into a home of their own and create instant equities of $500 - $2000.

We have saved $500 on this house, besides having better material than we could possibly have gotten at our home town. (J. P. Berck, Nebraska)

The house cost me $1410 and I am satisfied it would have cost me $2000 if I had bought the building materials in town. (John Bryan, Iowa)

My Sears Home cost less than $3000 and it is better than any house here that cost $5000. (Robert Blackwood, Nebraska)

A real estate dealer offered us $1800 more for our Vallonia than it cost us but we built it to be our home and we like it so well, we do not care to sell it. (J. W. Dilks, no city mentioned.)

I have had two offers to sell my home (The Mitchell) at a profit of about $2000. (W. R. Shipman)

I saved over $2000 on this house (The Puritan) and when it was completed, I was able to get a mortgage for more than the construction costs. (A. W. Fischer)

My home cost $5100 including a double garage and some extra work. Can list it for quick sale at $6500 but it is not for sale. (Max De Laney)

In some areas, these homes served as powerful advertisements for Sears.

My house has attracted a good deal of attention and favorable comment and has been visited by people from up to 120 miles away. Everybody is surprised at the quality of millwork. I saved $419 (by buying a Sears Home). (A. A. Ward, Kansas)

As soon as I get the curtains up, I will have a picture taken for you. There is someone at our house every Sunday looking at it. They call it the Sears Roebuck house. (W. Gregg, Kansas)

People are coming a long way to look at the Sears Roebuck house. Everyone who sees it is surprised at the low cost and high quality. (A. H. Mulle, Nebraska)

The home has been admired by hundreds of people. (Robert Stansfield, Riverside, New Jersey)

We are delighted with our home and everyone admires it. A great many people have come to see it inside and out. (Jefferson Adams, Michigan)

The house will stand the closest inspection and scores of people who come to see the so-called Sears Roebuck house have been favorably impressed with the plan and materials which they found while carefully looking over the building. (J. Berck, Nebraska)

We are much pleased with our Honor-Bilt home, the Vallonia. Inside and out, it was very much admired by everyone who inspected it. Judging from comments made, it is the most admired bungalow in this community. I dare say that three people who have seen my home have placed orders for Honor-Bilt homes. (Elwood Harvey, Pennsylvania)

An occasional testimony sounded almost like a backhanded compliment.

The Ready-cut material went together like a set of tinker toys. (Leon Henderson)

The longer I live in this house (The Ashmore), the better I like it. (James Humpal, Ohio)

Everyone is aghast at the low cost of our home. (Earl Suits, Michigan)

And a few testimonials demonstrate why it's so difficult to identify Sears homes today.

I changed the layout of the rooms and the house looks somewhat different from the original plans. (John Johnson, New Jersey)

Enclosed you will find a photo of my Sears Home, slightly modified from the original plans. (S. R. Wantz, Maryland)

We enlarged the house from the original plans and made other changes to suit the (southern) climate. (Josephus Autrey, Texas)

Many *builders* and *developers* were erecting these "Ready-Cut" homes all over the country, because they found them easier and cheaper to build than traditional stick-built homes. One had been building Sears precut homes since 1916; another reported that he'd now built 257 Honor-Bilt homes. Builder Emil Golke stated that he'd built 73 Sears homes.

In the last eighteen months, we have purchased material and millwork for sixteen houses, all of which have been erected in our subdivision, Wooster Place. (Brown and Martin Realty, Ohio)

I have built Modern Homes No. 108, 124, 16 and 168 from your plans and they are furnished throughout with your materials. I am a real estate man developing his own property. I hire my own men and built these houses by day work with Union Labor and I expect to build ten more. (W. W. Beckwith, Connecticut)

*We have just finished building seven of your homes and we have found a ready market for them all. They are the talk of everyone who sees them. Everyone who has purchased one of these houses from us has been entirely satisfied. (*No name or city listed)

Built by Lawrence Kaczmarek of Ohio

A few months after *The Houses That Sears Built* was first published, I received an email from Richard Herman in Ohio.

"On page 116, you mentioned a testimonial from Kaczmasek," he wrote. "Could that be a misspelling of the name Kaczmarek?"

Whilst writing the first edition of my book, I had randomly chosen several impossible-to-pronounce names off the pages of the Sears Modern Homes catalog to make the point that a large number of immigrants were achieving the Great American Dream of homeownership, thanks to Sears Roebuck and Company. I wasn't sure where I'd found the name "Kaczmasek." The idea of finding it again made me break out in a cold sweat.

Mr. Herman said that Lawrence Kaczmarek of Elyria, Ohio was his wife's grandfather and that he had built The Westly in 1919. The date helped me narrow the search. I started with my 1922 Modern Homes catalog.

I hastily scanned the names in the testimonials and found it.

"Built by Lawrence Kaczmasek, Ohio. He says, 'I saved about $1,000 on my Already Cut House.'"

And there was a picture of his stunning Westly, complete with a striped canvas awning over the dormer and flower pots on the porch. A real beauty. In the quiet of my small apartment, I danced a jig and made lots of happy noises. I called Richard right away and shared my news. He dropped the phone and excitedly passed the information along to his wife. (It's great to find people who share your excitement over inimitable historical tidbits found in dusty old catalogs.)

In 1974, Kaczmarek's Westly was slated for demolition. The city needed the property for a street extension. As the family faced the solemn chore of evacuating their life-long home, Richard Herman was asked to remove "non-essential items" from the basement and take them out to the back yard to be burned with all the other trash.

"I realized that some of the 'trash' included some interesting letters regarding the Sears kit home," Richard told me. "I put those aside and saved them from the burn pile."

Unfortunately, the house was razed. All that remains of Lawrence Kaczmarek's Westly are the documents that Richard saved and the photo in the 1922 Sears Modern Homes catalog.

Nearly 30 years later, Richard graciously shared those documents with me. It was one of the most remarkable finds of my career. For several nights, I tucked myself into bed with that binder full of old letters that had traveled back and forth between Sears and Lawrence Kaczmarek. I studied the Sears Roebuck letterhead, marveled at the old pica type with it's missing jots and tittles and nearly memorized every word on every document. It was a lovely way to drift off to sleep.

1922 Sears Modern Homes Catalog

This Westly is similar to the house Lawrence built in 1919. The home pictured above (located in Southeastern Virginia) still has its original railings on both the front porch and dormer.

Below is a summary of those letters which show, with incredible detail, the *process* of purchasing a Sears Modern Home. The first letter was a response to an initial inquiry from Lawrence. Sears replied with,

April 2, 1918

Due to the unsettled condition of the lumber market, as well as the market in all other lines, the price quoted in this letter is good for thirty days only. It will be to your interest to get your order in as soon as you conveniently can.

We have selected (electrical) fixtures suitable for this Modern Home. By looking through our Fixture Catalog, you may find fixtures which will meet with your taste better than the ones we selected and can change the list accordingly.

We also list gas and combination fixtures in this catalog, so in case you intend to use gas, the proper fixtures can be selected. The enclosed separate estimate on the plumbing for this house will show you what we will furnish for this item.

You certainly have selected a very attractive, well laid out home. The rooms in it are all large with plenty of windows to insure good light and the best of ventilation. The large pantry and plenty of closet room which this house has are features always appreciated by the housewife. The large front porch adds much to the appearance of this house, also to its comfort. It is indeed a home any man can well feel proud to own.

Remember, everything we furnish is guaranteed and you have the comfortable assurance in dealing with us of knowing that everything will be right.

We have a special reduced price on this house just now, and if you send your order to us before March 15, you may deduct $93 from the price quote in this letter ($2282.64).

I don't think Lawrence got his order in by March 15, 1918. Another letter from Sears - dated March 18, 1919 - states,

We acknowledge with thanks receipt of your order for material for our Modern Home The Westly, No. 2026, also bank letter from your banking company, advising us that you have deposited with them $2500 to our credit to pay for the material for this house. We note from your letter just what changes you desire made in the house.

The next letter is dated March 21, 1919 and reports that the house will soon be on its way.

We expect to ship your (railroad) car of lumber on or about March 29, and will advise you of actual date of shipment as soon as it goes forward. Other material for this house will be shipped in the order you will need it as possibly you have not room to store such material as is not immediately required.

If you do wish us to ship all material at once or if you wish us to delay the millwork until you instruct us to ship, please telegraph us and we shall be glad to arrange accordingly. The writer is going

to give your order personal attention and if you have occasion to write us about it, be sure to use the enclosed stamped envelope. Do not hesitate to call on us or write us for any information we can give you during the time you are putting up your building.

Please be sure to caution your carpenter should there be any part in our plans that he cannot understand that he should write us for any information that he may desire before attempting to cut or fit the material.

Sometime in late March, Lawrence apparently telegraphed Sears and asked how much it would cost to change from "Fire Chief Roofing to Slate Surfaced Shingles."

Sears responded with,

Changing from Fire Chief Roofing to Slate Surfaced Shingles will increase your order sixty dollars and fifty nine cents. Wire answer if OK to change.

Lawrence opted for the Slate Surfaced Shingles.

According to the 1921 Sears Building Materials catalog, Slate Surfaced Shingles were not slate shingles, but merely a good grade of asphalt shingles impregnated with crushed slate. The ad boasted, "Never needs painting!" Shingles were available in red and green and buyers were promised the roofing material was "practically fireproof!"

The Fire Chief Roofing was asphalt roofing that came in 36-foot rolls. The Fire Chief Roofing was a little cheaper than the Slate Surfaced Shingles.

The base-level Westly came with cedar roofing shingles. However, wooden shingles were falling from favor in the late 1910s. The 1921 building materials catalog explained why. "Sparks from a passing train or a chimney can destroy a wood-shingled building at any moment. With Slate Surfaced Roofing you are protected from this danger." (*Author's note: Eek.*)

The letter, dated March 29, 1919, continued,

The mill has been given instructions to ship the lumber at once and follow it by a special wire tracer so as to avoid any unnecessary delay while in transit. When the lumber is received, kindly check it carefully with the list sent with our previous letter so that you will know positively that you have received all the material. If you find any shortage, report it to us within five days. This is very important.

In addition to the lumber, we will ship the hardware, paint, building paper, so that it will reach you at about the same time. The balance of the material with the exception of the millwork will follow in the order needed. We are shipping the paint in the colors as per your selection.

March 31, 1919 is the date of the next letter from Sears.

We are enclosing a blue print of the working drawing for your Hercules Heating Plant. A copy of our instruction book has been mailed. If it should be necessary at any time during cold weather to leave the heating plant without fire in the boiler, be sure to drain the entire system, as explained in the instruction book.

When the heating plant arrives at your freight depot, please examine it carefully to see that it is in good condition. If there is anything you do not thoroughly understand or if there is any further information you desire, write us and your letter will have careful attention. (Rose's translation: "Please read the Hercules Heating instructions thoroughly so that you do not blow up yourself and your family and your Westly.")

On the ninth of April, Sears wrote to Lawrence with the good news that the house had been shipped.

The (railroad box)car of lumber for your Modern Home #2026 (The Westly) went forward from our yards on April 4th. On the blue print plans you have a list of the exact kind and number of pieces that were loaded into this car. This material was checked and rechecked when the car was loaded to make sure there would be no error of any kind.

As the car was sealed, you should receive everything in perfect order, but in your own interest we suggest that you carefully check over the lumber immediately upon arrival and if you should find any shortage or damage, write us promptly and give full description of the trouble and you shall have immediate attention.

For your own protection, it is absolutely necessary that you do this at once as any shortage or damage must have occurred on the way and the time for filing claim with the Railroad Company is limited.

Should any other shipment for this house arrive in bad order or with part missing, let us also know at once and send us your delivery receipt with agent's notation of the damage or shortage so that we can at once fix the matter up without trouble, delay or expense to you.

A wee problem arose, which was addressed in a letter dated June 9, 1919.

As you received some of the parts of your furnace in a damaged condition, we are glad you returned them. We are replacing them for perfect parts, which will go forward to you, by freight, as soon as possible. We regret the inconvenience you have been caused by the delay in getting this matter straightened out for you..

Only one letter from Lawrence appeared and it is dated June 19, 1919. In it, Lawrence writes,

I am sending you an order for a Gem Bathroom Outfit which I will use for my new Westly home, #2026 which I am now building. Please send me rough-in measurements for the bath fixtures. Also send me door and window screens for the Westly home, 2026 and later on, will send an order for furniture. Please rush the rough-in measurements as we are awaiting them.

Sears replied on June 24, 1919 with the measurements for the Gem Bathroom Outfit.

At this point, Lawrence was apparently getting low on funds. He inquired about purchasing a Hercules pipeless furnace for the Westly. Originally, he'd been interested in the Hercules Hot Water Heating Plant, which was a pricey little affair - $398.15, but well worth it. The pipeless furnace was $116.36.

"Pipeless Furnace" was a 1910s euphemism for a coal-burning, fire-breathing, soot-belching, behemoth space-heater that lurked in the basement, directly underneath the living room floor. It didn't have "pipes" (ductwork) because the hot air blew straight up – out of the furnace and into the living room area. From there, it

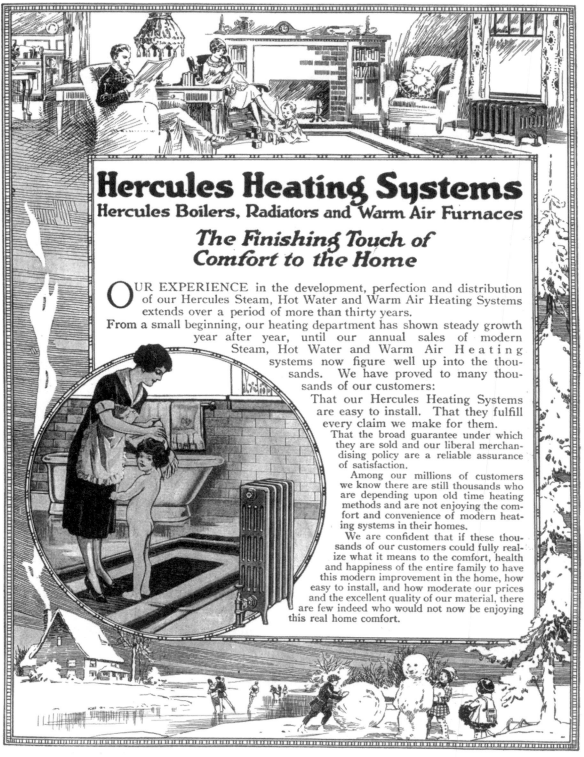

This advertisement (from the 1930 Modern Plumbing and Heating catalog) shows a family enjoying warmth and comfort while the winter winds howl outside. Furnaces were not part of the kit home package because heating needs varied so much region to region.

OUR GUARANTEE STANDS THE TEST IN THE SCALES OF JUSTICE

Mr. Laurence Kaczmarek   April 15, 20
Elyria, Ohio.   264*ELM*110

Dear Sir:

Your kind reply to our letter about the house is much appreciated.

Can you get us a picture of it? A small snap shot or postcard
view would do and we will be glad to pay whatever this costs
you. If you already have such a picture of the house, we would
be grateful to receive a copy. If not, will you have some
taken for us when the place looks its best and there are no
signs of building around the house or yard?

We would be willing for you to wait for the most favorable
weather to enable you to get the prettiest and most homelike
picture possible. Any time within the next few months will do
but please do not forget it.

When sending them, please be sure that your name and address
is on the back of the pictures and either use the enclosed
paster or else address them to the Modern Home Department.

We certainly thank you for your courtesy and appreciate the
interest you have taken in the matter.

With kindest regards.

                        Yours truly,

                        SEARS,ROEBUCK AND CO.

was hoped the 250-degree air would waft through the rest of the house. The result was unevenly heated homes. People in the living room were baking in the heat while the people upstairs struggled valiantly to break the ice in the toilet bowl.

Even Sears had to admit these furnaces had serious limitations. They departed from their characteristic puffery with this caveat on the Pipeless Furnace. "Keeps entire house comfortably warm if the doors between adjoining rooms are left open and registers are installed in the ceiling [below] so as to allow a reasonable amount of air circulation between the rooms."

Coal furnaces were nasty business. Ask anyone more than 65-years-old what they remember about tending the fire in the coal furnace. Most off them will shudder, shake their head, wince and reply, "Those things were awful."

Pipeless Furnaces were the lowest rung on the coal furnace ladder. But they were better than nothing and Sears offered them on the installment plan.

Sears wrote to Lawrence on July 7, 1919,

We would be glad to sell you this furnace on the time installment plan basis...In order that we might sell our goods on these [sic] basis we are compelled to add six percent to the price the material is listed at in our catalog.

On July 30, 1919, Sears wrote with news of another delay.

When we received your order for millwork, we notified you that we would ship it within 21 days, this being the usual time required. We have just received a letter from our factory stating that there has been a delay and they will ship your order August 20th or sooner. Delays of this sort are unusual with us, but for the past few weeks we have been receiving such a great number of orders that our factory has found it impossible to give their usual prompt service.

The next letter is dated April 15, 1920, nine months have passed since Lawrence received news that there was a delay. The house is apparently finished now.

Your kind reply to our letter about the house is much appreciated.

Can you get us a picture of it? A small snap shot or postcard view would do and we will be glad to pay whatever this costs you. If you do not already have a picture of the house, will you have some taken for us when the place looks its best and there are no signs of building around the house or yard?

We would be willing for you to wait for the most favorable weather to enable you to get the prettiest and most homelike picture possible. Any time within the next few months will do, but please do not forget it.

When sending them, please address them to the Modern Home Department.

The last letter from Sears is dated August 30, 1920.

We certainly appreciate very much your favor in sending us two pictures of your house. We are enclosing with this letter our check for $1.50 to cover the amount you paid for the pictures.

Reminiscences

Joseph Origer was born in 1914 on a farm near North Judson, Indiana in Sears Modern Home #101. His father had built the two-story kit house a year earlier, in 1913. Twenty-six years later, in the summer of 1940, Joseph and his new wife traveled to a Sears Modern Homes Sales Center in nearby Chicago to pick out another Sears kit home to build on the same farm.

The young couple chose The Hammond - a 1000-square foot, five-room Honor-Bilt bungalow with casement windows. On July 4th, 1940, two weeks after placing the order, their home arrived in one boxcar at the train depot. Joseph Origer shared some precious memories and wonderful details about the building of these two Sears homes.

My dad built a Sears kit silo in 1911 and he was so impressed with the quality of the lumber (all cypress) that he decided to buy and build Sears Modern Home #101.

Our farm adjoined the old Pennsylvania Railroad. Dad was working in the field when he saw a train pass by with building materials piled high on open flat cars and thought, 'I bet that's my house!' Dad went into the barn and hitched up the horses and went down to the depot to pick up his house. The story is that while Dad was at the depot unloading the building materials, the depot agent looked at the indoor plumbing fixtures and asked, 'What are those things?'

I remember my father telling me the kit home was all number one lumber and material. All the building materials cost $879 and the total expense, including all carpenter labor, was less than $1500. I still have the itemized list of materials for that house!

When I decided to marry and stay on the farm, my parents suggested we go to Chicago and pick out another Sears home. Dad said, "you know the material will be good."

It was 1940 when we bought the house. I think that was the last year they sold these homes. I had a 1939 Modern Homes catalog, so I sent for a 1940 catalog and found there had been a slight price increase. This was the time when Hitler was invading Poland and prices had gone up a little. I was excited about getting a house, but a friend of mine said, "Joe, you should wait a couple years until prices come down." I'm glad I didn't wait. It would have been a long wait.

We went to Chicago to look at Sears' housing displays and get a little more definite information. The Sales Center had samples of inside doors and millwork that we could look at. They had different samples of the inside fixtures and millwork.

The home we picked out – the Hammond – had a kitchen that was 8 x 10 feet so I asked the salesman (at the Sears Modern Homes Sales Center in Chicago) if we could make the kitchen bigger. He suggested that we make the back of the house two feet wider, so the kitchen, dining room and a back bedroom would all be two feet wider.

This of course changed all the precut lumber and the original plans. They had to make a new set of blueprints and specially cut all the material. My dad asked how much these changes would cost. We all held our breath while the salesman did the figuring and it seemed like it took him forever. Finally, he told us that the extra square footage would cost an additional $67. We went with the extra two feet.

The salesman said if we had it all sent in one shipment, it'd be cheaper then having it sent in several shipments, which was another option. The second option was for people who didn't have a place to store all the building materials. We went with one shipment to save a little money.

The house arrived about two weeks after we ordered it. The station agent called and said we had a carload of building material. We hauled it home on a truck and that took quite a few trips. Fortunately, we only had to travel 2 ½ miles. It all fit in one boxcar, but it was pretty tightly packed.

The plaster (for the walls) and cement (for the foundation) was included in the price that we paid. Sears placed the orders for those materials with a local lumber yard. I remember someone from the yard called me and asked, "when do you want your plaster and cement delivered?" I hadn't been aware that Sears did it that way.

We built The Hammond 400 feet away from Modern Home #101. We hired a retired carpenter that lived in town to help us build it. He charged us 50 cents an hour. He said the material was excellent quality and that you could pick up any 2 x 4 and use it as a straight edge.

The house arrived on July 4th and we were living in it by winter. When the house was completed, the total cost of my house, including everything - bathroom fixtures, plumbing, wiring, paint and varnish – was about $2,700. These 60-plus years The Hammond has been a wonderful house. I am glad I built it. This house has been well maintained inside and out, and it is still just as good as new.

Ruth Sward's mother died in the flu epidemic of 1918, leaving behind five children, ages 10, 8, 6, 4 and an 18-month old toddler. Ruth was four years old at the time of her Mom's death and she and her younger brother went to live with a German couple for two years until she was ready to attend first grade.

Ruth said that her father was living in a poor area at the time. "It was kind of a slum", she recalled. "To get us out of that, Dad decided to get us into a home of our own in a different neighborhood." Her father ordered a kit home from Sears Roebuck and Company.

My dad used to joke about our little Puritan (Sears House). He said the postman brought it. My dad and a good friend of his built two Puritans side by side at the same time.

In 1924, it was finished and we moved in. I remember I wrote March 1924 on the back of the china closet. I also remember the melting snow and the mud on those unpaved streets. It was in a part of Pittsburgh that was just being opened up for development.

We had six people – my father and five children – living in that little house and with one bathroom!

My dad was a civil engineer for the railroad and I'm not sure how much of the house building he had to hire and how much he did himself. As I recall, the foundation, plumbing and wiring was done by some-one else. Dad finished off the attic himself and put an extra bedroom up there for me and my sister, Margaret.

If it had not been for Sears and their kit homes, my Dad could never have afforded to have a home of his own.

The house is still standing - sturdy and in good shape. The same Puritan is still next door, too, but the two houses are not identical. When the houses were built, the two families decided that they didn't want the houses looking just the same, so they made some small changes.

Dad lived in that house from 1924 until he died in 1953. The next door neighbors moved out of their Puritan about 8 years after they built it and bought something bigger, but they stayed friends with my dad for their whole lives.

It was so good for us to have that little home. Everything in it was shiny and bright and clean.

The following is ©Reprinted by permission from Good Old Days Specials magazine, *September 2001 issue, House of White Birches publishers, Berne, IN 46711.*

Owner of a Mail-Order House
By Helen G. Gott

In 1928 my mother ordered a house from the Sears and Roebuck catalog. It was a five room, two-bedroom bungalow. I was only 7 years old and we were living across the street from the lot where our new home was to be built. I checked on the building progress every afternoon when I got home from school.

Soon the cement and granite-block foundation was ready, and the mail-order house arrived by rail in one big boxcar. After a few trips from the train station by horse and wagon, all of the lumber and materials were on the lot and ready to be put together like a big jigsaw puzzle. My grandfather built the house, and in September 1928 we moved into our sparkling new home.

Another Sears house was built in our town some time later, but ours was the first. It was a real novelty to all the townspeople.

I lived in this house until 1940, when I married, but I never did move too far from my hometown. The home was my mother's pride and joy, and she lived in it until her death in 1972. Being her only heir, I inherited the house. That's when my husband and I moved back to my hometown and the house where I grew up.

This mail order house is now 72 years old and just as sound as the day it was built. Everything is on one floor, which is really appreciated when one gets on in years. The living room, dining room, kitchen and breakfast nook are in the back of the house, facing south so there is sun all day.

The two bedrooms and bath are on the front of the house facing north. My husband and I have made a few renovations and changes to the house, such as a new oil furnace with baseboard heating, new bathroom and kitchen fixtures, some rewiring, lowering some of the ceilings, installing new siding and adding combination windows. Other than these changes, everything else is original, including the glass doorknobs.

When we put in the new furnace with baseboard heating, every piece of baseboard that had to be removed had a Sears and Roebuck tag on it.

If it sounds like I love my Sears mail-order house and feel very fortunate to own one, it is true.

Chapter 12

Fact vs. Fiction
Myths, Mistakes and Misinformation About Sears Modern Homes

If you cannot find numbers or letters stamped on the lumber, it can't be a Sears home.

Apparently, stamped numbers did not *consistently* appear on Sears lumber until after 1920. This alone suggests that at least *one-third* of Sears homes do not have stamped lumber. (By 1920, Sears had sold 25,000 homes.) And I've seen many post-1920 Sears homes (authenticated with blueprints or other paperwork) that didn't have a hint of stamped lumber. There are a variety of reasons for this. So yes, you may have a Sears home, even if there are no numbers on the lumber.

My house was built in 1905 and I *know* it's a Sears house because that's what all the neighbors told me.

Sears began selling building supplies in 1895, but they did not sell *kit homes* until 1908. Building supply catalogs from Sears offered almost everything you needed to build a house, but the first Sears Modern Homes catalog, offering the package deal, did not appear until 1908. Interestingly, Sears *did* sell house designs - blueprints - in the early 1900s.

In fact, both Sears and Montgomery Wards promoted and sold an identical 4 x 6-inch booklet titled *"Practical Homebuilder"* with 115 different blueprints priced from $2.50 - $8.00, for houses that would cost $500 - $3500 to construct. But these were not Sears Modern Homes or even a precursor to Sears Modern Homes. *Practical Homebuilder* was published by Frederick Drake & Company and imprinted with the Sears or Wards name on the cover page and sold through their general merchandise catalogs.

And there's also the age-old question – what *is* a Sears house? In my opinion – It is a kit home – blueprints and materials - purchased from the Sears Modern Homes catalog during their years of operation; 1908 - 1940.

The famous architect Frank Lloyd Wright worked for Sears for a short time.

Many people have asked me about Wright's affiliation with Sears Modern Homes. I seriously doubt that Frank Lloyd Wright ever drew a paycheck from Sears Roebuck and Company for services rendered as an architect. Furthermore, despite exhaustive research, I've never found a shred of evidence to support this bold claim – that Wright designed a few of Sears' houses. Sears did offer two "Prairie Style" houses, a fresh and new housing design attributed to Wright and perhaps, that is the source of this persistent legend.

I know my house is *not* a Sears house because a local contractor built it.

In the 1912 Sears Modern Homes catalog, Sears offered a matched set of six houses that had the same "footprint." These homes could be built on the same foundation and had similar floor plans, but each house

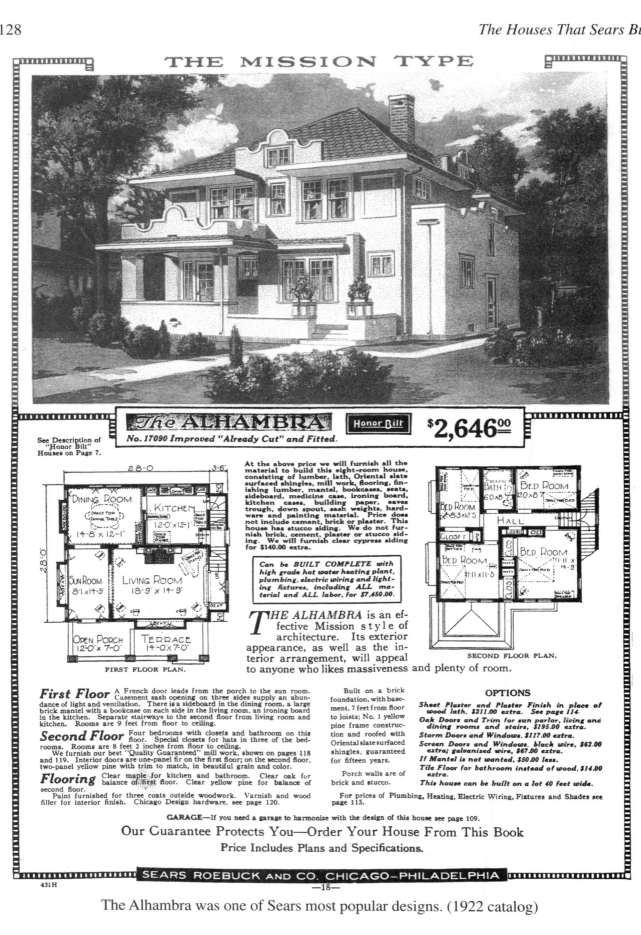

THE MISSION TYPE

The ALHAMBRA
Honor Bilt $2,646.00

No. 17090 Improved "Already Cut" and Fitted.

See Description of "Honor Bilt" Houses on Page 7.

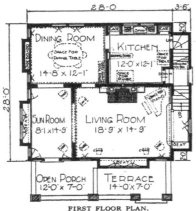

FIRST FLOOR PLAN.

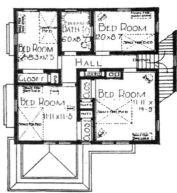

SECOND FLOOR PLAN.

At the above price we will furnish all the material to build this eight-room house, consisting of lumber, lath, Oriental slate surfaced shingles, mill work, flooring, finishing lumber, mantel, bookcases, seats, sideboard, medicine case, ironing board, kitchen cases, building paper, eaves trough, down spout, sash weights, hardware and painting material. Price does not include cement, brick or plaster. This house has stucco siding. We do not furnish brick, cement, plaster or stucco siding. We will furnish clear cypress siding for $140.00 extra.

Can be BUILT COMPLETE with high grade hot water heating plant, plumbing, electric wiring and lighting fixtures, including ALL material and ALL labor, for $7,450.00.

THE ALHAMBRA is an effective Mission style of architecture. Its exterior appearance, as well as the interior arrangement, will appeal to anyone who likes massiveness and plenty of room.

First Floor A French door leads from the porch to the sun room. Casement sash opening on three sides supply an abundance of light and ventilation. There is a sideboard in the dining room, a large brick mantel with a bookcase on each side in the living room, an ironing board in the kitchen. Separate stairways to the second floor from living room and kitchen. Rooms are 9 feet from floor to ceiling.

Second Floor Four bedrooms with closets and bathroom on this floor. Special closets for hats in three of the bedrooms. Rooms are 8 feet 2 inches from floor to ceiling.

We furnish our best "Quality Guaranteed" mill work, shown on pages 118 and 119. Interior doors are one-panel fir on the first floor; on the second floor, two-panel yellow pine with trim to match, in beautiful grain and color.

Flooring Clear maple for kitchen and bathroom. Clear oak for balance of first floor. Clear yellow pine for balance of second floor.

Paint furnished for three coats outside woodwork. Varnish and wood filler for interior finish. Chicago Design hardware, see page 120.

Built on a brick foundation, with basement. 7 feet from floor to joists; No. 1 yellow pine frame construction and roofed with Oriental slate surfaced shingles, guaranteed for fifteen years.

Porch walls are of brick and stucco.

For prices of Plumbing, Heating, Electric Wiring, Fixtures and Shades see page 115.

OPTIONS

Sheet Plaster and Plaster Finish in place of wood lath, $211.00 extra. See page 114.

Oak Doors and Trim for sun parlor, living and dining rooms and stairs, $195.00 extra.

Storm Doors and Windows, $117.00 extra.

Screen Doors and Windows, black wire, $62.00 extra; galvanized wire, $67.00 extra.

If Mantel is not wanted, $50.00 less.

Tile Floor for bathroom instead of wood, $14.00 extra.

This house can be built on a lot 40 feet wide.

GARAGE—If you need a garage to harmonize with the design of this house see page 109.

Our Guarantee Protects You—Order Your House From This Book
Price Includes Plans and Specifications.

SEARS ROEBUCK AND CO. CHICAGO—PHILADELPHIA

431H   —18—

The Alhambra was one of Sears most popular designs. (1922 catalog)

This Alhambra in Ohio looks much like it did when built in the 1920s.

There is an Alhambra hidden under all this aluminum. (in Wisconsin)

This Alhambra sits on a farm in Ohio.

A modified Alhambra in Missouri.

An unhappy Alhambra in Ohio.

looked a little different from the outside. It was a direct pitch to builders who wanted to build, "for renting, for speculation or for selling."

The 1912 catalog continued, "While laborers, horses, scoops and other utensils are on the ground, six basements can be excavated at a slight advance over a lesser number."

Sears promised that builders could make 15 - 50% additional profit by building kit houses (compared to traditional stick-built homes). The back pages of the Sears Modern Homes catalogs featured letters from contractors and builders bragging about the tidy profits they earned from building and selling Sears kit homes. According to these testimonials, many contractors built Sears houses speculatively (without having pre-sold the house, prior to construction).

Several of the advertisements that Sears placed in *American Carpenter and Builder Magazine* were headed with these captions: "To every carpenter and builder!" or "Carpenters – let us double your profits" or "Build this bungalow and make $849!"

A small book titled "Modern Carpentry" by Fred T. Hodgson (copyright 1918, published for Sears Roebuck & Co.,) stated that "over 100,000 people have asked us for our Book of Modern Homes *each year*. Among these people are architects, contractors, carpenters and builders in every state of the union."

And there were the Sears homebuyers who purchased a house from Sears, but did not feel carpentarily inclined. They *hired* builders to erect their home. (By the way, don't bother to look up *carpentarily* because I made it up. It's a great word, isn't it?)

I know this is a Sears home because I remember when it came in on the railroad and my brother and I helped our parents unload the boxcars!

People often send me photos of their "Sears home" and about 75% of the time, I have to reply with "That is a lovely home, but it is *not* a design of a Sears home that I recognize." And that simple statement could mean several things. It's possible that their Sears home was extensively customized, in which case I tell the letter-writers to look for shipping labels, stamped lumber, etc.

More frequently, I discover that their home is a design that was offered by another kit home company. These many years later, folks have forgotten the name of the other national kit home companies, such as Gordon Van Tine, Aladdin, Sterling Homes, Lewis Homes and Harris Brothers. However, they do remember that the house came in a kit and was shipped by boxcar. "Sears home" has become a generic name for all kit homes. Fewer than 25% of the photos I receive are readily recognizable as Sears kit homes.

Sears homes are often found in clusters.

For the most part, Sears homes are widely scattered across the 48 states. When corporate buyers like Standard Oil of Indiana built housing for their workers (as happened in Carlinville, Schoper and Wood River, Illinois), they *were* built in clusters. But corporate buyers probably made up a very small percentage of Sears home buyers. Occasionally builders or developers (as referenced above) built Sears homes in rows or even, entire neighborhoods. I have found several instances of Sears homes built in pairs, often by family members or close friends.

Sears homes were shipped in one or two railway boxcars and contained 30,000 pieces.

There were approximately 32,000 pieces of Sears house listed in the bill of materials. But on page seven of the Bill of Materials for Modern Home #111 (The Chelsea), was "20,000 shingles (for roofing and siding). Yes, an average Sears house contained 30,000 pieces, but *20,000* of those pieces were wooden shingles.

Sears homes are boxy, small and modest.

It's true that many of the homes that Sears sold were small and boxy and modest, but they offered a wide variety of houses for a wide variety of budgets. Some of the houses (such as The Magnolia) were spacious and elegant.

Sears houses were shipped by boxcar.

Before I began this research, I assumed that all Sears homes were shipped by train. And then I met Jane Booker, who told me that her uncle worked at the Sears Mill in Cairo, Illinois. When the lumber was all cut, stacked and numbered, it was loaded onto a flatbed truck and young Jane would drive the truck to the construction site. She also remembers hauling around that 75-page instruction book (which contained detailed information on how to assemble a Sears home). According to Jane, "That book weighed a ton." I've also heard that a few Sears homes were *floated* to their site on barges.

Sears houses were always located near rail lines.

For the most part, this is true. Hauling 30,000 pieces of house via one or two horsepower was logistically challenging, and the process usually took several trips. For this reason, Sears homes *were usually* located near (within a mile or two) of train tracks.

But you also have to think "historically." In 1930, there were 430,000 miles of railroad track in this country. Today it's half that number. Hundreds of thousands of miles of railroad track have been removed (and often turned into hiking and biking trails).

The largest collection of Sears homes is in Downer's Grove, Illinois.

Nope. Currently, Elgin, Illinois (a suburb of Chicago), has the largest *known* collection of Sears homes in the country. There are more than 200 Sears homes in that city. According to kit house historians Rebecca Hunter and James Chapa, Downer's Grove has fewer than 100 Sears homes.

Carlinville (Illinois) has 152 Sears homes in the Standard Addition neighborhood and many more in other parts of the city. And Carlinville certainly has one of the *most interesting and unique collections* of Sears homes, with 12 solid blocks of the little beauties, all lined up in neat rows. I know of no other community with this many Sears homes clustered together.

And then there's Wood River, Illinois (near St. Louis, Missouri), with more than 50 Sears homes in 25 different styles. For a city with 11,000 residents, this is a significant collection.

Having visited many cities that are heavy-laden with Sears homes, I'm quite sure there are cities with more than 200 <u>undiscovered</u> (as of yet) Sears homes.

However, this question – Who has the most Sears homes? – is a red herring. More importantly - what are individual cities doing to identify, cherish and preserve the Sears homes they *do* have? It's not what you have that matters; it's what you do with what you *have*.

Sears Roebuck was the first to offer mail order houses.

Sears promoted this in the 1919 Modern Home catalog. "When you buy from us," their ad said, "you are dealing with the *originators* of the mail order system of selling complete houses" (emphasis added). Aladdin sold kit homes from 1906 (two years before Sears) until 1981 (41 years after Sears picked up their framing members and went home). Sears was neither the first nor the last to sell kit houses through mail order.

Sears homes were prefab houses that were easily assembled.

So often, people interchange the terms "prefab" and "precut" as if they had the same meaning, but this is a mistake. Sears kit homes, sold out of the 1908-1940 Modern Homes catalogs were precut – not prefab!

Sears sold 100,000 houses.

This is an oft-repeated fact, but it is wrong! In 1931, Sears reported that they'd sold 57,000 homes. It took Sears 23 years to sell those 57,000 homes. But in the early 1930s, housing starts skidded to a stop nation-wide. Sears sold fewer than 75,000 Modern Homes in their 32 years in the kit home business.

Sears offered 447 designs.

"*Houses by Mail: A Guide to Houses from Sears, Roebuck and Company*" by Katherine Cole Stevenson and H. Ward Jandl lists 447 different house designs. I defined (and counted) "designs" in a slightly different way and (for that reason) came up with a different number.

The Barrington and The Cambridge are identical Sears homes, but The Barrington is a frame house and The Cambridge has a brick exterior. The *only difference* between these two "designs" is the different exterior sidings. There were several dozen Sears houses that were *identical in every way*, *but had different exterior sidings*. Where *Houses by Mail* counted that as two houses, I counted it as one. And there were a handful of houses inadvertently left out of *Houses by Mail*. Adding in those few designs, I came up with a number "around" 370.

There were no Modern Homes sales offices west of the Mississippi.

This is not true. There was a Modern Homes sales office in St. Louis (for about two years) and one in Kansas City, Missouri (for one year). For the geographically challenged, both St. Louis and Kansas City are *west* of the Mississippi River.

There were 12 Sears homes in Schoper (near Standard City) built by Standard Oil in 1918, but only one remains standing.

There were 12 homes in Schoper, built by Standard Oil in 1919. Regarding that last house: It's gone, chief. According to local residents, that last Schoper Sears house burned down in 1996 or 1997.

Sears sent along everything needed to build a complete home.

Not true. Masonry, blocks, bricks, plaster, etc., were not part of the package, because of shipping costs. Furnaces, plumbing and electrical equipment were also not part of the package, but could be ordered separately from Sears. These houses were shipped to Florida, Wisconsin, California and Virginia and different locales had different electrical, plumbing and heating needs.

Five and six panel doors are unique to Sears homes.

Wrong. Five and six panel doors are unique to homes that were built in the *first 50 years of the 20th Century*. In other words, they are not unique, but *ubiquitous*. (Love that word.) The other myth making the rounds is this: Sears homes have hexagon bathroom tiles. Yawn. So do hundreds of thousands of non-Sears homes.

If your bathroom fixtures have the letters "SR," it might be a Sears home.

I have seen "SR" stamped on bathtubs and sinks in 1930s Sears homes. The SR initials also appear occasionally on radiators, but even this is not incontrovertible proof that you have a Sears home, as Sears sold a lot of heating equipment in the early 1900s.

If it has an "S" on the chimney, that means it is a Sears home.

This nutty (albeit persistent) rumor is floating around on the internet and every now and then, the occasional reporter asks me if this is true. It is false! That wrought iron "S" on the chimney is a stylistic element that has no relation to the Sears Modern Homes department. None!

If it has a lot of built-ins (built-in ironing board, phone stand, etc.), it's probably a Sears home.

This is false. Built-ins were *very popular* and *very common* in the 1920s and 30s. Built-ins do not suggest or signify that you have a kit home.

Sears had a "dollar a knot" guarantee on the lumber in their kit homes.

Legend has it that Sears promised buyers a silver dollar if they found a knot bigger than a dime in their Sears house lumber. That's not true. Aladdin, one of Sears primary competitors in the kit home business, *did* make a similar promise. Aladdin's 1919 catalog stated:

The lumber in Aladdin Readi-Cut Houses is higher in grade throughout than any regularly carried by any seller in America. Further, we guarantee that you will receive clear and knotless siding, clear and knotless flooring, clear and knotless interior finish, for every Aladdin dwelling house.

Chapter 13

Frequently Asked Questions

Why did Sears stop selling houses?

Sears actually closed their Modern Homes department in 1934, after taking a long, hard look at their massive financial losses. According to *Catalogs and Counters*, Sears liquidated more than $11 million in mortgages in 1934 and that was also the year that the Federal Housing Administration came into being and it appeared that Sears biggest problem – financing – was now solved

In 1935, Sears re-entered the housing market, but sales were anemic. In 1929, Sears sold $12 million in homes. In 1930, that number dropped to $10 million and by 1933, it had dropped to $3.6 million. In subsequent years, sales of Sears Modern Homes never surpassed that $3.5 million mark.

Plus, in the words of Bob Dylan, the times, "they were a-changing." In 1908, when Sears opened their Modern Homes department, many folks probably remembered helping Mother and Father (or Grandma and Grandpa) build their log cabin or soddie on the family homestead. Building one's own home was an important part of America's heritage, especially in the wide-open spaces of the 19th Century Midwest.

By the 1930s, homes had become far more complex. Even modest homes now had plumbing, electricity, central heating systems and more. Homebuilding was increasingly becoming a technical trade, requiring not only contractors, but subcontractors and their unique skills and expertise. And when World War II ended (1945), American ideas about building would undergo another major shift, as developers like former Navy Seabee Bill Levitt turned a 1,000-acre potato field into a neighborhood full of 750-square foot homes.

And Sears did sell Homart Homes (small prefabricated homes) after World War II (see Chapter Eight), but 1940 seems to have been the end of the Sears Modern Homes department and their kit homes.

Didn't Montgomery Ward also sell homes through their catalogs?

Yes, Montgomery Wards sold kit homes, like Sears, through their mail order catalogs. There is very little information on Montgomery Ward homes, probably because their sales numbers were much lower than Sears.

Montgomery Wards began offering kit-home catalogs in 1910 and their last (Wardway) catalog was printed in 1932. Gordon-Van Tine supplied the kit homes for Wards. For that reason, it's impossible to distinguish a Gordon-Van Tine home from a Wardway home from the exterior. When interior moldings or millwork are removed, the shipping labels will read "Montgomery Ward" if it's a Wardway home. Differentiating Wardway from Gordon Van-Tine often requires a crowbar and a sacrificial baseboard. (*The Kenmore was the name of a modest Wardway home. That's an interesting name for a Montgomery Ward's house.*)

HOME No. 106

$1,047.00
HOME No. 106

For $1,047.00 we will furnish the material to build this home, consisting of all lumber, lath, shingles, finishing lumber, flooring, doors, windows, frames, trim, colonnade, sash weights, building paper, hardware, pipe and gutter, and paint and varnish. We absolutely guarantee the material we furnish to be sufficient to build the house according to our plans and specifications.

One of our most popular homes. It is a story and a half design, which makes it an economical home to build, but it represents an unusually good value for the reason that it has four bedrooms besides a very attractive layout of living rooms. Makes a pleasing appearance in any setting.

GENERAL SPECIFICATIONS

Built on a brick foundation, lattice under porches. Double first floors with one floor of good one inch lumber over which is laid finish floor. Outside walls have matched sheathing, building paper, and clear Cypress bevel siding. All framing lumber the best quality of Yellow Pine. Star A Star Cedar shingles. No. 1 lath. Excellent grade of hardware. Windows glazed "A" quality clear glass. Painted two coats best Tower Brand paint outside, your choice of colors, wood filler and varnish for interior. Catalogue number of each item shown on the Bill of Material with our plans, and you can read full description in our Building Material Catalogue.

By allowing a fair price for labor, brick, cement and plaster, which we do not furnish, this home can be built for about $2,275.00.

FIRST FLOOR

Bevel plate front door leads into reception hall, lighted by sash of leaded glass, Argyle design. Cased opening leads into living-room. In front is a large bay, with three windows, leaded Argyle Cottage design in center. Handsome colonnade opens into dining-room, which also has a bay with three windows. To the rear is a chamber and to the left a kitchen, with pantry located where it is most easily reached without going through. Porch in rear, and a stairway leads to grade entrance and basement stairs. Yellow Pine trim throughout. Ceiling, 9 feet high.

SECOND FLOOR

Choice Yellow Pine stairs, window at landing. Three large bedrooms and bath on this floor. Plenty of light and closet room. Yellow Pine trim and doors. Ceilings, 8 feet high, except for slight slope at eaves.

BASEMENT

Excavated under entire house. Cement floor. Lighted by three light cellar sash. Seven feet to joists.

Heating, Plumbing and Lighting

WRITE FOR DETAILED ESTIMATES

Warm Air Plant, complete........ $ 86.50
Steam Heating Plant, complete...... 172.00
Hot Water Heating Plant, complete.. $204.00
Plumbing System, complete......... 83.50
Acetylene Lighting System.... (See Page 79)

Size, exclusive of porches: Width, 25 feet, Length, 33 feet.

Read Our Free Plan Offer on Page Two

Montgomery Ward sold homes through mail order from (about) 1910 until 1932. For the most part, Wardway homes were supplied by Gordon-Van Tine, another national kit home company.

What about the other companies that offered houses by mail order?

Aladdin Homes of Bay City, Michigan, sold 75,000 homes between 1906-1981. In Alan Gowans' book, "*The Comfortable House*," he states that Aladdin and Sears considered a merger sometime in the 1910s. Gowans states, "…Aladdin's founders refused on the grounds that such arrangements too often ended with Sears owning the supplying company" (p. 50).

The other major contender in the kit home business was Gordon-Van Tine (based in Davenport, Iowa), who claimed in their 1939 catalog, "More than 270,000 people live in Gordon Van Tine Homes!" If you do the math and figure five people to a household, that means they had sold about 54,000 homes. Architectural Historian Dale Patrick Wolicki estimates that they sold 50,000 – 60,000 homes.

Lewis Manufacturing went into the building materials business in 1896 and started selling kit homes in 1913. In the mid-20s, they changed their name to Liberty Homes and continued selling houses until 1973. "Lewis-Liberty Homes" sold about 60,000 houses. (Thanks to Dale Patrick Wolicki for the stats on Aladdin, Gordon Van-Tine and Lewis-Liberty.)

In 1919, Pacific Homes (a regional company in Los Angeles) stated that they'd sold 5000 homes and 3000 of these were located in Southern California. There was also Harris Brothers (formerly known as the Chicago House Wrecking Company), R. L. Bennett, Sterling Homes and countless regional companies. National Refrigerators, a St. Louis company that manufactured and sold wooden ice boxes, issued a kit house catalog in the late 1910s called "Miller Ready-Built Homes" offering 28 of the nastiest little, non-descript cottages and bungalows that you ever saw.

The more research I do, the more I realize, almost every sizeable community had a regional kit home company for a time.

I found some stamps on the framing members of my old house; several digits – separated by a hyphen. What does that mean?

Gordon Van Tine (which includes Montgomery Ward) used a distinct numbering system for the framing members – several digits separated by a hyphen, such as 17-23-18-21-48. I've also seen a *word* stamped on each individual board, describing the placement of the lumber or board, such as "dormer roof" or "bathroom floor." Truly, little is known about the other kit home companies. I encourage and invite anyone who has found marks on their kit home to drop me a note and tell me what you've discovered.

Are any companies still selling kit homes today?

Yes. Log homes are the popular kit homes today, but there are also several regional companies selling conventional kit homes. To find them, look up "Kit Homes" on the internet. However, I seriously doubt they'll send you a full set of blueprints for $1, as Sears once did.

How did you get interested in Sears homes?

I was born and raised in Portsmouth, Virginia in a neighborhood filled with 1920s-era housing. I spent countless hours riding my three-speed Sears bike through the different neighborhoods, studying and comparing the wide variety of architecture. I have always had a deep abiding love for old homes.

In 1987, I purchased "*The Comfortable House,*" by Alan Gowans. It had quite a bit of information about kit homes and I found the topic fascinating. My love for mail order homes had been ignited. And then in 1999, while doing freelance writing for Old House Web, (www.oldhouseweb.com), I asked my editors if they'd like an article about the Sears homes in Carlinville, Illinois. They said, yes.

The drive from Alton, Illinois (my home) to Carlinville took about an hour, but once there, I lost all track of time. In subsequent days (and subsequent trips), I found myself spending hours upon hours at the Carlinville Public Library, reading countless newspaper and magazine articles about the building of those 156 Sears houses in Carlinville's "Standard Addition."

Several times, I returned to the library to get more information. Or I'd make the drive to Carlinville so that I could plop down on the curb and sit in speechless wonder, smack dab in the middle of those 12 blocks of Sears homes. Before long, I'd invested 40-50 hours in a single article.

I've heard it said that we find our life's work at the place where our personal talents intersect with the world's need for more truth (information) or more beauty or more love. For me - that intersection of my talent and the world's need - was a book about Sears homes.

Do you live in a Sears home?

No, but I wish I did! When our family moved (from the East Coast) to Alton, Illinois in March 1996, we rented a 1980s condo in the downtown area. One year later, we moved into a fixer-upper; a 1904 "Builder's Style" home in Upper Alton. ["Builder's Style" is a euphemism for a simple old house that does have a few nice features.]

For the next few years, my (now ex) husband and I restored the old house. In attempting to do a faithful restoration (period accurate), I learned how difficult (and costly) it is to bring a badly remuddled house back to its *original* condition. When I speak with passion about the need to restore these Sears homes to their original condition, I speak from experience.

In Spring 2002, when my marriage ended, I moved out of the house in Alton. Alas, even now, I do not live in a Sears home. One day – I'd love to have a Sears home to call my own.

Would you marry for a Sears home?

Okay, so this is not a *frequently asked question*, but it is a question I was asked at a lecture in Central Illinois. And I thought it was a great question, so I include it here. After a fine-looking gentleman asked me this, I paused for a moment and repeated his question, "*Would I marry for a Sears home?*"

"I guess it depends," I answered thoughtfully. "Which *model* are we talking about?"

What was the final cost of a Sears kit home?

The 1922 Sears Modern Homes catalog had an extra bit of information I've not seen in other Modern Homes catalogs. It listed "built complete" prices. For instance, The Puritan cost $1947, but Sears added this in small print: "Can be BUILT COMPLETE with plumbing, high grade warm air heating plant, electric wiring and lighting fixtures, including all material and all labor, for $4888."

The Betsy Ross cost $1504, but the "built complete" price was $4340. The Avondale was $2685, but the complete price was $6,250. The price of the house, multiplied by a factor of 2.3 – 3.0 would give a better idea of the "built complete" cost.

Why were the house prices so low?

The prices Sears quoted for these houses were for the building materials *alone.* And remember the story from Chapter Two, about the woman whose husband earned $8 a week? Wages in the 1910s and 1920s were a fraction of today's incomes. According to *American Carpenter and Builder Magazine (*December 1912*)*, skilled carpenters in Chicago were earning 65 cents and hour and plumbers were making 75 cents an hour.

How much money did people save by buying and building a kit home?

It's tough to say for sure, but apparently, you'd save about one-third by building your own kit home. Some of the kit home companies claimed homebuyers would save up to 50% by building kit homes, but that's probably somewhat unusual and so much depends on the local economies, as well.

Did Sears build these houses, too? Did they offer construction services?

In the beginning, no, Sears only sold the kit homes. However, in the late 1920s, they began to offer construction help. In *Business Week*, March 26, 1930, there was an article entitled, "Quality Production Reaches the Home Builder." It discussed this new construction service offered by both Sears and Wards, stating, "About all the customer has to do is to say, 'Build me such and such a house on such and such a lot.' The company does the rest."

The article went on to say that this new service was already proving to be "exceedingly popular." Both Wards and Sears offered the home builder as much or as little help as he wanted or needed with construction of the kit home.

How many people built these Sears homes themselves?

It's so hard to know for sure, but judging from the testimonials (an admittedly unscientific method), it would seem that about half the Sears homes were built by the homeowners and half were built by professional carpenters and builders. By the way, when I'm researching a purported Sears home and I find that the original owner was a carpenter, I always heave a little sigh. Frequently, the kit homes built by carpenters were *significantly* altered from the original designs and plans.

When I bought my house, the former owners told me it was a Sears house and they seemed confident about this. But I can't find a listing for it in *"Houses by Mail."*

Because the sales records from the Sears Modern Homes department are gone, we have no idea how many Sears homes were "customized" but I'm betting that 50% or more were customized when built; some extensively.

I've seen a number of authenticated Sears homes (with stamped lumber, shipping labels or blueprints) that *bear no resemblance* to the 370 designs offered in the 32-year history of Sears Modern Homes department. Last but not least, remember that Sears homes were built in the 1910s, 20s and 30s. Nothing stays the same – especially old houses!

Where did you get your old Sears Modern Home catalogs and how much did they cost?

In the last several years, I've purchased these catalogs through online auction sites and from online antiquarian book dealers. Prices for the original catalogs are $50 and up. For about $20, you can buy a reprint of the 1926 Sears Modern Homes catalog from Dover Publishing. Schiffer Publishing also offers a good quality reprint of the 1912 Sears Modern Homes catalog. Both are available at Amazon.com.

What about those little houses with tile walls and metal roofs. Are they Sears homes?

It's amazing how many people think that prefab steel houses are Sears homes. Many of the steel homes with "tile walls" are Lustron Homes; post-World War II prefabricated homes. Lustrons were made of 20-gage porcelain enamel steel tiles, and each tile measured 2 x 2 feet. The interior walls also were steel tile. If you wanted to hang a picture on the wall, you didn't use nails – you used magnets! There are only a few thousand Lustron Homes in the country and they're concentrated in the Midwest. *Lustron was not connected to Sears*. To learn more about Lustrons, read "*Lustron Homes*" by Tom Fetters.

What about Sears kit barns?

In the 1909 Sears Modern Homes catalog, a single sentence appeared which stated, "*Our architects are now preparing plans for several designs of good substantial up to date barns for which we will be able to furnish plans about July 1, 1910.*"

The 1918 Sears "Book of Barns" stated, "The much discussed difficult task of barn building has been reduced by us to a pleasing undertaking. If during the construction of your barn, you should fail to understand some detail, which is unlikely with our proved 'Already Cut' system, write us, stating just what the difficulty is. We will promptly set you right."

Sears barns were offered in traditional shapes (rectangular) but they also offered L-shaped barns, round barns and octagonal barns. And Sears sold every other outbuilding imaginable including silos, poultry houses, hog houses, ice houses, milk houses, outhouses and more.

In the Midwest, I've found several farms with both a Sears house and a Sears barn. The barns, like the houses, *should* have stamped lumber. And who knows how many Sears silos and other outbuildings are still standing throughout the Midwest!

How can I learn more about Sears homes?

Part of my joy and delight in writing about Sears homes is that there is so little currently known on this topic and yet such enthusiasm to learn more! I'm hoping to produce and release a video titled "*How to Identify Sears Homes*" along with a new book "*Quickie Field Guide to The 65 Most Popular Sears Homes*." (For more information, please see the back pages of this book.)

There are also a few websites (such as mine); searshomes.org; Rebecca Hunter and Jim Chapa's; searskithouse.com and the official Sears website is searsmodernhomes.com.

How many Sears homes are still standing?

Unfortunately, it's impossible to know, but based on what I've seen around the country and the letters I've received, probably <u>about</u> 90% of the 75,000 Sears homes are still alive and in reasonably good health.

Is it financially feasible to move a Sears home, to prevent its demolition?

Moving a house typically costs tens of thousands of dollars. Remember the story in Chapter One about a man in South Florida who paid $100,000 to move a Sears home? Not many communities and/or citizens are going to have the financial wherewithal to invest that kind of money in saving a modest bungalow. Many of these Sears homes are such simple and plain little homes that spending large sums of money to relocate them is simply not practical.

Do Sears homes have more value than traditional stick-built homes?

That's a tough question to answer. I think it depends on the community and the local economy. In the Midwest, where Sears homes are so common and real estate prices are so low, I don't think the "Sears home" designation automatically makes a house more valuable.

What are some common misconceptions about Sears homes?

Many people have the idea that Sears homes are lesser quality homes and/or they're very modest homes. Sears *did* sell "Simplex Cottages" which were true prefabs (shipped in sections to be bolted together at the site), and these were very small, modest houses that were considered temporary or portable houses. These homes probably didn't survive more than a few years. However, the bread and butter of the Sears Modern Home's program – the "Honor Bilt" home – was a remarkably solid house and came in hundreds of different designs, shapes and sizes.

Occasionally, I'm asked if these Sears homes are as solid as traditional stick-built houses, since it was often the homeowner who fulfilled the "some assembly required" component. My answer is, *absolutely.*

It's been my experience that when someone is creating something for the first time and for their own family, they tend to be zealots, making sure everything is "just so" and perfect. Whether it's creating meatloaf for the family meal or building a home, it's human nature to have the highest standards for those in our inner-most circle.

The instructions that came with your Sears kit home were incredibly detailed and even specified proper spacing of those 750 pounds of nails. Sears' promise was bold but true – "if you follow these instructions, you can *not* make a mistake."

In my freelancing days, I wrote an article about "Habitat for Humanity" and learned that during Hurricane Andrew in 1993, the modest homes built by Habitat withstood the hurricane, whilst the more expensive homes succumbed. There are two reasons for this. One, Habitat Homes were built by volunteers and homeowners and they worked slowly , carefully and thoughtfully. For instance, they worked with hammers and nails instead of nail-guns. If a nail missed the framing, the volunteer would stop, pull the nail out of the sheathing and try again. When a nail-gun misses the framing, it's hardly noticed. Novices also tend to overbuild and use more nails than are necessary. It seems likely that these same principles applied to the building of Sears kit homes.

Are Sears homes your full time job?

Yes, Sears homes are my full time job. I have no other occupation. And that's a good thing because I devote 60-plus hours a week to this work. A significant portion of my income comes from book sales, honoraria and the community surveys that are performed for cities that want to find their Sears homes.

If a community has a large collection of Sears homes, is there anything special they should do?

Yes! First – authenticate!!! Please oh please – don't promote your suspected collection of Sears homes until you've established that they truly *are* Sears kit homes! If you'd like help in authenticating, please contact me!

After you've authenticated your Sears homes, work toward getting a local historic designation for that area. Plaques, newspaper articles, museum exhibits and other promotional ideas will help increase public awareness as to the value of these old houses. Some communities have created brochures, calendars, driving tours, trolley tours and websites to help educate people about the importance and historical significance of kit homes. Work with the local historical organizations in your community, as you develop a plan for identifying and cataloging Sears homes.

How can I educate the folks in my community as to the value of Sears homes?

Begin with educating yourself. (If you've read this book in its entirety, presumably you know more about Sears homes than 99% of the population and you are now the local expert!) You might also want to familiarize yourself with the guidelines for historic rehab as outlined by the Secretary of the Interior. As I mentioned earlier, the gravest threat facing Sears homes is remuddling – decimation through insensitive remodeling! *For more information about the Secretary of Interior's guidelines, as well as generic information on the proper way to restore historic residential structures (homes), visit Old House Web (www.oldhouseweb.com).*

Identify a few Sears homes in your community and then contact the owners and tell them all about it. Use public forums – address your city council and historical societies. Contact the local media and try to get newspaper articles written about the Sears homes in your city; put together a few museum exhibits; contact the local civic groups and offer to give a short talk at a luncheon, etc.

The window of opportunity for finding Sears homes through personal reminiscences is fast closing. The people who built these Sears homes, for the most part, have passed on. Even the people who remember helping Mom and Dad build a kit house are quite elderly. I think it's imperative to find these people and record their stories (and learn about their Sears homes), before *they* pass on.

Also, buy more copies of this book for your public library. It's a great reference work and I hope it will be instrumental in getting people excited about the Sears homes in their community.

Chapter 14

The Lost Sears Homes

"Houses by Mail, A Guide to Houses From Sears, Roebuck and Company" is a wonderful field guide and I've recommended it because it contains most of the houses that Sears offered. However, the authors were unable to obtain a few of the original Sears Modern Homes catalogs. Because of this, there are a few "lost" Sears homes; house designs not included in *Houses by Mail*. Reprinted pages from the Sears Modern Homes catalogs showing these lost homes follows.

1) **Sears Modern Home #303**. This house presents a stunning rebuttal to that oft-repeated comment – "Sears homes were just boxy little affairs – really quite plain." Modern Home #303 was a massive trailing-edge-Victorian house and quite ornate. Modern Home #303 appeared *only* in the rare 1909 catalog.

2) **Modern Home #128** is listed in *Houses by Mail*, but *that* model number is assigned to a house that looks nothing like *this* Modern Home #128. Sears duplicated not only model numbers, but names, too. There were two Aldens, two Auroras, two Hawthornes, two Oakdales, etc. Different houses; same name.

3) **Modern Home #120** was listed in *Houses by Mail*, but again, *their* #120 and *this* #120 are completely different.

4) **Modern Home #108.** This is the only Sears house that featured this squared corner window. Modern Home #108 appeared only in 1908.

5) **Modern Home #138**. This house appears to have a very spacious third floor, but there's no reference to that in the floor plans. This home appeared in the 1908 Sears Modern Homes catalog and never again.

6) **Sears Modern Schoolhouse, #5008**. This "Modern" schoolhouse has *no indoor plumbing* and no bathroom. It does have something called "a future toilet." It's likely that Sears was marketing this "Modern Schoolhouse" toward smaller communities and reckoned that such locales may not have municipal water. Number 5008 only has six classrooms and the library is seven feet wide and eighteen feet long. Hardly enough room for the librarian and her desk. What if she wanted a "future toilet" in the library one day?

Was this schoolhouse ever built? I include a picture of this catalog page in my slide presentation as I tour the country, hoping someone somewhere will recognize this building and tell me its address! It's also possible that #5008 was built and subsequently torn down, given this nation's propensity for demolishing old school buildings.

7) **The Alden.** Sears had two Aldens. The Alden listed in *Houses by Mail* (and offered in the 1930s) is a snazzy looking and spacious Colonial. The second floor overhangs the first floor ever so slightly. But the "lost" Alden (which appeared *only* in the 1924 Modern Homes catalog) is a modest nondescript little two-story house. While writing this manuscript, I was searching for something in the 1924 catalog and spotted The Alden. I paused for a moment and thought, "I've never seen *that* house before." The Alden almost snuck past me and made it into *another* category: *"The Hopelessly Lost Sears Homes."*

8) **The Parkridge**. This small home appeared only in the 1930 Sears Modern Homes catalog and never again. It was described in the catalog as "an Americanized English type bungalow." I've seen at least six of these little houses which is surprising, because it was only offered for one year!

9) **The Westwood**. This house received an honorable mention in "*Houses by Mail.*" It was listed as being similar to the Collingwood and it *is* similar, but there are some (minor) differences. If I was asked to identify a Westwood based solely on the Collingwood model, I'd be a little hesitant to do so.

The Collingwood measures 24' by 46'9". The Westwood is 24'11" by 44'11". At first glance, I thought the difference could be explained by the brick walls (which are thicker than frame walls), but the room dimensions are different, too. And since room sizes can be helpful in determining if a house is a Sears home, this could be confusing.

Another point is the dining room window. In the Collingwood, the dining room has box window, with a separate hipped roof that adjoins the primary roof. The Westwood also has a box window, but it's integrated into the roofline. Lastly, the Collingwood has a breakfast nook off the kitchen and an enclosed stairwell (on the back of the house). The Westwood does not have a breakfast nook and the basement stairwell is on an interior wall in the kitchen.

10) **The Simple Sectionals**. Simplex Sectionals were not pictured in *Houses by Mail*. This is understandable, as most Simplex Sectionals were modest little houses and their big selling point was "easy assembly." Not exactly Scarlett's "Tara." Occasionally, these economical, temporary houses evolved into permanent homes. Once the first layer of substitute sidings came along, the sectional panels that distinguished these homes as different were covered and forgotten.

If you think you're living in a Simplex Sectional, you'll need to find the approximate date it was built and then hunt down a Sears Modern Homes catalog from that era.

11) **Summer cottages**. These were not pictured in *Houses by Mail* either, but then again, how many were sold? One hundred? Two thousand? I've not a clue. And most of these homes were quite modest. Many were primitive one-room shacks, but others, such as The Drake Woods featured three bedrooms, a living room and a bath. In 1938, Sears issued "Log Cabins and Summer Cottages," with eight summer homes and nine log cabins.

Sears began offering specialty catalogs devoted to summer homes in the late 1920s. Sometime in the early 1930s, Sears Home Construction Division issued a "Garages, Log Cabins, Play Houses and Cottages" catalog, which offered 12 garages, seven log cabins and eight summer homes.

In this early 30s catalog, Sears had this to say about log homes:

Log cabins were originally built of complete sections of trees with the bark left on. Modern construction, however, favors the use of log siding. Sears log siding, cut special from rugged 2 x 8 timbers, has all the bark removed, thus eliminating the possibility of insects getting beneath the bark. The flatness on the inside is another feature that simplifies construction, lowers cost and reduces shipping weight. Sears cabins have the appearance of cabins hewn from rough logs like our ancestors built them, but Sears construction means a big saving in cost of materials and labor. And instead of chinking the cracks between the rough logs with moss or clay, as in old fashioned cabins, Sears siding is precision-cut to form a weather tight lap joint.

It seems like Sears had come full circle. In 1908, their "Modern Homes" had amenities that made the old log cabin look primitive by comparison. Now, they were re-creating log cabins for kit homes.

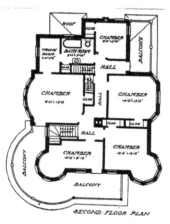

SECOND FLOOR PLAN

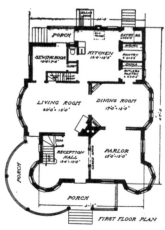

FIRST FLOOR PLAN

$2,073.00

For $2,073.00 we will furnish all the material to build this Eleven-Room Residence, consisting of Mill Work, Ceiling, Flooring, Finishing Lumber, Building Paper, Pipe, Gutter, Sash Weights, Mantel, Hardware, Painting Material, Lumber, Lath and Shingles.

By allowing a fair price for labor, cement, brick and plaster, which we do not furnish, this house can be built for about $6,700.00, including all material and labor.

For Our Free Offer of Plans See Page 2.

A MANSION of Colonial style of architecture. Large front porch, 7 feet 2 inches wide by 43 feet long, with Ionic porch columns. Large reception hall with opening to the parlor and living room and containing an open oak staircase of very unique design. All the rooms are large size. The dining room contains two small china closets, making the inside corners of the dining room correspond with the corners formed by the bay window, giving it the appearance of an octagonal room. Mantel in the living room. A door connects the living room and kitchen. Dining room and kitchen are also connected by means of the butler's pantry, which contains a neat china closet with leaded art glass. Rear stairs lead from the living room to the second floor and directly under them are inside stairs leading to the basement. Note the balcony on the second floor with door leading to it from the front and also from the side chamber. Balcony over the rear porch with door leading to it from the hall. By the towers and bay windows on both sides of the house you get a perfect view from practically any direction and perfect light and ventilation.

Our Superba front door, veneered oak. Queen Anne windows for first floor and attic. Oak interior doors and trim for the main rooms on the first floor. Sewing room, kitchen, pantry and entire second floor finished with cypress doors and clear cypress trim. Clear maple flooring throughout the entire house and gum or hazel wood flooring for the porches.

Built on a cement block foundation; brick construction and shingle roof.

Excavated basement under the entire house divided into rooms for fuel, boiler, vegetable cellar, fruit cellar, storeroom and laundry; 7 feet 6 inches from floor to joists, with cement floor. Rooms on the first floor are 9 feet 6 inches from floor to ceiling; second floor, 9 feet from floor to ceiling.

Modern Home #303 appeared only in the rare 1909 catalog. Oak doors, trim and woodwork were part of the basic package. It was designed to be built as a solid brick home.

$3,220⁰⁰ AND OUR BUILDING PLANS

Specifications and Complete Itemized Bill of Materials Will
Build this Large Modern Eleven-Room $5,200 Frame Residence with Bathroom.
DON'T PAY $150.00 FOR A SET OF BUILDING PLANS, FOR OURS WILL COST YOU
NOTHING, AS EXPLAINED ON PAGE 2.

MODERN HOME No. 128

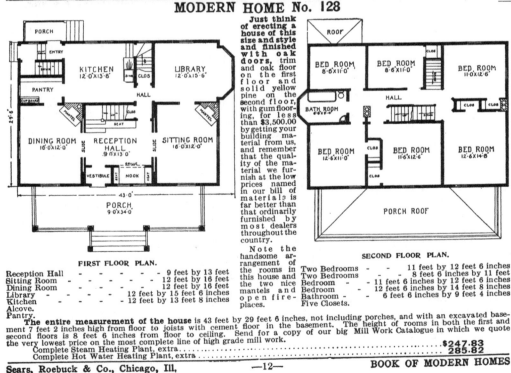

Just think of erecting a house of this size and style and finished with oak doors, trim and oak floor on the first floor and solid yellow pine on the second floor, with gum flooring, for less than $3,500.00 by getting your building material from us, and remember that the quality of the material we furnish at the low prices named in our bill of materials is far better than that ordinarily furnished by most dealers throughout the country.

Note the handsome arrangement of the rooms in this house and the two nice mantels and open fire-places.

FIRST FLOOR PLAN.

Reception Hall - - - - - - 9 feet by 13 feet
Sitting Room - - - - - - - 12 feet by 16 feet
Dining Room - - - - - - - 12 feet by 16 feet
Library - - - - - - 12 feet by 15 feet 6 inches
Kitchen - - - - - - 12 feet by 13 feet 8 inches
Alcove.
Pantry.

SECOND FLOOR PLAN.

Two Bedrooms - - - 11 feet by 12 feet 6 inches
Two Bedrooms - - - - 8 feet 6 inches by 11 feet
Bedroom - - - 11 feet 6 inches by 12 feet 6 inches
Bedroom - - - 12 feet 6 inches by 14 feet 8 inches
Bathroom - - - - 6 feet 6 inches by 9 feet 4 inches
Five Closets.

The entire measurement of the house is 43 feet by 29 feet 6 inches, not including porches, and with an excavated basement 7 feet 2 inches high from floor to joists with cement floor in the basement. The height of rooms in both the first and second floors is 8 feet 6 inches from floor to ceiling. Send for a copy of our big Mill Work Catalogue in which we quote the very lowest price on the most complete line of high grade mill work.

Complete Steam Heating Plant, extra..$247.83
Complete Hot Water Heating Plant, extra...285.82

Sears, Roebuck & Co., Chicago, Ill.   —12—   **BOOK OF MODERN HOMES**

Modern Home #128 - Note the large bay window on the far right side (Library) and also note the position of the second floor bathroom and the unusual window arrangement. This house appeared only in the 1908 Modern Homes catalog and never again.

$3,185⁰⁰ BUILDS THIS NINE=ROOM MODERN HOUSE

ACCORDING TO OUR PLANS, SPECIFICATIONS AND BILL OF MATERIALS WHICH WE SEND YOU FOR A TEMPORARY DEPOSIT OF $1.00 AND WE GIVE YOU BACK YOUR $1.00, MAKING THE PLANS COST YOU NOTHING, AS EXPLAINED ON PAGE 2.

THIS HOUSE WOULD ORDINARILY COST YOU OVER $4,200.00

MODERN HOME No. 120

The arrangement of this house is as follows:

FIRST FLOOR.
Reception Hall, 10 feet by 10 feet.
Vestibule, 3 feet by 7 feet.
Parlor, 12 feet by 16 feet 6 inches.
Dining Room, 14 feet by 14 feet 6 inches.
Kitchen, 13 feet by 13 feet 6 inches.
Stair Hall, 6 feet 6 inches by 14 feet 6 inches.
Pantry, 5 feet 6 inches by 8 feet 6 inches.

SECOND FLOOR.
Chamber, 12 feet by 22 feet 6 inches.
Chamber, 9 feet 6 inches by 19 feet.
Two Chambers, 10 feet by 15 feet each.
Bathroom, 5 feet 6 inches by 7 feet 9 inches.
Hall, 3 feet 6 inches by 20 feet.
Four Clothes Closets.
Balcony extending over the entire front porch.
Front Porch, 8 feet by 51 feet 6 inches.
The entire measurement of this house not including porch is 27 feet 8 inches by 47 feet. This has an excavated basement, 7 feet 4 inches in the clear. First story, 9 feet from floor to ceiling. Second story, 8 feet 6 inches from floor to ceiling. Attic, 7 feet between floor and collar beams.

To give you an idea of the quality and kind of material specified in this $4,200.00 house that you can build for less than $3,200.00, we name below a few of the items that are specified: Cement block foundation, fancy veneered oak doors, oak trim, oak stairs, etc., for the first floor. Also oak flooring for all the rooms on the first floor excepting kitchen, pantry, rear and side entrance and for these rooms we specify maple flooring. For the second floor we specify "A" grade solid yellow pine inside doors with yellow pine trim and gumwood flooring. **You can get the plans, blue prints and complete bill of materials itemizing all materials to be used in this house for nothing, as explained on page 2.**

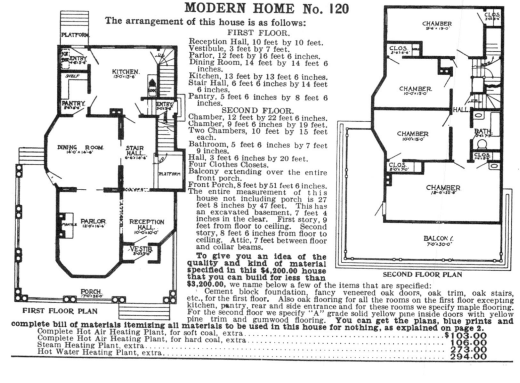

FIRST FLOOR PLAN

SECOND FLOOR PLAN

Complete Hot Air Heating Plant, for soft coal, extra......................................$103.00
Complete Hot Air Heating Plant, for hard coal, extra.................................... 106.00
Steam Heating Plant, extra... 273.00
Hot Water Heating Plant, extra... 294.00

Modern Home #120 - I've seen five of these #120s and all of them are in Alton, Illinois! Note the staircase window on the first floor right and the two bay windows on the first floor (living room and dining room).

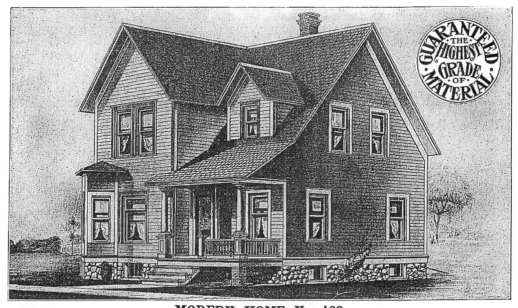

$1,586⁰⁰ Completely Builds This Magnificent SEVEN=ROOM $2,300.00 HOUSE

OUR BUILDING PLANS, SPECIFICATIONS AND BILL OF MATERIALS MAKE THIS LOW COST POSSIBLE.
WE ENABLE YOU TO BUILD WITHOUT A CENT OF COST FOR PLANS, AS EXPLAINED ON PAGE 2.

MODERN HOME No. 108

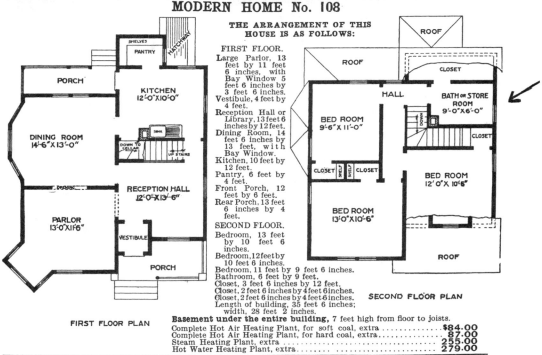

THE ARRANGEMENT OF THIS
HOUSE IS AS FOLLOWS:

FIRST FLOOR.
Large Parlor, 13 feet by 11 feet 6 inches, with Bay Window 5 feet 6 inches by 3 feet 6 inches.
Vestibule, 4 feet by 4 feet.
Reception Hall or Library, 13 feet 6 inches by 12 feet.
Dining Room, 14 feet 6 inches by 13 feet, with Bay Window.
Kitchen, 10 feet by 12 feet.
Pantry, 6 feet by 4 feet.
Front Porch, 12 feet by 6 feet.
Rear Porch, 13 feet 6 inches by 4 feet.

SECOND FLOOR.
Bedroom, 13 feet by 10 feet 6 inches.
Bedroom, 12 feet by 10 feet 6 inches.
Bedroom, 11 feet by 9 feet 6 inches.
Bathroom, 6 feet by 9 feet.
Closet, 3 feet 6 inches by 12 feet.
Closet, 2 feet 6 inches by 4 feet 6 inches.
Closet, 2 feet 6 inches by 4 feet 6 inches.
Length of building, 35 feet 6 inches; width, 28 feet 2 inches.

FIRST FLOOR PLAN

SECOND FLOOR PLAN

Basement under the entire building, 7 feet high from floor to joists.

Complete Hot Air Heating Plant, for soft coal, extra $84.00
Complete Hot Air Heating Plant, for hard coal, extra 87.00
Steam Heating Plant, extra 255.00
Hot Water Heating Plant, extra 279.00

Sears, Roebuck & Co., Chicago, Ill.   —40—

Model #108 - Notice the unusual box window on the left corner. This is the only Sears house that featured this squared corner window. Like many homes offered by Sears in these early catalogs, this house has a "bath or store room" on the second floor. City water and sewage was not available in many areas. Modern Home #108 appeared only in 1908.

$2,700⁰⁰ Will Build this NINE-ROOM HOUSE Finished with the Finest Material

OUR PLANS, SPECIFICATIONS AND ITEMIZED BILL OF MATERIALS TELL YOU HOW TO DO IT.

$1.00 (TEMPORARY DEPOSIT) BRINGS YOU THE COMPLETE SET OF PLANS AND WE GIVE YOU BACK YOUR $1.00, MAKING THE PLANS COST YOU NOTHING, AS EXPLAINED ON PAGE 2.

MODERN HOME No. 138

Contractors heretofore have been compelled to charge from $3,800.00 to $4,200.00 for a house of this kind, because of the unreasonably high prices they have been obliged to pay for the building material to be used in its construction, but because of the low prices we quote on the building material we put the contractor in a position to take a contract at the figure named above and to use a better grade of building material. Note the convenient arrangement and large sizes of all the rooms in this house, which are as follows:

FIRST FLOOR

Hall, 8 feet by 20 feet 6 inches.
Parlor, 12 feet by 13 feet 9 inches.
Living Room, 12 feet by 14 feet.
Dining Room, 12 feet by 12 feet 6 inches.
Kitchen, 12 feet by 9 feet 3 inches.
Pantry, 5 feet by 11 feet 6 inches.

SECOND FLOOR

Chamber, 16 feet 3 inches by 9 feet 6 inches.
Chamber, 16 feet 3 inches by 9 feet 6 inches.
Chamber, 8 feet 6 inches by 9 feet.
Chamber, 12 feet by 12 feet 6 inches.
Bathroom, 8 feet 3 inches by 5 feet.
Five Closets.
Front Porch, 34 feet by 8 feet.
Rear Porch, 10 feet by 4 feet.

The entire measurement of this house is 34 feet wide by 28 feet long, not including

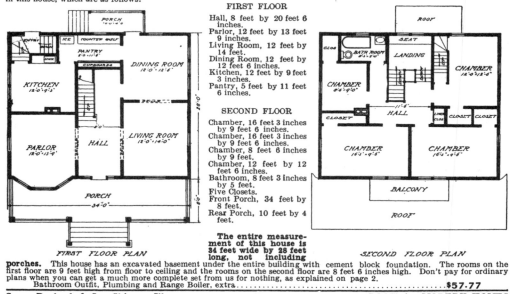

porches. This house has an excavated basement under the entire building with cement block foundation. The rooms on the first floor are 9 feet high from floor to ceiling and the rooms on the second floor are 8 feet 6 inches high. Don't pay for ordinary plans when you can get a much more complete set from us for nothing, as explained on page 2.

Bathroom Outfit, Plumbing and Range Boiler, extra...$57.77

Sears, Roebuck & Co., Chicago, Ill.   —62—   BOOK OF MODERN HOMES

Modern Home #138 - This house appeared only in the 1908 Sears Modern Homes catalog.

$11,500⁰⁰ WILL BUILD THIS LARGE MODERN BRICK SCHOOLHOUSE

ACCORDING TO OUR PLANS, SPECIFICATIONS AND ITEMIZED BILL OF MATERIALS, WHICH WE FURNISH YOU WITHOUT COST, AS EXPLAINED ON PAGE 2.

SCHOOLHOUSE No. 5008

If you were to buy a set of plans from your local architect that are as complete as those we furnish you, they would cost you at least $250.00. If you need a new schoolhouse in your locality, have your School Board send for a set of plans for this schoolhouse, as we can save them at least $5,000.00 on this building, and this means that you will have that much less taxes to pay.

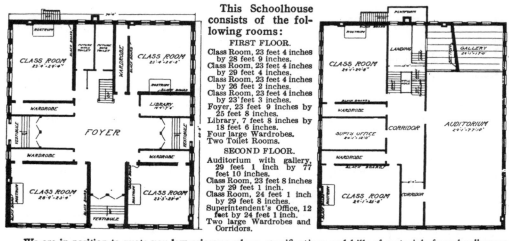

This Schoolhouse consists of the following rooms:

FIRST FLOOR.
Class Room, 23 feet 4 inches by 28 feet 9 inches.
Class Room, 23 feet 4 inches by 29 feet 4 inches.
Class Room, 23 feet 4 inches by 26 feet 2 inches.
Class Room, 23 feet 4 inches by 23 feet 3 inches.
Foyer, 23 feet 9 inches by 25 feet 8 inches.
Library, 7 feet 8 inches by 18 feet 6 inches.
Four large Wardrobes.
Two Toilet Rooms.

SECOND FLOOR.
Auditorium with gallery, 29 feet 1 inch by 77 feet 10 inches.
Class Room, 23 feet 8 inches by 29 feet 1 inch.
Class Room, 24 feet 1 inch by 29 feet 8 inches.
Superintendent's Office, 12 feet by 24 feet 1 inch.
Two large Wardrobes and Corridors.

We are in position to quote you low prices on plans, specifications and bills of materials for schoolhouses to be drawn up specially to your order and ideas of your School Board. Don't order a set of plans until you have written us and received our quotation.

Sears, Roebuck & Co., Chicago, Ill.   —64—   BOOK OF MODERN HOMES

Sears Modern Schoolhouse, #5008 - This school appeared only in the 1908 Sears Modern Homes catalog. It's likely that Sears was marketing this potty-less "Modern Schoolhouse" towards smaller communities and reckoned that such locales may not have municipal water and sewage systems.

The Alden - This cute little colonial appeared only in the 1924 Modern Homes catalog. This house has several unique features that distinguish it from many other modest two-story homes. Note the center chimney, the single window on the side wall of second floor and the unusual entryway with a tiny closet window (which may have been covered in siding by now). From the rear view (bottom left corner) you can see the intersecting gable and the unusual window arrangement.

THE PARKRIDGE is classed as an Americanized English type bungalow due to its many gables and the general treatment of the exterior. The walls are planned to be covered with our 24-Inch Royal Red Cedar Shingles laid with a wide exposure. A clear pine batten type front door with shutters to match, and good window arrangement are the features of the exterior.

THE SIZE of the plan is 24 feet wide and 38 feet 6 inches deep, with five good sized rooms conveniently arranged. Cement steps and small terrace form the approach to the front entrance.

INTERIOR

THE CIRCLE head front door is made additionally attractive by the use of ornamental iron hinges, and leads into the vestibule which has good wall space for outer wraps, etc. The living room is

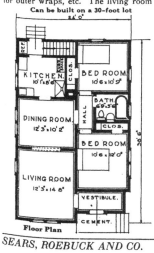

Floor Plan

Honor Bilt
The Parkridge
No. 3301 "Already Cut" and Fitted
For Complete Price Fill Out
Information Blank,
Pages 129-130

12 feet 3 inches wide by 14 feet 8 inches deep, and connects with the dining room and vestibule by the use of circle head plaster arches harmonizing in design with the front door. The dining room, 12 feet 3 inches by 10 feet 2 inches, is well lighted with two large sliding windows and contains good wall space.

THE SUCCESS of a kitchen depends on its being compact and designed to have a convenient place for all fixtures such as table, sink, range and cupboards. This kitchen is a success, and is size 10 feet 1 inch by 8 feet 6 inches.

THE REAR entrance is formed by a small hall sufficiently large for refrigerator and the cellar stairs.

BEDROOMS AND BATH

THE RIGHT side of this plan is devoted to the bath and the two good size bedrooms, the front one being 10 feet 6 inches by 12 feet, and the one at the rear 10 feet 6 inches by 10 feet 9 inches. The bedrooms are separated from the living quarters of the home by a small hall, which gives them the necessary privacy. Each bedroom has two windows and a good size closet. The bathroom is 6 feet 9 inches by 5 feet 6 inches wide and contains a built-in medicine case above the lavatory.

This home gives the maximum in comfort and convenience at the lowest possible cost.

HEIGHT OF CEILINGS: 8 feet 6 inches. Cellar, 7 feet.

SPECIAL FEATURES

COMPLETE description of the guaranteed specifications for this home are on pages 99 to 115. Special Features

Include: 24-Inch Royal Red Cedar Shingles for side walls; clear oak flooring for living room and dining room; kitchen and bath have clear maple; balance of house clear pine. Interior doors clear one-panel subframe design; kitchen cabinets consist of one counter unit "H" and one wall unit "A." All cabinets are constructed with lipped doors and drawers and offset hardware. Your choice of many color enamels. Wood medicine case, batten shutters, Shefton design hardware.

OPTIONS

STUDY carefully the options shown on pages 99 to 115 and indicate on Information Blank the options you desire us to include in **complete low delivered price.**

For Garages see pages 97 and 98.
For description of Heating, Lighting and Plumbing Fixtures see pages 106 to 112.

For Easy Payment Plan see pages 2 and 3. Information Blank on pages 129 and 130.

An Inviting Entrance of Unusual Charm

The Parkridge - This small home appeared in the 1930 Sears Modern Homes catalog and never again. It was described "an Americanized English type bungalow." Its distinguishing features are the twin gables (which comprise the whole width of the house), the round front door and the long, thin attic vent over the front windows.

THE COLLINGWOOD ..

Monthly Payments
as Low as
$50 to $55
Built Complete
on Your Lot

EXTERIOR

THE WESTWOOD is an unusual bungalow that is very practical because of its simplicity. This type of home, without question has the maximum convenience at the minimum cost. The inset front porch is of practical size and gives the necessary protection to the front entrance. Large dormer, exposed fireplace chimney and good window arrangement are other noteworthy features of the exterior. The plan is 24 feet 11 inches wide, by 44 feet 11 inches in depth. Red or cream face brick of either smooth or wire cut texture will give the proper affect. All exterior wood trim members and moldings are furnished in cypress, which is the best material obtainable for the purpose.

INTERIOR

THE LEFT side of the plan is devoted to the living room, dining room and kitchen. The living room is 12 feet, 5 inches wide by 16 feet, 5 inches long, contains good wall space and is well lighted by a triple window in the front wall and two small sash on each side of the fireplace placed high from the floor so the wall space under them is available for bookcases or other furniture. The opening between the living room and dining room is planned for a plaster arch.

The dining room is 13 feet, 11 inches by 10 feet, 10 inches and is relieved of the plainness of a square room by the bay projection in the left wall. It is lighted with two large sliding sash windows.

LOCATED between the kitchen and dining room you will find the stairs leading to the attic which has sufficient headroom so that it can be finished off for two additional rooms if so desired.

THE KITCHEN contains convenient place for all fixtures such as range, sink, cabinets and refrigerator. It is equipped with one counter unit "H," one wall unit "A" and one wall unit "B."

HonorBilt
The Westwood
No. 3299— "Already Cut" and Fitted
For Complete Delivered Price,
Fill Out Information Blank,
Pages 129-130

Can be built on a 35-foot lot

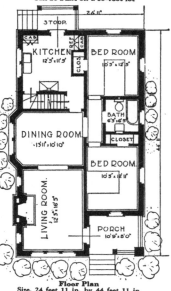

Floor Plan
Size, 24 feet 11 in. by 44 feet 11 in.

BEDROOMS and Bath. The right side of the plan is devoted to two large bedrooms with connecting bath. A small hall separates these rooms from the main part of the house. Each bedroom is well lighted by two large windows located to give cross ventilation and each has a good size closet.

BASEMENT is planned to contain heating plant, fuel, laundry and storage. Height of ceilings: First floor, 9 feet. Basement, 7 feet.

SPECIAL FEATURES

A COMPLETE description of the guaranteed specifications for this home will be found on pages 99 to 115. Special features include: Interior doors, clear one-panel sub-frame design. Clear oak floor for living room, dining room and hall; clear maple for kitchen and bath and clear pine for bedrooms.

Clear red cedar shingles for roof. High grade millwork consisting of flower box and exterior members of cypress.

Medicine cabinet with Venetian mirror. Brick mantel and fireplace. Kitchen cabinets consisting of one counter unit "H," one wall unit "A" and one wall unit "B." Cabinets are constructed with lipped doors and drawers and offset hardware. Your choice of many attractive color enamels. See page 115. La Tosca design hardware.

We also include all face brick for exterior walls, chimney and exposed part of foundation walls. We guarantee enough material to build this home but do not include cement, plaster or common brick required.

OPTIONS

CAREFULLY study the descriptions of all the options shown on pages 99 to 115 and indicate on Information Blank the options you desire us to include in **complete low delivered price.** You may want one of our many attractive colors of asphalt slate surface shingles fully guaranteed for 17 years instead of wood shingles; or sheet plaster and plaster finish instead of wood lath. Every item of material and equipment is fully guaranteed as to quantity and quality.

For Garages see pages 97 and 98.

For description of Heating, Lighting and Plumbing fixtures see pages 106 to 112.

For Easy Payment Plan see pages 2 and 3.

For Information Blank see pages 129 and 130.

The Westwood - This house received an honorable mention in "Houses by Mail." It was listed as being similar to the Collingwood and it is similar, but there are some (minor) differences. (1930 Sears Modern Homes catalog) [small inset: Collingwood]

Simplex Sectional SUMMER COTTAGES

The SILVERHORN
55C186 Four-Room Sectional House With Two Porches $648.00
Size, 18 feet 3 inches by 24 feet 3 inches.

Note the attractive paneled walls. The gable is finished Sea Green Crushed Slate Surfaced Siding, giving a stucco effect. Porch extends across entire front. If porch is wanted 8 feet deep instead of 6 feet as shown in floor plan, can be furnished at small additional price shown below. Bedroom contains clothes closet; pantry is provided for kitchen.

Catalog No.	Price, Cottage	Shipping Weight, Cottage, Pounds	Price, Wall Board for Lining	Shipping Weight, Wall Board, Pounds	Price, Screen Sections and Door for 6-Foot Porch	Price, 8-Foot Porch With Screen Sections and Door	Price, Shutters for Windows, Clover Design	Price, Screen Doors and Half Window Screens	If Foundation Posts Not Wanted, Deduct
55C186	$648.00	12,500	$116.00	2,400	$45.00	$76.00	$29.00	$19.50	$10.00

The BOWER
55C189 Five-Room Sectional Cottage With Large Porch and Bathroom $1,007.00
Size, 24 feet 3 inches by 30 feet 3 inches.

For economy and convenient arrangement of rooms, the square type affords the least waste of space. Note large rooms and porch shown in floor plan. Note kitchen pantry and closets in bedrooms. Regular house contains porch 6 feet deep. If wanted 8 feet deep, with screen sections, it can be furnished at the small extra charge shown below.

Catalog No.	Price, Cottage	Shipping Weight, Cottage, Pounds	Price, Wall Board for Lining	Shipping Weight, Wall Board, Pounds	Price, Screen 6 ft. Sections for Porch With Door	Price, 8-Ft. Porch with Screen Sections and Door	Price, Screen Doors and Half Window Screens	Price, Shutters for Windows, Clover Design	If Foundation Posts Not Wanted, Deduct
55C189	$1,007.00	18,000	$186.50	3,900	$49.00	$87.00	$21.00	$36.00	$11.00

The WASHINGTON
55C136 Four-Room Sectional Cottage With Screened Porch $746.00
Size, 32 feet 3 inches by 20 feet 3 inches.

This cottage is arranged with the greatest economy of floor space. This is really a five-room cottage as the screened porch can be used as a sleeping porch. Arranged to give excellent ventilation and comfort. Note 20-foot living room extending entirely through center of house. All rooms light and airy. Price includes screened porch, as illustrated.

Catalog No.	Price, Cottage	Shipping Weight, Cottage, Pounds	Price, Wall Board for Lining	Shipping Weight, Wall Board, Pounds	Price, Screen Doors and Half Window Screens	Price, Shutters for Windows, Clover Design	If Foundation Posts Are Not Wanted, Deduct
55C136	$746.00	14,000	$131.50	3,350	$15.50	$33.50	$8.00

For General Specifications See Pages 96 and 97 SEARS, ROEBUCK AND CO.

Simplex Sectionals - Sears offered simplex sectionals and summer cottages in many different designs. The walls of these homes consisted of 36-inch wide panels which made assembly quick and easy. These individual panels are what caught my eye and enabled me to discover a Simplex Sectional in Wood River, IL. (1924 Sears Modern Homes catalog)

No Sawing — No Nailing — Easily Handled

WINDOWS AND DOORS—Good quality, hung in frames constituting part of sections. Inside doors five-cross panel. Outside doors upper half glazed clear glass. Doors made of fir, size 2 feet 6 inches by 6 feet 6 inches, 1⅜ inches thick, complete with hardware, including mortise locks. French doors, where specified on following pages, will be 4 feet wide by 6 feet 6 inches high, ten lights of glass in each door. Unless otherwise illustrated, all windows are two-light glazed, size 24x26 inches, hung complete with spring bolt locks. French windows, where illustrated, will be 2 feet 4⅛ inches by 4 feet 10 inches, ten lights of glass to each sash.

INSIDE PARTITIONS—Made of No. 1 yellow pine or fir, matched and beaded ceiling, in sections 3 feet wide, 7 feet 10 inches high.

PAINT—Entire outside of Garages and Summer Cottages, including porch floors, are painted one coat of gray paint trimmed in white, with the exception of the Mount Vernon Cottage, which is painted white.

WALL BOARD—Sectional Garages and Cottages are quoted without wall board, in which manner they are popularly used. Customers desiring to line these buildings with wall board, thereby forming a double wall with air chamber between, as illustrated to the right, will find prices of complete wall board, cut to proper sizes, quoted as options. When wall board is ordered, it is shipped complete for walls and ceiling with necessary lumber accessories, consisting of 2x4-inch ceiling joists, baseboards, moldings, panel strips and nails. Wall board is our 4-ply plain, light tan finish Fibre board.

SCREENS—When ordered will be shipped with 14-mesh **galvanized wire** netting, proper sizes to fit windows and doors of building for which they are intended.

SCREENS FOR PORCHES—When ordered, we will omit porch railing and balusters, also columns, and will ship instead regular screen sections (see illustration to the right) made of 1x6-inch No. 1 yellow pine or fir drop siding, with screen frame fitted, covered with 14-mesh galvanized wire netting.

Triple Sliding Garage Doors
Fully Illustrated and Described on Pages 94 and 95.

Simplex Garages are furnished with triple doors, equipped with special patented hardware, permitting them to slide on a curved track on the inside of the garage. These doors are vastly superior to regular hinged doors, which swing out, as the opening of our doors cannot be interfered with by snow drifts, ice and obstacles in the alley. By sliding around on the inside of the garage, they are entirely out of the way of the car in entering or leaving the garage, and out of the wind, which often causes great annoyance, as well as damage to the machine and doors, by blowing swinging doors backward and forward against the car. While all three of the triple doors slide, one of them also folds so that it can be used as a service door, so as to allow entrance to the garage without opening the other two doors. Size of opening for single garage, 8x8 feet. Double garages have two sets of triple sliding doors. Doors are substantial and strong, and conform to illustration shown with each building.

COMPLETE INSTRUCTIONS AND PLANS EXPLAINING SIMPLE METHOD OF ASSEMBLING FURNISHED WITH BUILDINGS.

Masonry items, steps and plumbing not included in price of building.

Shipment of Frame Sectional Buildings

Wooden Sectional Garages, Resort Cottages and Poultry Houses **shipped complete from our factory in SOUTHERN ILLINOIS.** Steel garages **shipped from factory in OHIO.**

TERMS.

Sectional Resort Cottages sold only for cash. Garages sold for cash or easy payments. See order blank.

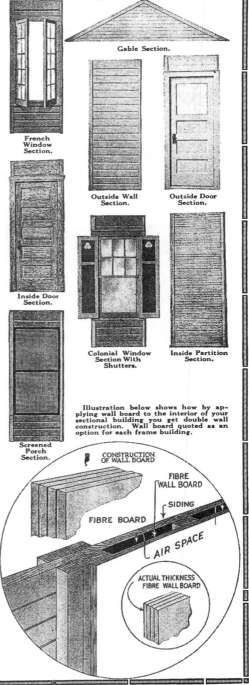

Sections of Simplex Sectional Buildings.

Gable Section.

French Window Section.

Outside Wall Section.

Outside Door Section.

Inside Door Section.

Colonial Window Section With Shutters.

Inside Partition Section.

Screened Porch Section.

Illustration below shows how by applying wall board to the interior of your sectional building you get double wall construction. Wall board quoted as an option for each frame building.

CONSTRUCTION OF WALL BOARD

FIBRE WALL BOARD

SIDING

FIBRE BOARD

AIR SPACE

ACTUAL THICKNESS FIBRE WALL BOARD

SEARS, ROEBUCK AND CO.   2d Ed   *Page 97*

Simplex Sectionals - Under the heading Summer Cottages, this page from the 1924 Sears Modern Homes catalog offers a good description of Simplex Sectional Cottages. The doors and windows came in pre-hung, pre-assembled sections. Under the heading "Wall Board" is this interesting statement: "Sectional garages and cottages are quoted without wall board . . ." The interior walls were made of pine or fir beadboard, three feet wide and almost eight feet tall.

Chapter 15

What Did George Bailey and Sears, Roebuck Have in Common?

The man who owns his own home is not liable to drift around. He has something definite, something very dear to keep him on the job. He is an integral part of the community.

It is foolish and useless to preach economy, prudence and the obligation of citizenship to a man if he belongs nowhere and is not permanently attached to the community in which he lives. What a solace, comfort and source of satisfaction it is for man and wife, father and mother, to know in the declining years of their lives that they are secure in a home of their own.

> *American Carpenter and Builder*
> *June & August 1920*

Sears may have exaggerated some of their money-saving claims, such as the cost of hiring an architect or the savings that resulted from precut lumber or the promise that your kids would be healthier if you bought them a home, but the fact is, their generic designs *did* meet a broad range of needs and made housing affordable for the masses.

Sears offered 15-year, 75% loan-to-value mortgages in 1930, four years before the FHA was even a glimmer in Roosevelt's eyes. During this era, many conventional lenders were offering less favorable terms on home mortgages, such as a maximum of seven years to repay, steep renewal fees, penalties and other unpleasant and expensive terms. Loan-to-value ratios usually did not exceed 50%.

Sears asked potential buyers only one major financial question on their mortgage application: What is your vocation?

Who knows how many African-Americans, single women, new immigrants and other "undesirables" - who would have otherwise been "red-lined" by the mortgage companies of the day - were able to obtain a mortgage and build a home of their own because of Sears?

Testimonials received from new Sears-homeowners bare names that suggest immigrants constituted a fair percentage of their customers. A sampling: Eckbloom, Elsesser, Engelfried, Ensor, Fitzjearl, Harrar, Hauser, Humpal, Jung, Kaczmarek, Kromp, Letzerich, Lichtenwalter, Mackrodt, Mommaerts, Olpp, Owry, Papay, Schlag, Sechler, Skogsburg, Siennicki, Soderquist, Streitlein, Von Lehmen and Waldhier.

And who knows how much stability "a home of their own" brought to these working-class families and their surrounding communities? These testimonial letters frequently stated that the new homeowners saved thousands of dollars by building their own home. This sweat-equity probably gave thousands of struggling families a nest-egg and some security they'd not otherwise have known.

In one of my favorite movies, *"It's a Wonderful Life,"* George Bailey gets to see what his town, Bedford Falls, would have looked like if he'd never been born. Without George's positive influence and his ever-fledgling Building and Loan, the modern subdivision of Bailey Park would never have been developed and countless citizens would never have had the opportunity to become homeowners.

Without the Bailey Building and Loan, George finds that Bedford Falls is full of substandard *rental properties*. And because there are so many rental properties, there is less stability in the family structure and in a broader context, there is less stability in the whole community. In this alternate sans-George world, Ernie the cab driver does not live with his family in their own "nice little home in Bailey Park," but instead, his home is a decrepit shack in Pottersville and it's implied that this hardship is partly to blame for the fact that Ernie's wife "ran off three years ago and took the kid."

The streets of this alternate-Bedford Falls (now named Pottersville) are lined with liquor stores, night clubs, pawnbrokers, striptease shows and pool halls. Gaudy neon signs flash "girls, girls, girls" and illumine the night-time corridors of Main Street. Citizens are neither calm nor law-abiding and brusque policemen struggle to keep peace and order.

George's revelation that he really had a "wonderful life" stemmed in part from the realization that his meager efforts to give people the chance to become homeowners gave them a feeling of accomplishment, prosperity, security and pride. By extension, the whole community benefited in important, significant and enduring ways.

The early Sears Modern Homes catalogues stated this basic philosophy in different ways, but there was an elementary core truth therein: *Homeowners have a vested interest in their community and communities with a large percentage of homeowners will enjoy a greater proportion of prosperity, stability and peace.*

Perhaps Sears was, to small communities in the Midwest, what George Bailey was to Bedford Falls. Sears empowered and enabled tens of thousands of working-class and immigrant families to build their own home. What would countless Midwestern towns have become without Sears homes? How many towns in the Midwest were spared the fate of becoming a Pottersville? Probably many.

Sears Modern Homes made a significant difference in many communities throughout the Midwest. I'm sure of that.

Why do we love Sears homes?

In my career as a Sears house historian, I've stood in the living room of several different Sears homes, with an opened catalogue in my hands and realized, "I'm *in* the living room that is pictured in a 1920s catalog." These 1920-era homes were in original condition and *no changes* had been made to the interior. In several cases, these homes were "featured" in the Modern Homes catalogs, meaning they had detailed interior shots of the houses.

Holding the catalog in my hands and gazing up at the real living room that matched the photo, it was as though I had walked *into the pages* of an 80-year old catalog. It was my dream come true. There is something awesome about that and it's got kind of a "Twilight Zone" feel to it. I love it!!

That's the reason I love Sears homes. They make the past come alive. The past that is represented within the brittle and browned pages of an old catalog <u>comes alive</u> when you can walk into those pages – physically walk – into a living room that is pictured in a 1924 Sears Modern Homes catalog.

Sears homes are like that. They pry open the fourth dimension and let you step into a different time.

What is Sears-rosis?

Sears-rosis: An inordinate love of mail order kit homes, specifically, kit homes offered through Sears, Roebuck and Company.

As your love affair with these interesting and historical homes develops, and you find yourself spending hours of spare time driving the streets, looking for Sears homes, you'll pass through three stages of developing thought.

First, you'll declare with great joy that *everything* is a Sears home. You've studied *"Houses by Mail"* long enough to notice that Sears Modern Homes look like every house in your community. This stage doesn't last too long.

The second stage of Sears-rosis is the sad declaration that there are *no* Sears homes in your community. You've now looked at *"Houses by Mail"* long enough to understand that even if there *were* Sears homes in your community, isolating them and identifying them as Sears homes is impossible because *every* house looks like a Sears house.

It is at this point that you'll find yourself dreaming of Sears homes and seeing them in your mind's eye, every time you close your eyes. Your relatives and loved ones will complain incessantly about your driving, as you spend a large percentage of your time, staring out the driver's side window, staring at rooflines, studying front doors and porches, scanning the horizon for the subtlest hint that you're near a Sears home.

The words, "Honey, let's take a little detour and look for Sears homes on our way to the store," will bring a cacophony of sobs from the little ones in the back seat, disgruntled groans from your spouse and a rolling of eyes and a plea "to let me out, so that I can hitchhike home," from the teen in your midst.

This stage lasts a bit longer than the first stage and it is not an especially pleasant stage for you or the family, as they all try to adjust to the fact that you've become a little too interested in early 20th Century mail-order architecture.

The third stage is the final stage. It's a peaceful place where you've learned that your house-cruising time is not family time. You've memorized the subtle nuances that distinguish a Sears home and you're learning how to spot these architectural details at 50 paces. This third stage is where you realize that everything is *not* a Sears house, but conversely, you realize that there are a few Sears homes in your community. In summary, the third stage is where you strike a balance between the first and second stages.

It's at this stage that the spouse realizes that dabbling in Sears homes is probably pretty harmless and has learned to simply smile and say, "That's nice, dear," when you come running in the door, jumping, panting, twitching and yelling, "I just saw my first Fairy!" *("The Fairy" was a very modest Sears home. The first time I made this loud and enthusiastic proclamation, my (then) husband thought sheer lunacy had set in.*

He was quite concerned that I'd slipped over the edge, as he imagined that my "fairy" was a small ethereal being with wings, a little wand and sprinkles of magic dust.)

At this stage, the children under 13 can readily identify Sears houses and the children over 13 simply refuse to get in the car with you.

When relatives and friends want to kill a few hours of time, they simply ask, "seen any Sears homes lately?" Police in surrounding communities now recognize your car and stop knocking on the driver's side window to ask why you're parked in front of the blue house on Lorena Avenue again tonight. When teens want to distract you, they'll ask, "Mom, did you know Trudy's mom lives in a Sears home that her grandfather ordered from the 1931 catalogue?"

I've been at this third stage sometime now. My children could speak extemporaneously for two hours on Sears homes and no one asks questions when I announce, "I'm going out to look for Sears homes."

Conclusion

Three years ago, when I began the search for contemporary information about Sears homes - when I wrote that first article about Sears homes in Carlinville - I found very little. Yet I *did* find many people who, like me, craved information about these fascinating old houses. And that's why I decided to write this book. I wanted to share what I've learned. And it's my hope that these interesting and awesome mail order homes will be re-discovered, preserved and protected – throughout the country. I hope this book, and increased awareness of the architectural value of Sears homes, helps further that goal.

In closing, I hope that this book has lived up to its title. I hope it's been a "fun read" for you and above all, I hope that you've learned *everything* you ever wanted to know about Sears homes.

☺

Bibliography

Books

Asher, Louis E. & Edith Heal. *Send no Money*. Chicago: Argus Books, 1942

Bruce, Alfred and Sandbank, Harold. *A History of Prefabrication*. Raritan, NJ: The John B. Pierce Foundation Housing Research Division, 1945.

Carlinville and Macoupin County Sesquicentennial, Inc. *The Story of Macoupin County, 1829-1979,* Carlinville, IL: Carlinville and Macoupin County Sesquicentennial, Inc. 1979.

Chase, Stuart. *A Generation of Industrial Peace*. New Jersey: Standard Oil Company, 1947.

Clark, Clifford Edward, Jr. *The American Family Home, 1800-1960*. Chapel Hill: The University of North Carolina Press, 1986.

Dedmon, Emmett. *Challenge and Response, A Modern History of Standard Oil Company (Indiana)*. Chicago: The Mobium Press, 1984.

Dover Publishing. *Small Houses of the Twenties, The Sears Roebuck 1926 House Catalog, An Unabridged Reprint*. New York: Dover Publications, Inc. 1991.

Emmet, Boris & Jeuck, John E. *Catalogues and Counters, A History of Sears, Roebuck and Company*. Chicago: The University of Chicago Press, 1950.

Giddens, Paul H. *Standard Oil Company, Indiana, Oil Pioneer of the Midwest*. New York: Appleton-Century-Crofts, Inc., 1955.

Gowans, Alan. *The Comfortable House, North American Suburban Architecture, 1890-1930*. Cambridge, Massachusetts: The MIT Press, 1986.

Hodgson, Fred T. *Modern Carpentry; A Practical Manual*. Frederick J. Drake & Company, 1918.

Hoge, Cecil C., Jr. *The First Hundred Years Are The Toughest: What We Can Learn From the Century of Competition Between Sears and Wards*." Berkeley: Ten Speed Press, 1988.

Katz, Donald R. *The Big Store, Inside the Crisis and Revolution at Sears*. New York, Viking Penguin Inc., 1987.

Morse, Sidney, *Household Discoveries and Mrs. Curtis's Cook Book*. Petersburg, NY: The Success Company, 1908.

Nye, David E. *Electrifying America, Social Meanings of a New Technology*. Cambridge, Massachusetts: The MIT Press, 1990.

Schiffer Publishing Ltd. *Homes in a Box, Modern Homes From Sears Roebuck*. Atglen, Pennsylvania: Schiffer Publishing Ltd. 1998.

Schlereth, Thomas J. *Victorian American, Transformations in Everyday Life*. New York, HarperCollins Publishers, Inc., 1991.

Smith, LaWanda. *The History of Wood River, Illinois*. Wood River, Illinois: Ron Snyder & Associates, 1985.

Books

Sorensen, Lorin. *Sears, Roebuck and Co. 100ᵗʰ Anniversary 1886-1986*. St. Helena, California: A Silverado Publishing Company Book, 1985.

Stevenson, Katherine Cole and H. Ward Jandl. *Houses by Mail, A Guide to Houses From Sears, Roebuck and Company*. New York: Preservation Press, 1986.

Worthy, James C. *Shaping an American Institution; Robert E. Wood and Sears, Roebuck*. University of Illinois, 1984.

Time Life Books, *This Fabulous Century*, 1900-1910, New Jersey, Time, Inc., 1969.
Time Life Books, *This Fabulous Century*, 1910-1920, New Jersey, Time, Inc., 1969.
Time Life Books, *This Fabulous Century*, 1920-1930, New Jersey, Time, Inc., 1969.

Weil, Gordon, L. Sears, Roebuck, U.S.A. *The Great American Catalog Store and How It Grew*. New York: Stein and Day Publishers, 1977.

Magazines

American Carpenter and Builder Magazine, Chicago, Illinois.
Advertisement for Sears and Roebuck, June 1910, p. 95.
Advertisement for Sears and Roebuck, February 1911, p. oops.
Advertisement for Sears and Roebuck, February 1912.
Advertisement for Sears and Roebuck, March 1912.
Advertisement for Sears and Roebuck, June 1912, p. 119.
"England and Chicago Builders: At Work and At Play," December 1912.
"Decorating the Home," June 1913, p. 46.
"Agents Earn $45 a Week Selling Folding Bathtubs," September 1913.
Advertisement for Aladdin Homes, April 1914, p. 105.
"Contractors! Build This Bungalow" (Advertisement), April 1914, p. 117.
"Free Book of Bungalows Sent Upon Request!" (Advertisement), April 1915, p. 137.
"$298 Buys the Material For This House!" (Advertisement), July 1915, p. 115.
"Bungalows Only; A Novel Building Restriction at Gary, Indiana," May 1915, p. 40.
"Dealers and Contractors Need Good House Plan Service," December 1916, p. 42.

American Builder (Note: *American Carpenter and Builder* was renamed *American Builder* in 1917.)
"Reducing the Cost of the Workman's House," December 1917, p. 40.
"Industrial House Problems," January 1918, p. 46.
"Practical Plans for Industrial Housing," November 1918, p. 30.
"Practical Plans for Industrial Housing," December 1918, p. 28.
"Uncle Sam is Backing Up the Building Industry," May 1919, p. 23.
"How the Contractor Can Help Finance Home Building," June 1919, p. 73.
"Building Boom is Here," August 1919, p. 46.
"The Fort Madison, IA., Industrial Housing Project," September 1919, p. 140.
"Cypress; The Wood Eternal" (Advertisement), March 1920, p. 21.
"Home Ownership Means Security," June 1920, p. 73.
"Housewife Commanding Figure in the Home," August 1920, p. 72.
"Miracle City (Wood River) Builds Modern High School," December 1920. p. 120.
"Building Conveniences That Appeal to Housewife," April 1921, p. 96
"Auto Company Combats Housing Shortage," May 1921, p. 108.
"Every Woman's Message to Architects," June 1923, p. 66.
"Electric Handsaw cuts costs," February 1925, p. 236.

Business Week, New York City, New York.
"New Installment Plan for Home Building," January 29, 1930, p. 10.

Magazines

Business Week, New York City, New York.
"Two Mail Order Houses Now Are Building Homes," March 5, 1930, p. 17.
"Quantity Production Reaches the Homebuilder," March 26, 1930, p. 25.
"Mail Order House Links Up Realtors," April 23, 1930, p. 16.
"Sears, Roebuck Joins Promoters to Erect Group of 100 Homes," Sept. 10, 1930, p. 7.
"Sears-Ward Merger Talk Again Revives," September 2, 1931, p. 13.
"Sears' House Plan: General Houses, Inc., Makes Houses; Sears Sells Things to Go in Them," May 2, 1936, p. 17.
"Sears Prefabricates: Mail Order Company to Sell House Assembled on Lot," August 31, 1934, p. oops. Can you believe I forgot to get a page number for this one? I could make up a page number and you'd probably never know the difference. After all, who reads bibliographies?
"Sears and Housing," September 2, 1939, pp. 27-28.

Fortune, New York City, New York.
"The Great American Salesman," February 1932, p. 124.
"The Catalogue as Historian," February 1932, p. 130-something.
"Mass-produced Houses in Review," April 1933, pp. 52-58.
"A Vision in Kilowatts," April 1933, p. 35.

Good Old Times Specials Magazine, Berne, IN
"Owner of a Mail-Order House," September 2001.

Old House Journal (Yearbook), Brooklyn, New York
"Barber's House 'Kits,'" December 1980, p. 190.

Stanolind Record, Whiting, Indiana.
"Brief Review of the Growth of Wood River Refinery," October 1919, p. 30.
"Safety Work at Whiting," October 1919, p. 31.
"Enter Standard Oil, And It's Different," December 1919, p. 14
"Model Mine and Miners' Homes at Carlinville, Illinois," December 1919, p. 17. "Industrial Harmony," December 1919, p. 32.
"Wood River," January 1920, p. 13.
"Company Built Houses, Wood River," February 1920.
"Carlinville Mines Hit," May 1920, p. 4.
"Human Spiders Complete Giant Stack," October 1920, p. 10.
"Where Comes Standard Oil, Comes Prosperity," March 1921, p. 9.
"Mine One-A, Carlinville, Discontinued," March 1921, p. 11.
"Carlinville/Schoper," March 21, 1921, p. 49.
"Carlinville," April 1921, p. 48.
"Carlinville," June 1921, p. 44.
"Carlinville," July 1921, p. 47.
"Standard Oil (Indiana) and The Community," August 1921, p. 36.
"Carlinville," August 1921, p. 46.
"Carlinville," September 1921, p. 53.
"Carlinville," October 1921, p. 49.
"Ardent Advocates of the Full Dinner Pail," February 1923, p. 6.
"Carlinville," May 1923, p. 40.
"Carlinville," June 1923, p. 39.
"Carlinville," August 1923, p. 42.
"Standard Addition, Carlinville, Illinois," September 1923, pp.19-21.
"Carlinville," September 1923, p. 41.
"Carlinville," December 1923, p. 42.
"Carlinville," August 1924, p. 36.

Magazines

Stanolind Record, Whiting, Indiana.
"Carlinville," September, 1924, p. 40.
"Carlinville," October 1924, p. 43.
"Carlinville," November, 1924, p. 40.
"Carlinville," December, 1924, p. 40.
"Carlinville," January 1925, p. 40.
"Carlinville," June 1925, p. 46.
"Carlinville," July 1925, p. 41.
"Carlinville," August 1925, p. 40.
"Wood River Opens Community Center, Gift of Standard Oil," August 1926, p. 29.

Newspapers

Cairo Citizen, Cairo, Illinois.
"Census Figures for 1900 and 1910," January 13, 1911.
"Over 100 Autos In Cairo," March 25, 1911.
"Sears and Roebuck Closed Deal for Site," May 19, 1911.
"Sears and Roebuck to get $3500 Bonus to Locate Here," May 23, 1911.
"Sears and Roebuck Bought 30-acre Tract in North Cairo," May 26, 1911.
"Police Pick up Demented Woman; Claims Husband Drove Her Insane," July 8, 1911.
"Building Switch at Sears and Roebuck Plant," July 8, 1911.
"Sears and Roebuck Officials in Cairo," July 28, 1911.
"Half a Million to be Cost of New Sears and Roebuck Plant," July 29, 1911.
"Cairo Given Another Boost," March 14, 1912
"Levee District Scene of Destruction; Factories and Homes Inundated," April 5, 1912.
"Sears and Roebuck to Stay in Cairo," April 12, 1912.
"Vanalstine quits Sears and Roebuck," August 26, 1912.
"Property of Lumber Plant is Sold Here," December 10, 1955.

Chicago Tribune, Chicago, Illinois.
"Some Illinois Coal Miners' Homes and a Typical Family," November 3, 1919.
"Sears Roebuck Addition; $250,000 Plant to be Built at Cairo," May 21, 1911
"Looking Ahead With Business: Sears Roebuck," January 22, 1931.

New York Times, New York City, New York.
"Sees Future Homes Bought Like Autos," May 25, 1932
"Boy Escapes Death Under Fast Train," May 25, 1932 [just kidding. I didn't really use this one.]
"Fordized Housing Plan of New Group: General Houses, Inc., Formed to Market Ready-Made Steel Homes Like Automobiles," June 23, 1932.

Wall Street Journal, New York City, New York.
"Sears Will Expand Home Construction," January 22, 1932, p. 5.

Alton Evening Telegraph, Alton, Illinois*
The Carlinville Democrat, Carlinville, Illinois*
The Macoupin County Enquirer, Carlinville, Illinois*
*Write me a note, send me a nice gift and I'll give you the precise dates. It'd take another book to list all the dates in these newspapers, as I used bits and pieces from three years worth of newspapers. No fooling.

Catalogs
1908-1940 Sears Modern Homes Catalogues.
1908 General Merchandise Catalogue
1912 Successful Building Book (promotional booklet for Sears Homes)
1914 Building Materials Catalogue
1935 Honor-Bilt Building Materials catalog
1910 (approximate date) Seroco Paint Catalogue
1915 (approximate date) Seroco Paint Catalogue
1929 (approximate date) Instructions for Installing Modern Plumbing Systems
1930 Modern Plumbing and Heating Systems Catalog
1910 Heating Equipment Catalogue
1933 (approximate date) Garages, Lob Cabins, Playhouses, Cottages catalog
1931 Summer Cottages
1948 and 1951 Homart Homes Catalogs
1910 and 1914 Montgomery Ward Book of Homes
1918, 1924, 1928, 1931 Montgomery Ward "Wardway" Catalogs
1920, 1926 and 1929 Gordon Van Tine Book of Homes
1919 Pacific Homes Catalog (courtesy- *Dale Patrick Wolicki, Bay City, Michigan*)
1916 Sterling Homes Catalog

Honor Bilt Homes (Sears Roebuck and Company) Brochures
(undated) Air-Sealed Walls (brochure)
(undated) Cypress, The Wood Eternal (brochure)
(undated) Honor Bilt Homes Make Happy Homes (brochure); (courtesy - *Dale Patrick Wolicki, Bay City, Michigan.*)

Would you like to contact
Rose Thornton?

Or learn more about hiring Rose to find the
Sears homes within your community?

Or check her availability for addressing your group?

Or share information about a Sears home?

Email: thorntonrose@hotmail.com

or
Rose Thornton
P. O. Box 1392
Alton, IL 62002

Reorder information

To order
The Houses That Sears Built
Please send $19.95 + $3 shipping and handling, to:

Gentle Beam Publications
P. O. Box 1392
Alton, IL 62002

This book can also be ordered online, through:
www.oldhouseweb.com or www.amazon.com

This book is available at quantity discounts for bulk purchases.

But wait! There's more!

Finding the Houses That Sears Built is an easy-to-use field guide which identifies Sears' 60 best-selling designs. Nationally-known kit-home expert Rose Thornton states that mastering these 60 designs will enable you to find about 90% of the Sears Homes in your community. *Finding the Houses That Sears Built* features original pictures and information from Sears Modern Homes catalogs, compared side-by-side to approximately 120 contemporary photos of Sears Homes as they appear today. Each photo has a 100-word caption, explaining tips and techniques for finding these houses in the field. Price is $24.95 plus $3 shipping.

California's Kit Homes: A Reprint of the 1925 Pacific Ready-Cut Homes Catalog. Pacific Ready-Cut Homes was a Los Angeles-based company that sold about 40,000 kit homes throughout California in the early 1900s. This high quality reprint of their 160-page catalog contains more than 100 housing styles, dozens of vintage photos, a plethora of historical information and a 15-page introduction (written by Rosemary Thornton and Dale Patrick Wolicki). Price is $24.95 plus $3 shipping.

Gentle Beam Publications
P. O. Box 1392
Alton, IL 62002

gentlebeam@hotmail.com
www.oldhouseweb.com

About the author: Since the publication of the first edition of *The Houses That Sears Built* (Gentle Beam Publications, 2002), Rose has appeared on PBS's *History Detectives*, CBS's *Sunday Morning News*, A&E's *Biography* and WGN News. In Summer 2004, *The Houses That Sears Built* was featured on *Jeopardy!*. Rose and her book have also appeared in the *Christian Science Monitor*, *The New York Times*, *L. A. Times*, *Dallas Morning News*, *The Washington Post, Old House Journal* and about 100 other publications.

Her other books include this newest revision of *The Houses That Sears Built* (Gentle Beam Publications, 2005), *Finding The Houses That Sears Built* (Gentle Beam Publications, 2004) and *The Reality of Real Estate* (Hampton Roads Publishing, 1993). She's the co-author of *California's Kit Homes* (Gentle Beam Publications, 2004).

From the *Smithsonian* in Washington, D.C. to *Bungalow Heaven* in Pasadena, California, Rose has traveled extensively in the last three years, studying and researching kit homes, giving more than 200 lectures in 11 states. In addition to researching, writing and lecturing on kit homes, Rose is also a contributing editor at Old House Web (www.oldhouseweb.com).

Rose in front of The Fullerton in Washington, D. C.
(Also known as the "Jesse Baltimore" House)

Photo credit: Mary Rowse